READING JOHN IN EPHESUS

BY

SJEF VAN TILBORG

E.J. BRILL

LEIDEN · NEW YORK · KÖLN

1996

The paper in this book meets the guidelines for permanence and durability of the Committee on Production Guidelines for Book Longevity of the Council on Library Resources.

ISSN   0167-9732
ISBN   90 04 10530 1

READING JOHN IN EPHESUS

SUPPLEMENTS TO
NOVUM TESTAMENTUM

VOLUME LXXXIII

CONTENTS

INTRODUCTION

The completion of the edition of *Die Inschriften von Ephesos*[1] in which the epigraphic data so far known of Ephesus are brought together, is a milestone in the Ephesus research. For the first time since T.T. Wood began his search for the remnants of the Artemision, and started the shipping away of archaeological Ephesus in bits and pieces into museums from all over the world, the Ephesian texts have been brought together in one place. In this way researchers are given the chance to gain insight in the history of historical Ephesus, this gold-mine of archaeology which attracted so many people.

This edition is (only) the temporary result of the efforts of archaeologists to make their findings available for others. The research goes on and new inscriptions are being published all the time.[2] As is clear from the critical remarks by Horsley (1992), there are a number of *desiderata* regarding the main edition of the *Inschriften*. For the kind of research which exegetes have to do, the dating of texts is very important. Precisely in this, more precision or at least more attention would have been desirable, although I do not want to imply that the editors have not done anything in this regard. As long as a researcher does not possess the means to date texts more precisely—and this is seldom possible with printed texts—one has to be content with the dating proposed in the main edition. That is also what I have done in this study. To keep the argumentation as clear as possible I organized my own 'archive' of

---

[1] Hrsg. von H.Wankel - C.Börker - R.Merkelbach et al., Bonn, I-VIII, 1979-1984, R.Hebelt Verlag. As abbreviation I will use the number of the volume + the number of the inscription. If this is still unclear I will add IE.

[2] These become, albeit at a somewhat later time, easily available in the yearly edition of the *Supplementum Epigraphicum Graecum* (SEG).

what is provable first century Ephesian, based on the epigraphical material from Ephesus, supplemented with historical data from as much contemporary literature as possible (such as preserved in e.g. the fragments of the Greek historians, in Strabo, Acts, Josephus, Tacitus, Suetonius, Pausanias, Strato, Artemidorus, Xenophon of Ephesus, Ignatius, Philostratus etc.) and supplemented with prosopographic, political, social, economic, and art-historical studies about first century Ephesus. When I say 'first century Ephesian', I mean from the beginning of the century (the time of Augustus from the beginning of our era) till about 130 AD (the foundation of the emperor-temple for Hadrian in Ephesus is in 129 AD); the main interest of the research lies in the Vespasian-Trajan period (69 AD—117 AD).[3]

For contemporary Johannine research such attention to the location and situation of John's Gospel in Ephesus seems rather unwarranted. There are always new attempts to show that John's text should be situated in or near Palestine. And if this is not true for the final text, it is said to be true for, at least, aspects of the historical development of the text. Within Johannine research the former unanimity on the situation of the text has been superseded by a multiplicity of opinions, which will go on for some time to come. The location in Ephesus is no longer 'innocent'. Hengel[4] saw this as a challenge and, in a wide-ranging study, gathered all texts which lie behind the ecclesiastical tradition's situation of the Gospel of John in Ephesus. But his study is not beyond criticism,[5] and this makes clear that the discussion is not yet closed.

In the following study one can find a number of arguments which make the traditional location of the Gospel in Ephesus

---

[3] This means that I have not used undated inscriptions in this 'archive'. Unless specifically mentioned I have not used such inscriptions. With rather less pretension of completeness I have set up similar 'first century archives' for the surrounding and competing cities, Smyrna, Magnesia, Sardis, Pergamum, and Miletus, in order to be able to compare and to control the uniqueness of Ephesus.

[4] See esp. the German study from 1993 in which not only the source material but also the secondary literature is discussed and evaluated in an apparently exhaustive way.

[5] See esp. the serious criticism by Davies 1992, 249ff treating Hengel's edition 1989; further Culpepper 1994, 107-138 and 304-307.

defensible. In my own vision the Gospel of John, or at least the final version of this Gospel originated in a Jewish quarter of a Hellenistic city. It may be true that John's Gospel cannot be imagined without Jewish influence, and that it is unintelligible without knowledge of Jewish theology and Jewish customs. It is equally true that it cannot be imagined without the influence of Hellenistic thoughts and customs and that it is unintelligible without knowledge of Hellenistic philosophy, religion, and culture. It is this marvellous mixture which makes John's Gospel so fascinating. Historically speaking, this presupposes a location where such a combination is imaginable and possible. Every major Hellenistic city where a fairly large group of Jews has settled would do. There are many. Ephesus, at least, is one of those.

Yet, in this study I am not going to try and *prove* that the Johannine Gospel belongs in Ephesus. To avoid the danger of circular argumentation it is necessary to find a way in between. I believe I have found it in the supposition that—notwithstanding the existence of many different opinions—it is important to study how John's text was read or could have been read in first century Ephesus. On the one hand, such a supposition is not devoid of probability —after all, there is the long and now epigraphically provable connection between Ephesus and *Joannes*[6]; on the other hand, such a supposition fits in with the paradigm-change within literary-theoretical research in which attention to the origin of a text and the sources which played a role in it has moved towards an interest in reader-reception.

Concretely this means that texts are compared with texts: the texts from and about Ephesus with the text of the Johannine Gospel. The process involved is in this study called 'interference' , the

---

[6] That is to say that the name *Joannes* is found in Ephesus more than any other biblical name and more than in other cities: the apostle, theologian, and evangelist John is mentioned in the Ephesian inscriptions at least 18 times (compare this with Paul, 4 times; Peter once; Mary 4 times); furthermore, the name *Joannes* appears in some variations another 30 times as the name of a particular person: Ἰωάννης (23 times); Ἰοάννης (once); Ἡοάνης (4 times); Ἡοάννης (twice); compare the fact that the name *Joannes* appears in Smyrna only once, and not at all in Pergamum and in Magnesia—but the lists of names are not so trustworthy as the one from Ephesus.

exchange which spontaneously originates between reader and text when a typical similarity or dissimilarity is seen. In our case, these similarities and/or dissimilarities deal with city-interferences: all texts about the history, culture, architecture, and social environment of first century Ephesus which positively or negatively 'interfere' with the reading process of John's Gospel. The word 'interference' is used, therefore, in its most neutral meaning, more or less analogous to the use of the word in the world of physics where 'interference' means "the mutual influence which two systems exercise on each other if they come together".[7] In our case we have two language-acts which, on the basis of the denotative function of language, come into contact with each other via the reader and influence the process of giving meaning. I will develop this systematically for the process of signification of John's text. The opening and closing texts of the various chapters (sometimes of individual paragraphs) verbalize the difference in meaning between understanding the Johannine texts without the Ephesian influence and the same texts read from the point of view of interference with the Ephesus-texts.

I base myself in this study mainly on the equality of words which evoke semantic similarities or dissimilarities because of the differences in co-text: the use of names in John and in Ephesus; the similarities and differences in function and use of the titles for the emperors and for Artemis in relation to the titles used for Jesus in John; the social embedding of John seen against the city life of Ephesus; the comparison with the teaching activity of Jesus and the formation of a group around his person with what is known about such realities in Ephesus; the appearance and the function of the high priests in relation to the imperial cult and how this influences the meaning of the appearance of the high priests in John. The study is about this kind of contextual interferences. Obviously, many aspects of the content of the Johannine text will thereby remain undiscussed; but what we gain is an insight into the concrete embedding of the text in the history and life of the city of Ephesus.

---

[7] See the description in the Oxford English Dictionary: "the mutual action of two waves or two systems of waves, in reinforcing or neutralizing each other, when their paths meet or cross".

CHAPTER ONE

THE PROSOPOGRAPHY

It is not all that natural to begin with the study of the use and significance of names. Even if one reads John's Gospel many times, one does not have the impression that the text pays much attention to names. This is the result of the fact that—apart from the first chapter, where eight different persons appear in short order—the individual characters are linked to long and similar narratives. This reduces the index function of the used names: that names point to extra-narrative realities. I hope to show, nevertheless, that this function has not completely disappeared.

That I want to start with a comparison of the names as used in John and Ephesus, is primarily linked to the special archaeological situation of Ephesus. It is a city of names. Hundreds of pedestals for statues and innumerable inscriptions of decrees and governors have ensured the preservation of thousands of names. The inscriptions which can be traced back to the first century contain some 900 different names of which 425 date from the time of Vespasian-Trajan. That is quite an archive and a real treasure trove of information.

1.1 *The system of names in John*

I start with a catalogue of the personal names in John:

1. Ἀβραάμ: 8:33,37,39,40,52,53,56,57,58
   ὁ πατὴρ ὑμων / ὁ πατὴρ ἡμων: 8:39,53,56
2. Ἀνδρέας: 1:40,44; 6:8; 12:22
   ὁ ἀδελφὸς Σίμωνος Πέτρου: 1:40; 6:8
   ἀπὸ Βηθσαϊδά, ἐκ τῆς πόλεως Ἀνδρέου καὶ Πέτρου: 1:44
3. Ἄννας: 18:13,24
   ὁ πενθερὸς τοῦ Καϊάφα: 18:13

4. Βαραββᾶς: 18:40
   λῃστής: 18:40
5. Δαυίδ: 7:42
   ἀπὸ Βηθλέεμ τῆς κώμης ὅπου ἦν Δαυίδ: 7:42
6. Ζεβεδαῖος: 21:2
   οἱ τοῦ Ζεβεδαίου: 21:2
7. Ἠλίας: 1:21,25
8. Ἠσαΐας: 1:23; 12:38,39,41
   ὁ προφήτης: 1:23; 12:38
9. Θωμᾶς: 11:16; 14:5; 20:24,26,27,28; 21:2
   ὁ λεγόμενος Δίδυμος: 11:61; 20:24; 21:2
10. Ἰακώβ: 4:5,12
    ὁ πατὴρ ἡμῶν: 4:12 <4:5>
11. Ἰησοῦς: 237 times, but notice:
    ὁ υἱὸς τοῦ Ἰωσὴφ ὁ ἀπὸ Ναζαρέτ: 1:45
    ὁ υἱὸς Ἰωσήφ οὗ ἡμεῖς οἴδαμεν τὸν πατέρα καὶ τὴν μητέρα:
    6:42
    ὁ Ναζωραῖος: 18:5,7; 19:19
12. Ἰούδας: 6:71; 12:4; 13:2,26,29; 18:2,3,5
    Σίμωνος Ἰσκαριώτου:6:71; 13:2,26 (resp. Σίμωνος Ἰσκαριώτης)
    ὁ Ἰσκαριώτης: 12:4
13. Ἰούδας: 14:22
    οὐχ ὁ Ἰσκαριώτης: 14:22
14. Ἰωάννης: 1:6,15,19,26,28,32,35,41; 3:23,24,25,26,27; 4:1;
    5:33,36; 10:40,41
    βαπτίζων: 1:28; 3:23; 10:40
15. Ἰωάννης: 1:42; 21:15,16,17
    Σίμων ὁ υἱὸς Ἰωάννου: 1:42
    Σίμων Ἰωάννου: 21:15,16,17
16. Ἰωσήφ: 4:5
    ὁ υἱὸς Ἰακώβ: 4:5
17. Ἰωσήφ: 1,45; 6:42
    ὁ πατὴρ Ἰησοῦ: 1:45; 6:42
18. Ἰωσήφ: 19:38
    ὁ ἀπὸ Ἀριμαθαίας: 19:38
19. Καϊάφας: 11:49; 18:13,14,24,28
    ἀρχιερεὺς τοῦ ἐνιαυτοῦ ἐκείνου: 11:49,51; 18:13
20. Κλωπᾶς: 19:25
    Μαρία ἡ τοῦ Κλωπᾶ: 19:25

21. Λάζαρος: 11:1,2,5,11,14,43; 12:1,2,9,10,17
    ἀπὸ Βηθανίας: 11:1
    ἐκ τῆς κώμης Μαρίας καὶ Μάρθας: 11:1
    ὁ ἀδελφὸς Μαρίας καὶ Μάρθας: 11:1
    ὁ φίλος ἡμῶν: 11:11
22. Μάλχος: 18:10
    ὁ δοῦλος: 18:10
23. Μάρθα: 11:1,5,19,20,21,24,30,39
    ἡ ἀδελφὴ Μαρίας: 11:1,5,28
    ἡ ἀδελφὴ Λαζάρου: 11:21,23,39
24. Μαρία: 11:1,2,19,20,28,31,32,45; 12:3
    ἡ ἀδελφὴ Μάρθας: 11:1,5
    ἡ ἀδελφὴ Λαζάρου: 11:19
25. Μαρία: 19:25; 20:1,11,16,18
    ἡ Μαγδαληνή: 19:25; 20:1,18
26. Μαρία: 19:25
    ἡ τοῦ Κλωπᾶ: 19:25
27. Μωυσῆς: 1:17,45; 3:14; 5:45,46; 6:32; 7:19,22,23; 9:28,29
28. Ναθαναήλ: 1:45,46,47,48; 21:2
    ὁ ἀπὸ Κανὰ τῆς Γαλιλαίας: 21:2
29. Νικόδημος: 3:1,4,9; 7:50; 19:39
    ἄρχων τῶν Ἰουδαίων: 3:1
30. Πιλᾶτος: 18:29,31,33,35,37,38; 19:1,4,6,8,10,12,13,15,19,21,
    22,31,38
31. Σίμων: 6:71; 13:2,26
    Ἰουδάς Σίμωνος Ἰσκαριώτου: 6:71; 13:2,26
32. Σίμων Πέτρος: 31 times but notice:
    ὁ υἱος Ἰωάννου: 1:42; 22:15,16,17
    ὁ ἀδελφὸς Ἀνδρέου: 1:40,41
    κληθήσῃ Κηφᾶς: 1:42
33. Φίλιππος: 1:43,44,45,46,48; 6:5,7; 12:21,22; 14:8,9
    ἀπὸ Βηθσαϊδά (τῆς Γαλιλαίας) : 1:43 <12:21>
    ἐκ τῆς πόλεως Ἀνδρέου καὶ Πέτρου: 1:43

1.2 *First observations*
This list needs to be set in order because not all the data are equally relevant and some need to be analyzed.

1.2.1
First of all it seems that a clear distinction is made between the names of persons who actually play a role in the story and the names of those who belong to the world of the story as told: Abraham, David, Elijah, Isaiah, Jacob, Joseph Jacob's son, and Moses. They are not introduced. Occasionally there is an apposition —Abraham, our father, in opposition to Abraham your father; David, native of Bethlehem; Isaiah, the prophet; and Jacob, our father. However, these appositions are always in the service of the concrete discussion in which these personages play a role. Sometimes no explanation is given, as in the case of Elijah and Moses. These people are supposed to be well-known for the intended reader and need no introduction.

1.2.2
We see the same thing with some characters in the story itself: John (the Baptist), Pilate, and in a way also Jesus. All three are main characters and the lack of apposition shows that the book deals with narrative characters which are well known in the reading community.

The lack of any apposition (family, birth place, and function) is most clear in the case of John (the Baptist). The word βαπτίζων (in 1:28; 3:23 and 10:40) is in the Gospel of John not an indication of title but a description of function. Because of the Synoptics we are used to speaking about John *the Baptist*, but one should not really do this in the Gospel of John. The simple mention of the name should be enough.

It is symptomatic for Pilate's reputation in the supposed own milieu as well possibly also for the fact that there is no Latin name system in John that Pilate is never called by his own proper Latin name in John's text. Luke is the only evangelist who uses the full name.[1]

---

[1] Luke 3:1 Πόντιος Πιλᾶτος, see also Acts 4:27; there is some doubt in the tradition of the text in Matt. 27:2. Luke also provides full Roman names in Acts. In Luke's Gospel there is doubt: Κυρήνιος (Luke 2:1) is

In the case of Jesus' name the situation is the most complicated. For the moment I do not want to go beyond the family names and the indications of place which make this name parallel to other names in the list. The interference of Jesus' titles (in the plural) with the situation of Ephesus will be treated extensively in the next chapter.

1.2.3

The names 'Malchus' and, possibly, also 'Barabbas' are a category apart. In accordance with the prosopography of the time—where the use of a simple name indicates that it is the name of a slave, as will be explained further on—one can say that these names are without family indication, without mention of the father or of the place of birth, because they do not belong to an *oikos* through descent, because they are 'slaves' or 'bandits'.

1.2.4

The rest of the names—about half the list: Andrew, Annas, Zebedee, Thomas, Judas, John, Joseph (twice), Iscariot, Caiaphas, Clopas, Lazarus, Martha, Maria (three times), Nathanael, Nicodemus, Simon (twice), Philip (and Jesus)—all accompanied by some apposition, are the subject of our next consideration.

We can describe the prosopography used in four categories:

indications of relationship:
   —paternity: the sons of Zebedee; Jesus, son of Joseph; Judas, son of Simon Iscariot; Simon, son of John;
   —brother and sister relationship: Andrew and Peter; Lazarus and Mary and Martha; Mary and Martha;
   —father-in-law: Annas and Caiaphas;
   —marriage (?): Mary, the wife of Clopas—it could also have the meaning "Mary, the daughter of Clopas".

---

written in its short form (see Tac. Ann. II,30; III,48; Jos. Ant. XVII. 355; XVIII. 1); Καίσαρ <Αὐγούστος> (Luke 2:1) and Τίβεριος Καίσαρ (Luke 3:1) are the names of emperors as found on coins (cf. Meshorer, 1967, 136ff; no. 79,81A,83,84; 170ff: no. 216,220,221A,222A,223A, 224,225,226,228,230,231).

indications of place:
—Bethsaida: the city of Andrew and Peter; the city of Philip;
—Iscariot: it is an old manuscript problem with which name
'Ἰσκαριώτης has been conjugated: with Judas or with Simon,
Judas' father. There are two possibilities:

if 'Ἰσκαριώτης is the indication of a place, it could be a
Greek version of the Hebrew 'ish Qeryyot', the man from
Keriot, a small town in the south of Judea; and it then fits
Judas as well as Simon as apposition;
if it is indicative of a person, it could be linked with the
Hebrew-Aramaic 'shiqra/sheqarya': the cheat. Then, it
can only be seen as an apposition for Judas[2].

—Nazareth: Jesus, the son of Joseph from Nazareth; Jesus the
Nazorean. I do not think there is the same doubt about the term
Ναζωραῖος as there is about the term 'Ἰσκαριώτης: the first
time it is used in John (in 18:5,7), it is clearly an identification
of Jesus. Narratively it must refer there to Jn 1:45 and
6:42—else the soldiers would be looking after a person who had
not yet appeared in the story at all—notwithstanding maybe the
original meaning of the term.[3]
—Arimathea: Joseph of Arimathea;
—Bethany: the village of Mary, Martha, and Lazarus;
—Magdala: as apposition for Mary;
—Cana: the city of Nathanael.

epithets:
—Didymus: Thomas "who is called Didymus";
—Iscariot: cf. what has been said above about Judas in the
second possible interpretation: Judas, the cheat; and for the other
Judas who is called "not the Iscariot" (both meanings possible);
—Cephas: for Peter: "you will be called Cephas".

indications of function:
—Nicodemus, an *archon* of the *Ioudaioi*;
—Caiaphas, the high priest of that year.

---

[2] Brown 1966, 298; Schnackenburg 1971, 113f.
[3] See Schaeder, TWNT s.v. Ναζαρηνός-Ναζωραῖος, who anyway
keeps the meaning 'from Nazareth'.

Since, apart from Annas and Caiaphas, they are all people who are gathered around Jesus or have been attracted by him, these characteristics give a first vision of the 'group around Jesus' as the author wants to introduce them to his readers:

a group of men and women who, in several cases, are mutually related to one another;

a group of men and women who know each other—if one sees it in the context of chapter 1: John (the Baptist) knows Jesus; two disciples of John follow Jesus; Andrew brings his brother to Jesus; Philip comes from Andrew's and Peter's village; Philip calls Nathanael who comes from nearby Cana;

a group which is composed of people from all over Palestine: those not mentioned by name such as the woman from Samaria and the blind man from Jerusalem who is cured, have to be taken into account too;

a group of people who, in the person of Nicodemus, have relations with the leaders of the country.

1.3 *The formal characteristics of the system of names in Ephesus*

If one wants to know how this system was read and understood in Ephesus, one needs to compare it with the system in use there. Several names appear literally:

—Philippos: V-1687, (twice), in the time of Tiberius; II-509 and VI-2048, in the time of Domitian.

—Nikodemos: IV-1030, in the time of Hadrian

—Didymos as *cognomen* in SEG 1984, 1121, in early imperial time; and as *nomen* in I-20, in the time of Nero.

—Andreas: according to the reconstruction in SEG 1984, 1132, IE VIII-I-3222 should be read as $M\eta\tau\rho\hat{\alpha}$ vac ς 'Ανδρήα in which 'Ανδρήα should be seen as the genitive of 'Ανδρίας or of 'Ανδρέας.

Because these are only a couple of names—which are clearly good Greek—the comparison between John and Ephesus should be primarily concerned with the formal similarities and differences. I use the same categories as in the Johannine system.

1.3.1 *The indications of relationship*

It is good to start with this because they are abundant in Ephesus. To say that in every inscription a family relationship is expressed would be an exaggeration, but not by much. Time and again, sons and daughters mention their father; fathers call to memory their children; spouses indicate with whom they are married; longer or shorter genealogies are given. The *oikos* as a community of relatives and friends and as image of the *polis* is a living reality, as can be seen in the inscriptions. Formally we find, therefore, a real similarity with the names in John. This is true for the mention of descent, of being brother or sister, of marriage, and of friendship. It is even true for the double form to express descent: the form Σίμων Ἰωάννου as well as the form Σίμων ὁ υἱὸς Ἰωάννου appear so frequently that there is no need to develop this here.

I need to add one observation though. As has been presupposed in the foregoing text, the inscriptions of Ephesus use a double name system:

—the Greek system, where we find a combination of the name with the genitive of the father's and/or the grand-father's name (sometimes in combination with the name of the mother)—as in the case mentioned above from John and in Ephesus, e.g. Δημήτριος Παμφίλου; Ἀνθέστιος ὁ υἱὸς Ποπλίου; Ἐπίγονος Ἐπιγόνου τοῦ Βακχύλου; Κλαυδία Φιλίππου καὶ Μελίσσης θυγάτηρ—;

—and the much more complicated Roman system.[4] In principle we have there three names: the *praenomen*, the *nomen* of the *gens* and the *cognomen*. Sometimes there is the addition of the father's name and the name of the *tribus* and in our period often one or more *agnomina*. In its fullest form we get: Γάιος Λικίννιος Μενάνδρου υἱός Σεργία Μάξιμος Ἰουλιανός (Μένανδρος is the father; Σεργία is the φυλή and Ἰουλιανός is the *agnomen*). This is quite common with the richer families: Sextilius Pollio, Ofilius Proclus; with the Vedii; the Flavii Pythius; the Vibii, with Celsus Polemaeanus; with Valens Valerius etc. This is the most certain indication that the person has Roman citizenship. Often only three names are mentioned: Γάιος Ἰούλιος Φῆλιξ, or sometimes only two: Ἀγελήιος Κόιντος. Especially in this last case we cannot be completely certain that such a person is a Roman citizen. Maybe the family has only adapted the developing name system. (In the Johannine Gospel Σίμων Πέτρος seems to belong in this category). Whether people are Roman citizens or not is even less certain when the name is some kind of combination of the two systems, like

---

[4] Doer 1974/1937; Thylander 1952; Kajanto 1964; Weaver 1972.

Θεόφιλος Δημητρίου Μᾶρκος, or Δημήτριος Μητροδώρου Πλουτίων. It is not easy to imagine that the name Μᾶρκος is used as a *nomen* or *cognomen*. The mention of just a simple name, as for example Τρόφιμος or Τρύφων, usually indicates a slave status. For the names of women this is less frequently so, especially when they are mentioned in the context of a family relationship. Yet in some cases real slaves are indicated.

To demonstrate how this system in all its complications is used in Ephesus, I will give one example of an inscription of *kouretes* (IV-1010):

ἐπὶ πρυτάνεως Τιβερίου Κλαυδίου Νυσίου υἱου Κυρεινα Νυσίου	three *nomina* + name of the father + name of the φυλή; certainly a Roman citizen
κουρῆτες εὐσεβεῖς·	
Θεόφιλος Μενάνδρου	name + name of the father; Greek name system
Λυσίμαχος (Λυσιμάχου) τοῦ Λευκίου Μουνδίκιος ἀγνεάρχης διὰ βίου	two *nomina* + name of the father and grandfather; combination of the Greek and Roman systems; Roman citizenship ?
Λεύκιος Μούκιος Μενεκράτης,	three *nomina*; Latin system; Roman citizenship probable
Μᾶρκος Γεριλλανὸς Ἀλοφόρος	three *nomina*; Latin system; Roman citizenship probable
Εἰκατίδας Ἡρώδου τοῦ Ἀρτεμιδώρου	name + name of the father and grandfather; Greek
Μᾶρκος Λωρέντιος Ἀγαθόπους	three *nomina*; Latin system; Roman citizenship probable
Μᾶρκος ἱεροσκόπος	one *nomen*; probably a slave
Μηνόδοτος ἱεροκῆρυξ	one *nomen*; probably a slave
Ἀττικὸς ἐπὶ θυμιάτρου	one *nomen*; probably a slave
Παρράσιος σπονδαύλης	one *nomen*; probably a slave

These variations make it possible to analyze the used names to some extent. I distinguish the names of the Romans (from Rome or more generally those from the West) from the people from Ephesus. With the latter we have the difference between the Latin and the Greek system, inclusive of the problems mentioned. In fact, I have placed the people with a double name under the heading 'Latin names'—as also the persons who combine the two names with the genitive of the father's name. As long as one accepts that these people are not necessarily Roman citizens,[5] one cannot say that this is not allowed. The forms of these names contribute to the romanising of the Greek names. The group 'uncertain' is about those names which cannot be fully reconstructed and which, therefore, are not open to a single conclusion at this stage of the excavations. In setting up the archive I have used a fairly arbitrary method for these names. If only a few letters of the name were preserved—where it is also unclear whether these letters belong to the beginning or to the end of the name—I left them out. One can reasonably assume that it is a name, but one cannot say much more about it. The totals are thus relative: additions are always possible.

As for the dating, the presentation is not as definitive as it might seem. I use the names of the emperors as indications for dating. That is generally correct, but sometimes the dating is more vague: 'the beginning of the first century', 'the middle of the first century', 'the end of the first century/the beginning of the second century'. In my computation I have always taken the first date as decisive. In this way the indication 'under Augustus' contains the names from the period of Augustus but also the names which are dated by IE as 'the beginning of the first century', 'first half of the first century', 'first century'; the indication 'under Nero' contains the period 54-68 AD but also 'the middle of the first century', 'the second half of the first century' etc. Because this research is about a tendency, this inaccuracy is not all that important.

---

[5] Contra Knibbe 1981, 98ff and cf. the critique of Llewelyn in New Docs 1992, 147ff and Horsley 1992, 133 who warn against too quickly taken conclusions on the basis of prosopographical data.

	Aug	Tib	Calig	Claud	Nero	totals
Romans	33	9	1	11	32	86
Latin names	54	95		23	50	222
Greek names	55	48		17	35	155
slaves	7	0		2	4	13
uncertain	10	16		3	4	33
totals	159	168	1	56	125	509

	Vesp	Tit	Domit	Nerva	Traj	totals
Romans	12	5	16	3	38	74
Latin names	10	4	98	1	138	251
Greek names			29	1	31	61
slaves			6		5	11
uncertain	1	1	5		21	28
totals	23	10	154	5	233	425

To obtain a good overview and to show the percentages of the development of the name system of the inhabitants of Ephesus within these two periods—Augustus to Nero and Vespasian to Trajan—one should not count the category of the names of the Romans. We then get the following:

	Augustus-Nero period		Vespasian-Trajan period	
	names	percentage	names	percentage
Latin names	222	52.4 %	251	71.5 %
Greek names	155	33.6 %	61	17.9 %
slaves	13	3.0 %	11	3.1 %
uncertain	33	7.8 %	28	7.9 %
totals	423	96.8 %	351	99.8 %

D.Knibbe[6] showed from the lists of the inscriptions of the *kouretes* that historically there is a shift. While in the first century the relationship between the Roman and the Greek name system is one to one, in the second century this becomes one to two. When we look at the larger sample of names which belong to the first century it becomes clear that this shift takes place already in the first century. The relation between the Greek and the Roman system in the time of Augustus-Nero is about three to five (i.e. for three names in the Greek system we find five in the Roman system) and in the time of Vespasian-Trajan it is about one to four (for every name in the Greek system we find four in the Roman system). As an historical trend this seems clear enough.

1.3.2 *The indications of place*
Because only the *oikos* and the *polis* are important in a name, further indications of place are rare. Partly they are taken up in the system of epithets, as for example Σάμιος, ᾿Εφέσιος, (particularly relating to native citizens of Ephesus, but it is used also for people outside of Ephesus who win a prize and obtain citizenship in Ephesus), ᾿Αλεξανδρεύς, ᾿Ασιατικός etc. In fact, they always function as a *cognomen* in the Roman system.

Related to the system of indications of place is the mention of the φυλή and the χιλιαστύς for the Greek names to indicate

---

[6] 1981, 98.

whether and how one has become a πολῖτης of Ephesus, parallel to the mention of the Roman tribal name with the people who are Roman citizens. In Ephesus the φυλαί are subdivided into six χιλιαστεῖς (thousands). The names appear so frequently that one can put together complete lists from which one can also reconstruct the development and the expansion of the inhabitants of the city. Because the number of citizens is always increasing, there is a need for ever more names. Of the φυλὴ Σεβαστή (in the time of Augustus) the names of at least four χιλιαστεῖς are preserved and of the φυλὴ Ἀδριανή (in the time of Hadrian) at least one.[7] The readers of John in Ephesus will have seen the indications of place in this way: as (fairly inaccurate) indications of citizenship of such a place: Jesus as a citizen of Nazareth; Andrew, Peter, and Philip as citizens of Bethsaida; Joseph as citizen of Arimathea; Lazarus, Mary and Martha as citizens of Bethany, Nathanael as a citizen of Cana. The fact that several times in John a κώμη is mentioned, will not have left a deep impression in the *polis* of Ephesus—unless one is to suppose that contemporary readers hardly participated in "city"-life, or not at all.

Real geographical names appear in the list of the *cursus honorum* of the Romans who are present: in military careers especially, and we find quite a few of those in Ephesus, including two who were *chiliarch*/tribune of the legion X Fretensis—the legion which served in Palestine (VII-1-3032, Tib. Cl. Priscus under Vespasian; and VII-2-4112, Fl. Iuncus under Trajan)—but also in civilian careers, in which context the administration in Egypt is mentioned several times, but naturally also various other areas. This has little in common with the name-system in John, neither formally nor as to content.

1.3.3 *The epithets*
The actual system of name-giving makes the use of epithets almost superfluous. There are enough possibilities in the system to distinguish and to prevent confusion. But they are not completely absent. Three linguistic forms are used:
    —to the name is added   ὁ καὶ + the added name: ὁ καὶ Ἐφέσιος (III-688);   ὁ καὶ [Σε]κοῦννδος or [Ἰου]κοῦνδος (IV-

---

[7] Knibbe RE Suppl s.v. Ephesus, 275ff.

1015); ὁ καὶ Ἀρτεμιδῶρος (VII-1-3005); ὁ καὶ Ἰσχυρίων (VII-2-4113). In John this system does not exist.

—to the name another apposition is added: e.g. νεώτερος (in IV-1028); or γεραιός (in III-907), but also, as already mentioned, determinations of place such as Σάμιος (II-510) or Καρχηδόνιος (II-511) which practically function as *cognomen*. This form does not appear in John either.

—to the name is added ὁ (καλούμενος) + the epithet: Tiberios Klaudios Agathopous ὁ Ἀλεξᾶ (IV-1012); Asklas Artemōnos ὁ καλούμενος Τρόφιμος (IV-1005). It is a form which we see several times in John: with the name Thomas which several times carries as addition ὁ λεγόμενος Δίδυμος; with the Mary, who in distinction from the other Mary is called ἡ Μαγδαληνή; with the one Judas who needs to be distinguished from the other Judas οὐχ ὁ Ἰσκαριώτης and with Simon Peter to whom Jesus says: κληθήσῃ Κηφᾶς; maybe the disciple for whom there is always the special apposition—ὃν ἠγάπα ὁ Ἰησοῦς—also belongs in this scheme. It is surprising that in John Πέτρος is never seen as an added name in contradistinction to e.g. Matt. 4:18; 10:2; Luke 6:14; Acts 10:5,18,32; 11:13. In John there is a continuous exchange between the names Σίμων, Σίμων Πέτρος, Πέτρος and ὁ Πέτρος. Finally, one might ask whether the name Ἰησοῦς Χριστός, which is used twice (Jn 1:18 and 17:3), belongs here too. The combination makes clear anyway that Χριστός is not just a title but has become also a name so that—just like Simon Peter—Jesus also was given a latinising double name.

1.3.4 *The indications of function*

The reasons for the inscriptions—publishing the liturgies, recording the popular decrees, preservation for posterity of the name and importance of certain people etc.—ensured that a very large number of function descriptions have been preserved. The inscriptions in Ephesus show the fun people in antiquity had, to find for each function a separate name. Sometimes they are quite important functions, like the ἀνθύπατος (the proconsul), the πρύτανις (the presiding officer of the βουλή) and the ἀρχιερεύς τῆς Ἀσίας (the high priest of Asia): the yearly leaders of the Roman government, the city-council and the provincial temple of the imperial cult, but there is also the σπονδαύλης (a flute player), the ἀκροβάτης (a dancer in the procession of Artemis) and the ζυγοστάτης (the man in charge of weighing the statues which Vibius Salutaris had given to the city): people who play a simple but enjoyable role in the yearly processions of the statue of Artemis. It is a fact that only very few inscriptions do not give an honorific title for some reason or other and that there is an enormous variety (for the more or less 425 names from the Vespasian-Trajan period, there are at least some 100 different titles).

Two of those have some importance for our study because of the literal similarity with titles and functions in John:

ἄρχων

The title ἄρχων is used for various functions:

—During the neocorate under Domitian (89/90), (the) *archontes* come from different Greek cities to Ephesus: two *archontes* from Hyrkanis (V-1498); the πρῶτος ἄρχων of Aizanoi (II-232; 232A) and the πρῶτος ἄρχων of Philadelphia (II-236)—which seems to indicate that in these cities there is a college of *archontes*;[8]

—If VII-1-3157 comes from the early imperial period (—and the exclusive use of the Greek name system points in that direction), an ἄρχων was active when the road was built between Ephesus and Magnesia under M. Caecilius Numa, the procurator of Augustus (see also V-1799). But it is not clear whether this ἄρχων comes from Ephesus or from Amyzon;

—In an inscription from a slightly later time (III-710, the time of Hadrian), (the) *archontes* from Ephesus are mentioned. Two *archontes*, called by name, have a vote taken about the erection of a statue for Gn. Pomp. Quartinus, which is to be paid for by his friend.

All in all this means that, from the inscriptions in Ephesus, one cannot conclude that the archonate there had a function as important as e.g. in Miletus[9] where we find always lists of five or six names. This is not without significance for the understanding of John where ἄρχοντες (in the plural) play an important role in the acceptance and refusal of Jesus (Jn 7:26,48;12:42). If the political institution of the *archontes* did exist in Ephesus, giving direction to all kinds of

---

[8] Cf. for Aizanoi, Le Bas-Waddington II-860.

[9] Cf. I.Miletus, Südmarkt 230;231;232 p. 312/13; and Rathaus 20 p. 95-96.

decisions, the readers in Ephesus will have seen the connection with the *archontes* in John. One should remember also what meaning the character ὁ ἄρχων τοῦ κόσμου (τούτου) and the fact that Jesus won victory over him (Jn 12:31; 14:30; 16:11) has against this background. But if such an institute did not exist in Ephesus, one would rather have thought of 'leaders in general'—an interpretation which is common in contemporary exegesis.

Apart from this (city-) political meaning, there is another way to understand the title, a use which is linked directly with the title which Nicodemus carries in John: he is ἄρχων τῶν Ἰουδαίων (Jn 3:1). There are other institutions which carry such a title:

—IV-1122 (between 97 and 102 AD) where an ἄρχων is mentioned at the Balbilleia, the games instituted by Tib. Cl. Balbillus;

—III-719 (the time of Trajan) where L. Attilius Varus is called the ἄρχων τῶν ἰατρῶν;

—VII-2-4101 (the time of Trajan) where L. Attilius Varus is again called ἄρχων in the context of a decree about doctors.

The genitive added to the title ἄρχων, indicates how we must understand the genitive τῶν Ἰουδαίων in Jn 3:1: the Ἰουδαίοι are organized as a group led by one or more *archontes*. Nicodemus has thus been qualified as a very important man, especially if a connection is drawn with the Jesus title βασιλεὺς τῶν Ἰουδαίων.

ἀρχιερεὺς τοῦ ἐνιαυτοῦ ἐκείνου

In Ephesus high priests are mentioned on various levels.

—In the inscriptions which mention emperors, almost all emperors (except Tiberius and Nero) have the title. They call themselves "pontifex maximus" and in the Greek versions ἀρχιερεὺς μέγιστος (Nero is called ἱερεὺς μέγιστος in II-410). It is a title for life and it indicates that they are at the head of the other Roman high priestships (like those mentioned in III-695B and in I-17-19).

—In IV-1124, the well-known Olympic winner Tiberios Klaudios Artemidoros is called ἀρχιερεὺς ξυστοῦ. He probably took part in the Olympic Games in Ephesus—organized by Domitian and continued under Nerva, probably under another name.[10]

---

[10] On these Olympic Games see now Friesen 1993, 117ff.

—In the story about Ephesus in Acts 19, seven sons of a *Jewish* high priest are even mentioned. They lose the battle with Paul, when they meet him as travelling exorcists (Acts 19:13-20).

Common to the mention of these high priestships is the fact that the people mentioned exercise their function only incidentally in Ephesus or not at all.

The opposite is true for all the people who, as high priest, are part of the developing imperial cult in this period. Every year, a high priest is elected and/or appointed in the province who, in the name of the province of Asia, is responsible for the functioning of the emperor's temple. That means that, from the foundation of the temple for Augustus and Dea Roma in Pergamum (29 BC), every year imperial high priests are appointed. Originally these people are called "high priests of Augustus and Dea Roma". Later in the century they are called "high priests of Asia". The change in title probably has its origin in the fact that at that time there are more provincial temples of the emperor. Because the title is given for life, they are mentioned more frequently. Apart from the high priest in function, one finds sometimes mention of "the high priests" in the plural.

This difference in designation is not without importance for the interference with the text of John. In John's Gospel the 'high priests' play an important role, together with the 'high priest of the year'. The inscriptions in Ephesus have two ways of indicating that a certain person is the 'high priest of the year': via the expression ἐπὶ ἀρχιερέως τῆς Ἀσίας, followed by the particular name,[11] and via the use of the present tense of the verb ἀρχιερατεύω.[12] The use of this verb in the aorist indicates the past time.[13] A high priest is in office for one year only. Therefore, someone can be a high priest several times, as was the case with Tib. Kl. Aristion who is called τρὶς ἀρχιερεὺς τῆς Ἀσίας (II-425). We may even know how the rite of installation took place. In the edict of Vibius Salutaris (I-27 line 203), we read that on the first full moon of the year of the high priest a procession takes place from the Artemision

---

[11] As in II-234-241; V-1498 and its variations in I-17 line 68; IV-1017; VII-2-3801.2; 3825.

[12] As in IV-1404, a text which cannot be easily dated.

[13] As in VI-2063; in II-428 the aorist of the verb ἀρχιεράομαι is used.

to the theatre where a sacrifice is offered at a popular assembly. That could be the first official act of the new high priest.

That the title is meaningful even after the term of office, is clear from the honorary inscriptions in which a number of people call themselves high priest or are so called by others: in the honorary inscription by others;[14] on the occasion of their own activities[15] and in the genealogies of Tib. Kl. Joulianos (III-674 lines 4 and 6) and of the Pompeii (III-708). These are inscriptions which explain how other texts about the functioning of high priests can be in the plural: 'the high priests' who in Pergamum give a contribution so that the birthday of Augustus can be celebrated even after his death (IV-1393) and the 'high priests' who somehow co-sign the edict of Paullus Fabius Persicus (I-17 line 71). In Ephesus there are high priests in the plural and there is a 'high priest of the year'. As we will see in the following study, this interference between John's text and Ephesus is a very important one.

1.4 *John's name system in the context of Ephesus*

How are these data relevant for a description of the way John's Gospel is embedded in the city culture of Ephesus? We see a remarkable mixture of similarity and differences, i.e. we see a potential for reference which is present as well as absent. I think they each create their own literary effect.

1.4.1 *The literary effect of the similarities*
The similarities exist on various levels. Literally, when similar names are used: Philip, Nicodemus, Didymus, Andrew (maybe); or when functions are discussed which exist in Ephesus as well as in the Gospel as is the case with the ἄρχων Nicodemus and the ἄρχοντες; with the ἀρχιερεῖς and the ἀρχιερεὺς τοῦ ἐνιαυτοῦ ἐκείνου especially; but also formally when a known name system is used: family indications, indications of place and appositions. It gives concrete readers the chance to understand the story against the background of a world which is known and understood.

Further on I will discuss the meaning of this in relation to the way the political and religious leaders are embedded. Here it is

---

[14] II-428; III-688; 644A; VI-1061/2/3/9.
[15] II-424/4a/5/5a; VI-2037.

relevant that John uses the Greek name system almost exclusively (with the only exception—and that is not entirely sure—of the names of 'Simon Petros' and 'Jēsous Christos'). Looked at from the viewpoint of similarity, this means that the author links up with the people who use that also: those citizens in the city who are not Roman citizens, although they belong to an *oikos* and to the *polis*. The constancy with which this happens in John's text, is otherwise unique to Ephesus: even in the list of those making sacrifice to Dionysus from the beginning of the second century (V-1601/02), we find (exceptionally) Latin names, the same as, and to an even greater extent, in the lists of contributors under Tiberius (V-1687 and SEG 1987, 883; 1989, 1176) and in the lists of the people who made a contribution for the toll house of the fishermen under Nero (I-20) and particularly in the lists of the *kouretes*. It is clear that the author of the Gospel does not situate his narrative characters in the main street of Ephesus.

1.4.2 *The literary effect of the differences*
In a way one can say that there are more differences than similarities. This is certainly so as regards the names which are used. The majority of these are unknown in Ephesus. The names have their life from the fact that they are known within the own reader's group. For outsiders they must have caused admiration and possible readers must have been introduced into an exotic world where people have strange although recognizable names.

More important is the fact that the name system used is historically over the hill. As we have shown, the Roman system is winning out over the Greek system, a change which is noticeable already in the first century. For the literary effect this means that for the concrete readers the names which are used get a 'historical' meaning: a process that is unavoidable and which makes the story progressively less realistic and more imaginative: it becomes more and more a story from the past. In the city culture of Ephesus one can say that, the higher a possible reader stands on the social ladder, the farther away he or she is from the world about which John is talking. The story can then be more attractive, more interesting and more beautiful, but it loses in realism.

CHAPTER TWO

JESUS AND THE AUTHORITIES IN EPHESUS

Jesus plays a central role in John's Gospel. The demarcation which I introduced before, by linking him only to the place of birth and the family name, obviously does not do justice to the role which is given him in the Gospel. The name Jesus is a short version of a whole series of titles. A number of them play a role also in the city life of Ephesus:

—the title 'king' with important figures of authority from the past, some of whom have an ideological role in the actuality of the first century, kept alive by the relations which the city maintains with royal families from neighbouring countries;

—the titles attributed to the emperors: 'God', 'son of God', 'Lord', 'Saviour', all of which have their own ideological implications;

—the titles which belong to Artemis and which largely coincide with the titles of the emperors: 'God', 'Goddess', 'Lady', 'Saviour' and which keep the religious impact of the imperial titles alive.

These specific titles play a role in the story of John. They do not exhaust the titles of Jesus—but then, this is true also for the emperor's titles (see later) or for Artemis[1]—but because of the similarities they give the readers in Ephesus access to the text of John in the context of the political and religious life in the city.

2.1 *The titles of Jesus in John's Gospel*

Scientific research into the Johannine Gospel shows that the various titles used for Jesus in John's text influence each other mutually in

---

[1] Oster 1990, 1700ff.

meaning and function.[2] The titles are often given an explanation in the text which brings them closer semantically: Jesus as a king who receives his authority from God; Jesus as son of God who is sent to the cosmos by the father as an emissary; Jesus as *kyrios* in whom God as *kyrios* becomes visible. This technique creates a certain *Verschmelzung* of the titles which the individual reader must recognize, while at the same time he/she must be careful not to lose the feeling of the possible different meanings of the titles in John's text. That Jesus is called 'son of God' means something different than when he is called 'Lord' etc. This study, which is concerned to show the interferences between the text of John and the socio-political context of Ephesus, endeavours to discuss this in a special way. It focuses on the similarities and differences and in this way makes certain semantic fields operative; fields which independently of this contextualization would not become clear, or at least not in this way.

Regarding the Gospel the following data are important:

2.1.1 *Jesus as king*

Two different appositions are added to the regal title of Jesus: Jesus is called βασιλεὺς τοῦ Ἰσραήλ[3] and βασιλεὺς τῶν Ἰουδαίων.[4] Exegetes sometimes presuppose that the title 'king of Israel' expresses more clearly national-religious dimensions than the title 'king of the Jews',[5] while sometimes it is suggested that they are simply parallel expressions.[6] It appears that 'Israel' always has a positive connotation in the text of John,[7] while this is certainly not so with *Ioudaioi*. The ease with which exegetes separate the title βασιλεὺς τῶν Ἰουδαίων from this ambiguous use of the name *Ioudaioi*, is contradicted by Jn 18:35 where Pilate rejects the suggestion that he might have anything to do with the *Ioudaioi*; and even more by 19:14,15 where Pilate tells *the Ioudaioi*: "see here your king"; and "should I then crucify your king?" at a point in the

---

[2] See e.g. the studies of J. Ashton, J.-A. Bühner, M. Hengel, M. de Jonge, W. A. Meeks, F. J. Moloney.

[3] Jn 1:49; 12:13,15.

[4] Jn 6:15 (undefined); 18:33,37,39; 19:3,12,14,15,19,21.

[5] See Brown 1966, I, 461.

[6] See Culpepper 1983, 142; Carson, 1991, 162.

[7] Jn 1:31,49; 3:10; 12:13.

story when all the negative connotations of the name *Ioudaioi* become reality. I.e. when—in a negative way—the *Ioudaioi* are seen as the representatives of the cosmos representing deceit, lies and hatred of the cosmos, and when they express this in a conclusive manner by clamouring for Jesus' death as *Ioudaioi*, and when Jesus at that moment is presented to them as 'king of the *Ioudaioi*', it seems to me not simply self-evident that this Johannine title for Jesus would not carry some of the ambiguity which is attached to the lexeme *Ioudaioi*. It means that, at least in these texts, the author is sensitive to this negatively associated concept of the people: among the *Ioudaioi* Jesus is the king, but not with their support and certainly not on their authority.

2.1.2 *Jesus as the son of God*

The impression one is left with, when reading John's Gospel—that Jesus is called son of God on just about every page—is not based on the constant use of the title. Rather the contrary. From the concordance it becomes clear that the lexeme 'son of God' is used only nine times. Even when one includes the texts which speak about 'the son'—which historicizing exegetes would not allow, because language about 'the son' and 'the son of God' originates from two originally incompatible traditions[8]—one does not find more than 27 (or 29) texts.[9] The impression of such omnipresence of the use of this title comes about, because Jesus (or the evangelist) constantly speaks about 'the father' and 'my father' implying that Jesus speaks about himself as the son of this father:

> 'the father' 81 times;
> 'my father', together with the expressions 'his', 'our', 'your' father and the address 'father' in the various prayers of Jesus, 44 times.

---

[8] Hahn 1964, 307; Ashton 1991, 318.
[9] 'Son of God' in Jn 1:34,49; 3:18; 5:25; 10:36; 11:4,27; 19:7; 20:31; 'the son' in Jn 3:16,17,35,36; 5:19 (twice),20,21,22,23 (twice),26; 6:40; 8:35,36; 14:13; 17:1 (twice); in Jn 1:18 and 9:35 the manuscript tradition is not clear.

Because of the focus of this study I limit myself to those texts which explicitly speak about Jesus being the son. Some things are remarkable:

—In the text of John the traditional distinction between speaking about 'the son' and 'the son of God' does not exist any more.
   —in 3:16-18 and 5:19-26 the two lexemes are used interchangeably without a real difference in meaning.
   —both lexemes are connected with the important Johannine ideas:'eternal life' and 'glorification':
      'eternal life' in the texts about 'the son' in 3:16-17; 3:36; 5:26; 6:40 and in the texts about 'the son of God' in 5:25 and 11:4;
      'glorification' in the texts about 'the son' in 14:13 and in the texts about 'the son of God' in 11:4 and 17:1.
   —important—and literarily very interesting—is that both concepts are used by Jesus himself: Jesus who speaks about himself in the third person singular as 'the son' and 'the son of God' in relation to 'father God' who is his own father.
—This does not mean that the two lexemes are used without any distinction at all.

Exclusive to the lexeme 'the son' is the connection with 'Jesus-as-the-one-sent', 'Jesus-as-the-envoy-of-his-father': 3:16-17 and connected with this the transfer of the functions of God the father to Jesus, 'the son of the house':[10] the father gave everything into the hands of the son (3:35) and he showed the son the functions of king and judge and then transferred them to him (5:19-23).

Exclusive to the lexeme 'son of God' is the fact that it is used as a real title: as expression of the believing insight and the testimony of John (the Baptist) (1:34), of Nathanael (1:49), of Martha (11:27), and of the future readers (20:31). There are believing persons who confess that Jesus is the son of God. Remarkable is that apart from Jn 1:34 (but the text tradition is not totally clear: apart from the lexeme ὁ υἱὸς τοῦ θεοῦ, we find in the mss ὁ ἐκλεκτός; ὁ ἐκλεκτὸς υἱός or ὁ μονογενὴς υἱός), the title 'son of God' never appears alone, but is always accompanied by other titles:

---

[10] Bühner 1977, passim.

1:49: + ʿΡαββί; + βασιλεὺς τοῦ ʾΙσραήλ;
11:27: + ὁ Χριστός; + ὁ εἰς τὸν κόσμον ἐρχόμενος;
20:31: + ὁ Χριστός.

The argument Jesus enters into with the *Ioudaioi* in 10:22-39 about his name, belongs in a way in this series: "if you are the *Christ*, tell us clearly" (10:24) and "how can you say to me 'you blaspheme', because I say 'I am *son of God*'" (10:36). Jn 10:22-39 is a scene which antithetically prepares Martha's testimony in 11:27, where Martha positively affirms this double name of Jesus. It also prepares the accusation against Jesus in the proceedings before Pilate, where the *Ioudaioi* say that Jesus must die according to their law, because "he made himself son of God" (19:7). Jn 10:22-39 is an argument that even more than other texts makes clear that the title 'son of God' is not identical with the messianic Christ-title. It contains messianic connotations—the son of David as the son of God; the just one as the son of God; the people as sons of God—but it also goes beyond that.

2.1.3 *Jesus as God*
In the argument with the *Ioudaioi*, further clarification is given as to what it means that Jesus is (the) son of God. That Jesus is the son of God, contains a whole range of implications. It implies that Jesus belongs with God; that he has a divine origin; that he is God's equal; that he is God. Twice the *Ioudaioi* hold this against him:

5:18: The *Ioudaioi* wanted to kill him ..., because he was speaking of God as his own father, thus making himself God's equal;

10:33: We want to stone you, ... because you, a man, make yourself God.

That Jesus is divine, or is God's equal, or is God, is an implication of the way Jesus speaks about God as his father (and of the attribution to Jesus or the acquisition by Jesus of the 'divine' names: I am the life, I am the truth, I am-who-am; Jesus as king, as judge over life and death etc.). But Jesus himself does not come to that conclusion; i.e. he does not say anywhere, "I am God".

In fact, the Johannine text does not simply leave it to the *Ioudaioi* to give expression to these marvellous implications. Three texts express direct, literal statements:[11]

—1:1: the opening sentence of the prologue which, in all its illogical ambiguity, says about the logos that it is πρὸς τὸν θεόν as well as θεός;

—1:18: the closing sentence of the prologue which (probably because there are many text variations) addresses the logos again as θεός, "who is nearest to the father's heart";

—20:28: the confession of Thomas after he has seen the resurrected Jesus with the wounds and the open side: "My Lord and my God".

This last sentence is most directly related to Jesus and—from now on without contradiction—gives witness to the divine reality of Jesus in the circle of his disciples. How important this confession of faith is for the author of the book, becomes clear in the closing sentences: the beatification of the people who have not seen and yet believe and the sentences about the author's intention of the book. (20:29,31). Even if a whole chapter still follows, in a way Thomas's confession closes the book.

2.1.4 *Jesus as the Lord*

As we have said, one title evokes the other. Thomas's confession is twofold and links the God-title with the title 'the Lord'. *Kyrios* is, obviously, a name for God but it also has other functions: it is a mode of address in contexts of dependency and it is used to designate male authority figures in various roles (the lord of slaves; the lord of the *oikos*; the teacher who is the lord of his pupils). Maybe the title *kyrios* plays a role in other circumstances. This is a short résumé of the use of the title in the Johannine Gospel.

kyrios as mode of address:

It is the most used in John[12] and, obviously, mostly for Jesus. A couple of times also for others: for Philip (by the Greeks in 12:21), for God (by Isaiah in 12:38), and for the gardener (whom Mary

---

[11] Cf. Mastin 1975-76 as one of the few exegetes who speak about this reality of the text.

[12] 32 times out of a total of 51.

thinks she is addressing in 20:15). It is a kind of etiquette. The narrator plays with it, because the only time Peter does not use *kyrie* addressing Jesus (and he does it ten times in all) is when he protests against Jesus wanting to wash his feet.[13]

kyrios as authority figure

The Johannine text is part of the culture of the time in which authority figures were seen as *kyrioi*: the lord of the house who rules the *oikos*, i.e. the members of the family, the friends of the family and the slaves (13:16; 15:15,20); and the teacher who is the master of his disciples (13:13,14). It expresses the ideology of the time and gives the author the chance to verbalize some theological insights: that the fate of the slave will not be different from that of the master; that, if Jesus serves his disciples, they too must be willing to serve.

kyrios as name for God

Via quotations from the Old Testament, God is introduced a couple of times as *kyrios*: in the absolute sense of the word where *kyrios* simply means God: the way of the Lord (1:23); the name of the Lord (12:13); the power of the Lord (12:38).

Jesus as *the kyrios*

We need to understand the texts which speak of Jesus as *the kyrios* against this background. The texts are expressed in language which expresses a mixture of distance and nearness. That is so for the two times that the lexeme /the kyrios/ is used *before* the Easter events:

6:23: "from Tiberias .... near the place where the crowd had eaten the bread, after *the Lord* had given thanks";

11:2: "This Mary was the one who poured perfume on the feet of *the Lord*".

The same is true for the remaining nine times the title is used in the narration of the story *after* Jesus' resurrection: Mary Magdalene who is searching for *her Lord* (20:2,13); the disciples who see *the Lord* (20:18,20,25; 21:7,12). It culminates in the profession of Thomas who, even though he addresses Jesus, does not use a vocative but the third person singular, tempered however by the

---

[13] Jn 13:8 over against 6:68; 13:6,9,36,37; 21:15,16,17,20.

addition of the possessive *"my* Lord and *my* God (cf. 20:13!); and
in the statement of the beloved disciple—the only one from him: "it
is *the Lord*" (21:7), surrounded with all the mystery and wonder
which characterize the closing chapter of this Gospel.

2.1.5 *Jesus as the saviour of the world*

At the end of the Samaria story, the Samaritans speak in a rather
unexpected way about Jesus who is "really the saviour of the
cosmos" (4:42). As with the title 'king of the Jews'—in which the
apposition 'the Jews' has probably not completely lost its
ambiguous meaning—it seems not improbable that in this title also
one can hear the ambiguous way in which John looks at the
cosmos: in this cosmos which resists God, Jesus is the saviour. If it
is true that the Samaria story (apart from other meanings) imagines
that, for the period of Jesus' and his disciples' stay in Samaria, the
ancient unity between Judea and Samaria has been restored, a
restoration of the time when there was as yet no conflict and
division between the sons of Jacob, the faith expression of the
Samaritans points to a future which is still further away. The
restoration of unity in Israel in its ancient glory is the beginning of
the 'salvation of the world'. By his active entry into the course of
history, Jesus saves the world.

2.2 The use of these titles in Ephesus

This first presentation of the way in which people see Jesus in the Johannine Gospel, can be compared with the way in which in Ephesus people dealt with their political and religious authority figures. We find similarities and differences. This presentation of the question has determined the choice of material.

2.2.1 βασιλεῖς in Ephesus

Ephesus came into contact with kings in the course of its history in many different ways. To give some background and colour to the texts in our era which speak about 'kings', I have to dig a little deeper into this history, because earlier kings play a role in a late era, as happens so often in the history of countries and cities.
—Androklos

The figure of Androklos is a good example of this re-use. He is the legendary founder of the city. The tradition says that he is the son[14] or the grandson[15] of the mythical king of Athens, Kodros.[16] Even though Androklos is not called king in the extant inscriptions, Strabo gives as tradition that the "royal seat of the Ionians" was situated in Ephesus,[17] and even—and it seems he is then speaking from his own contemporary situation (first century AD): "and still now the descendants of his family are called kings (βασιλεῖς); and they have certain honours, I mean the privilege of front seats at the games and of wearing purple robes as insignia of royal descent, and staff instead of sceptre, and of the superintendence of the sacrifices in honour of the Eleusinian Demeter" (14.1.3).

From the inscriptions (and coins) which have been preserved, it seems almost certain that in the Hadrian—Marcus Aurelius period this myth about the foundation enjoyed a popular revival. A number of inscriptions can be dated to this era:
—III-644 (after 129): Tib. Cl. Marcianus is honoured because "on the day of Androklos" he donated oil to all the gymnasia. There is

---

[14] Strabo 14.1.3.
[15] Pausanias 7.2.5/6.
[16] See also Ephoros, FGH 70, Fr 126; Kreophylos FGH 417, Fr 1.
[17] Cf. Anth. Pal. 9.790.

no proof at all that this was a feast day "seit altersher";[18] from the
coins which are preserved it seems more probable that the feast was
of fairly recent origin.

—IV-1064 (Marcus Aurelius era): in a prayer for the *prytanis*
Tullia, the demon of the "city of Androklos" is invoked;[19] i.e.
Ephesus and Androklos are seen as a personal unity;

—VII-1-3079 (after 129): the union of traders, called Androkleidai,
erect a statue for P. Vedius Papianus; are these Androkleidai the
same as the βασιλεῖς from the Strabo-text?

—It is probably necessary to link these texts with statues erected in
this period: the statue of Antinous in the image of Androklos,[20]
but also with the inscriptions on the statue of Androklos as a bear-
hunter which was rehabilitated by the city guards (II-501) and on
the statue in the Arkadiane street (II-557); on a mosaic (II-501A);
on a relief (II-557A); and on the relief on Hadrian's gate which was
probably added at a later time but which, not without reason, has
become part of this temple.[21] The coins, especially, indicate that
the myth of Androklos was revitalized in the period of Hadrian.
Precisely in the era from Hadrian to Marcus Aurelius a series of
coins was minted with varying images of Androklos.[22]

The successors of Alexander
There are many more king-inscriptions. In the more historical era
we find inscriptions of the kings who, since Alexander the Great,
have influenced the situation in Ephesus: Alexander, Lysimachos,
some Ptolemies, Seleucids and Attalids.

> —Alexander: There is only one inscription about Alexander
> preserved and it is from the period which is covered by this
> study. He is mentioned as a cult object in the curious address of
> T. Statilius Crito, Trajan's personal physician and "priest of the
> Anaktores (=Gods, Heroes), of Alexander the king, and of Gaius
> and Lucius, the grandchildren of Augustus" (III-719);

---

[18] Knibbe 1968, 68.
[19] Cf. the poem by Antipater in the Anth. Pal. 9.790.
[20] Inan 1966, I. 37; Clairmont 1966.
[21] See also Oster 1990, 1682/3, even though he makes no attempt at
all to date these inscriptions.
[22] Karwiese RE Suppl, s.v. Ephesus 335.337.340.

—Lysimachos: the successor of Alexander in this area and the much disputed second founder of the city. He is mentioned several times in the inscriptions but it is not certain that he is ever mentioned as king:

> —in the foundation-text of Salutaris a silver statue of Lysimachos is mentioned with the statue of the clan of the Tēioi (I-27 line 187; I-29 line 18), but it is not entirely clear that Lysimachos the king is meant here;
>
> —a similar uncertainty exists about the Hellenistic decrees about the way citizen's rights were given in IV-1407 and V-1464;
>
> —in IV-1407 the noun 'king' is missing and so it remains uncertain;
>
> —in V-1464 the person mentioned (Artemidoros Apollodorou) was an officer at the court of Lysimachos,[23] but in the published text the name and the title of Lysimachos have been added by the editors.

—From the ongoing history of Ephesus under the Ptolemies, the Seleucids, and the Attalids a number of names of kings are preserved in the inscriptions:

> —king Ptolemaeus Philadelphos and queen Arsinoe (II-199);
>
> —the Attalids Apollonis, the queen and the wife of Attalos I (VII-1-3408); king Eumenes II Soter (II-201; IV-1101) and king Attalos II (II-2020);
>
> —the enumeration of the genealogy of king Antiochos Epiphanes (II-203): king Antiochos Epiphanes Philometor; queen Laodike and king Mithradates Kallinikos.

—To these texts a number of other Hellenistic texts could be added, in particular texts about giving citizen's rights where now the names of the kings are lacking or are not sufficiently fully given to date them precisely (IV-1408; 1422; V-1452; 1453). They speak about kings and about services to be given to kings and services to be rendered.

Kings have played an important role in the political history of Ephesus. The last king in this line—although no successor of Alexander, but one who develops his policy from this ideology— is king Mithridates, about whose influence we find only veiled mention in the history of Ephesus in I-8. Originally, Ephesus took the side of Mithridates and murdered all the citizens from Italy who

---

[23] Cf. note to the text in IE.

were in the city. But after the capture of Athens by Sulla, the people of Ephesus quickly took the side of Rome (86 BC). In I-8 the city writes about this: "While the people remained loyal to the Romans, king Mithridates broke the pact with the Romans and tried to become *kyrios* over land which was not his .... and then the city fell through deceit and superior strength, the people decided to declare war on Mithridates in favour of the power of Rome and the common freedom." This turn-around did not prevent the punishment from the Romans (84 BC).[24] In the memorial for Memmius, Sulla's grandson in Ephesus (II-403; the time of Augustus), this Roman victory by Sulla was commemorated in a permanent and glorious way.

The presence of kings in the Augustus—Trajan era

After Mithridates, the political role of kings in Ephesus came to an end. As is clear from the above texts, this does not mean that there is no memory of it, especially when favours are to be granted: see the letter of L. Pomp. Apollonios, asking whether proconsul Mestrius Florus is willing to participate in the *mysteria* and sacrifices for Demeter and the Sebastoi (II-213, in 88/89 AD). The writer of the letter points out that this service has had the support of "*kings*, Sebastoi, and the successive proconsuls"—"as is clear from the enclosed"—(but, sadly enough, these are not preserved). Kings play a (humble) role in Ephesus in the first century AD. The awareness that kings played a role in the surrounding countries seems, therefore, to have been present. This is obviously important for the interference with the Johannine text.

In addition, there are also a number of texts which speak of the physical presence of kings in Ephesus. That will rarely have been without pomp and ceremony, keeping the awareness of a real kingship alive:

—VI-2018 (the time of Augustus) is a difficult text to interpret. It deals with rights in the distribution of water. Someone—of whom only the father's name—Σώπατρος—has been well preserved—is called ὁ καὶ αὐτὸς βασιλεύς. Is this one of the βασιλεῖς about whom Strabo speaks, and is this the reason why the editors of IE

---

[24] Magie II, 1103, note 36.

call him "priest of Demeter for life" in a lacuna? The name Σώπατρος appears also in other texts, but these are rather fragmentary and do not give a basis for further conclusions.

—II-565; SEG 1982, 1130; III-615; 615A; I. Smyrna 614; I. Tralleis 87 (first century): the royal family from Pontus. Many branches and several generations of the family tree of the royal house of Pontus can be reconstructed.[25] Some members of the family have left traces in Ephesus:

—in III-615 M. Ant. Pythodoros is being honoured because of his mother (Antonia, the daughter of Mark Antony or Kallinoe);

—in III-615A Kallinoe, Chairemon's mother, is honoured as priestess of Artemis;

—in II-565 we find the inscription about the famous bust of Pythodoris, the last known member of the family. Because the face is so manly, the female name does not seem very certain and people have even thought it might be a fake.[26]

Notwithstanding all this hesitation about the texts, we may take it for granted that throughout the whole of the century there was contact between Ephesus and the kingdom of Pontus. From the fact that the priesthood of Artemis was given to a member of the family, it appears at least that the city did what it could to maintain this contact and to strengthen it by granting favours.

—V-1537 (the time of Vespasian) is in a way the closest text to the history reported in the Johannine text. It is an act of homage by the council and the people of Ephesus (this mode of address makes clear that it happened before the neocorate under Domitian) for G. Julius Agrippa, king Alexander's son, because of his εὔνοια for the city. In this family too, many kings play a role. Alexander was made king of Cetis in Cilicia by Vespasian. He married Jotape, the daughter of the king of Commagene. He was the son of Tigranes, the king of Armenia and, not unimportant, he was the grandson of yet another Alexander, who himself is the grandson of Herod the Great, the king of all Palestine.[27]

Josephus remarks that this branch of the family set aside contact with the Jews in favour of Greek customs (Ant. 18.141), but in our

---

[25] See esp. the notes in I. Smyrna 614 and I. Tralleis 87.
[26] Inan 1977, II, 129.
[27] Jos. Ant. 18.138-40; Halfmann 1979, 119 nr. 25.

discussion it is important to remember that king Herod himself[28] played an important role in the history of the survival of the Jewish community in Asia, and especially in Ephesus. In 14 BC he followed Agrippa, the son-in-law of Augustus and the governor of Asia, not without political intentions and probably not empty-handed: "and many indeed in every city were the benefactions bestowed by the king on applicants in accordance with their needs".[29] In Samos, the last stop on this shared journey,[30] the rhetor Nicolas of Damascus spoke in favour of the Jews in Asia, "in the presence of the Roman officials and kings and persons in authority". This speech was very important, because it laid down in writing many decrees in favour of the Jews in Asia, in Cyrene, and also and especially in Ephesus.[31] Herod's journey to Asia was extremely important to the Jews and many of the formulations in Nicolas' speech can be found also in the decrees of the Roman authorities. Maybe this says more about Josephus' influence on the words of Nicolas than it does about Nicolas' historical speech. It does, however, show what people at the end of the century were thinking about rights acquired by Jews.

2.2.2 The titles of the emperor
ὁ υἱὸς τοῦ θεοῦ; θεός; κύριος; σωτήρ

Every emperor has his own identifying titles. Indeed, in the case of some defective inscriptions very often the emperor can be identified by the titles which still remain visible. Functions are mentioned which are sometimes for life such as the titles αὐτοκράτωρ, ἀρχιερεὺς μέγιστος, καῖσαρ, πατὴρ πατρίδος, σεβαστός, and τειμητής διηνεκής (=censor; in Ephesus it is only used by Domitian) and which are sometimes linked to a certain time such as the titles αὐτοκρατώρ τὸ α', δημαρχικῆς ἐξουσίας τὸ α', ὕπατος τὸ α', in which the τὸ α' is the variable which indicates how many times one has been honoured in Rome as imperator and how many times one has had the function of tribune and consul. Proper names

---

[28] 'King of the Jews' according to Jos. Ant. 16.311.
[29] Jos. Ant. 16,24; cf. Jos. Ant. 16.146ff.
[30] For the journey, see Halfmann 1986, 163ff.
[31] Jos. Ant. 16.31ff and 16.167; 16.172.

are the ones which the emperors assume after a victory or when they have won some territory: Brittanicus and Germanicus in the case of Claudius, Germanicus in the case of Nero and Domitian, a whole series in the case of Trajan: Germanicus, Dacicus, Optimus, Parthicus,[32] or in the case of Hadrian the Zeus-titles Olympios, Sotēr, Panionios and Panhellenios. All these titles recur regularly; they are not unimportant for the dating of inscriptions; they were certainly protected and regulated via the imperial local administration headed by the proconsul.

Much more important for the context in which this is being discussed—the possible interferences with the Johannine text—is the way in which the relationship with the preceding emperor(s) is expressed. Names are mentioned then: Augustus, the son of Caesar; Hadrian, the son of Trajan, grandson of Nerva etc. Sometimes we find the addition that this deceased king was God; and then the present king may call himself 'son of God':

—Augustus: "son of God": II-252; 253; 401; V-1522; VII-1-3006; 3409; VII-2-3825 (each time without mentioning that it is about Caesar);
—Nero: "son of God Claudius and descendant of God Caesar Augustus": V-1834; "son of God Claudius": SEG 1989, 1178;
—Titus: "son of God Vespasian": II-263B
—Domitian: "son of God Vespasian": II-263B (probably, but the inscription is fragmentary);
—Trajan: "son of God Nerva": II-470; 660C; V-1500;
—Hadrian: "son of God Trajan and grandson of God Nerva": II-266; 274-276; 278; 280; 430; 441; V-1486-88; VII-1-3433; VII-2-4333/34; 5114.

That means that a number of emperors were addressed as θεός. This can be seen also in inscriptions of a different order. If people indicate their functions in a *cursus honorum*, they show that they were in service to an emperor who became God; or in honorary decrees they speak of a divine emperor; or sometimes also in dedication texts in which the preceding emperor has his own special mention as θεός.

---

[32] Campbell 1984, 122-133.

This custom is directly related to the performance of the rite of apotheosis when an emperor dies. It is linked to the cremation of the emperor and the flight of the eagle up to heaven. Cassius Dio (56,41,9ff) describes the apotheosis of Augustus, initiated with a speech of Tiberius:

'It was for all this, therefore, that you, with good reason, made him your leader and a father of the people, that you honoured him with many marks of esteem and with ever so many consulships, and that you finally made him a *divus* and declared him to be immortal. Hence it is fitting also that we should not mourn for him, but that, while we now at last give his body back to nature, we should glorify his spirit, as that of a god, for ever.'

Such was the eulogy read by Tiberius. Afterwards the same men as before took up the couch and carried it through the triumphal gateway, according to a decree of the Senate. Present and taking part in the funeral procession were the Senate and the Equestrian Order, their wives, the Praetorian Guard, and practically all the others who were in the city at the time. When the body had been placed on the pyre in the Campus Martius, all the priests marched round it first; and then the knights, not only those belonging to the Equestrian Order but the others as well, and the infantry from the garrison ran round it; and they cast upon it all the triumphal decorations that any of them had ever received from him for any deed of valour. Next the centurions took torches, conformably to a decree of the Senate, and lighted the pyre from beneath. So it was consumed, and an eagle released from it flew aloft, appearing to bear his spirit to heaven. When these ceremonies had been performed, all the other people departed; but Livia remained on the spot for five days in company with the most prominent knights, and then gathered up his bones and placed them in his tomb. (transl. Hannestad 1986, 94/95).

As appears from Herodianus' description of Severus' apotheosis by Caracalla (IV.2), the custom remains through the whole of the imperial period. In Ephesus the frieze of the main altar of the Antonines gives a pictorial version of this event. It is the

Apotheosis Divi Traiani et Divae Plotinae. Vermeule[33] describes this work of art in this way:

> The cuirassed imperator mounts the quadriga of torch-bearing Helios who, with parazonium-bearing Virtus, leads the procession. Nike helps the imperator to mount. Tellus, accompanied by a child with a cloak of fruits, reclines beneath; she holds her characteristic cornucopia ... Hadrian, Antoninus Pius, Lucius Verus and Marcus Antonius take the votes for the reign ...Sabina and Faustina are portrayed as the goddesses Hera and Demeter... Plotina, the wife of Trajan as Artemis-Selene, in short hunting garb, steps into a chariot drawn by two stags. She is conducted by Hesperos who flies at her left, in the background. At the right and beneath the biga, Oceana (Thalassa) reclines to the left, with a rudder in her left arm. She leans on a marine monster, who swims to the right...

The relief can be admired in the Kunsthistorisches Museum in Vienna and it was undoubtedly erected in opposition to the altar of Zeus in Pergamum of which it has copied not only the style but also the imagery.[34] The frieze makes clear, in any case, that in Ephesus the divinization of the emperor was seen as an important political issue through to the middle of the second century.

As we said, this finds expression in Ephesus in the first century in a number of inscriptions. I give the list in historical sequence:

Augustus is called God:
—in the decree of the high priests of the emperor's temple in Pergamum concerning the celebration of his birthday after his death (IV-1393);
—in the decree concerning the celebration of the birthday of Tiberius in the time of Claudius, in the titles of the high priest G.I. Anaxagoras (in the more probable supposition that he is ἀγωνοθέτης of 'God Augustus Zeus' and that this is not about Tiberius: VII-2-3801.2);

---

[33] 1968, 109ff.
[34] Schober 1951; Schmidt 1961; for a more critical evaluation of the image in Ephesus, see Hannestad 1986, 201-204.

—in the edict of Paullus Fabius Persicus, again in the time of Claudius (I-17 line 41; 57; 58; I-18D line 14);
—in the honorary inscription for Ti. Cl. Balbillus of the time of Nero or later, who had some function in the *aedium divi Augusti* (if this is Augustus and not Claudius VII-1-3042);
—in the foundation text of Vibius Salutaris under Trajan (I-28: a statue of God Augustus).

Claudius is called God:
—in the *cursus honorum* of Ti. Cl. Balbillus: "ad legationes et respon[sa] divi Claudi"; "donis donato in triumpho a divo Claudio" (VII-1-3042);
—in the text on the south wall of the agora, dedicated to Artemis Ephesia and the God Claudius, to Nero, Agrippina and the city of Ephesus (VII-1-3003);
—in the *cursus honorum* of C. Rutilius Gallicus in the time of Vespasian: "legatus divi Claudi" (III-715);
—in the *cursus honorum* of M. Helvius Geminus of whom it is said on his tomb that he is "adlectus inter patricios a divo Claudio" (III-683);
—in the inscription for [   ] Arnesia, procurator of the God Claudius; and of Nero, the son of the God Claudius (SEG 1989, 1178).

Vespasian receives the title of God:
—in most inscriptions which deal with the neocorate under Domitian in the version after his 'condamnatio memoriae' (II-232, 233, 235, 237, 238, 240, 241, 242; V-1498; VI-2048);
—on the equestrian statue of Celsus Polemaeanus (or of Tib. Aquila, resp. of Hadrian) who calls himself in his *cursus honorum* πρεσβευτὴς Θεοῦ Οὐεσπασιανοῦ (VII-2-5102/03);
—in the *cursus honorum* of (probably) Gn. Pompeius [...] who is called νεωκόρος ναοῦ Θεοῦ Οὐεσπασιανοῦ (VII-1-3038);
—in a much later inscription about the family of the Pompeii where the same Pompeius is mentioned again as νεωκόρος ναοῦ Θεοῦ Οὐεσπασιανοῦ (III-710C line 12/13).

Titus is called God:
—in the *cursus honorum* of Ti. Cl. Classicus, one emancipated of the emperors who has been with the God Titus ἐπὶ τοῦ κοιτῶνος καὶ

ἐπίτροπος καστρήσιος (a cubiculo et procurator castrensis) (III-852);[35]
—on the equestrian statue of Celsus Polemaeanus (or of Tib. Aquila, resp. of Hadrian) who, apart from having been *legatus* of the God Vespasian, has also been in various functions πρεσβευτὴς Θεοῦ Τίτου (VII-2-5102/03; in the Latin text the two Gods, Vespasian and Titus, are linked in the expression "legatus Augustorum divorum Vespasiani et Titi").

Nerva is called God:
—in the text on a statue erected for him—Θεὸν Νέρβαν—which probably stood near the Nymphaeum of Trajan (II-420);
—in the *cursus honorum* of Alexander Capito: "procurator Divi Nervae" (III-684A);
—in the *cursus honorum* of Tib. Cl. Classicus, the emancipated of the emperor who was under the God Nerva ἐπίτροπος ἐπὶ τῶν ἀπολαύσεων (procurator a voluptatibus) (III-852).
—in a fragmentary inscription L. Cusinius Messalinus is called [ ]ος θεοῦ Ν[έρουα] (III-660C).

Hadrian is called God in two inscriptions which speak about his temple—apart from the fact that he is honoured as Zeus Olympios, but more about this in the history of his temple in Ephesus:
—in the honorary inscription for Ti. Kl. Pison Diophantes who was actively involved in the construction of the temple for Hadrian: καθιερώθη ὁ Θεοῦ ʾΑδριανοῦ νεώς, ὃς πρῶτος ἠτήσατο παρὰ Θεοῦ ʾΑδριανοῦ καὶ ἐπέτυχεν (II-428);
—in the honorary inscription for M. Antonios Aristides Euandros: ὑμνωδὸς Θεοῦ ʾΑδριανοῦ ναοῦ (III-921).

Two observations are important. These texts call an emperor θεός only after his death, or better even, after his official apotheosis. If one asks whether they can be called thus while still alive, the authors give varying answers. In Ephesus the two following texts are relevant as far as inscriptions are concerned:

---

[35] Although Weaver 1972 does not mention him, as far as I can see, Ti. Cl. Classicus belongs to the freedmen of the emperor who made a remarkable career in imperial service, see Weaver's list on p. 273/5.

II-252 is an inscription which is made by the θίασος τῶν νέων, when Herakleides Passalas is gymnasiarch. Augustus is here called: "Autokratōr, Caesar, son of God, God, Sebastos, the Founder". The Passalas family is actively involved in the promotion of the imperial cult. In 19/18 BC Apollonios Passalas erected a statue of Augustus together with a τέμενος (III-902). This Apollonios is the father of Alexander Passalas who erected a group of statues for the family of Germanicus (II-257, probably 17/18 AD). From I-9N line 1, it appears that the father and the grandfather are both called Apollonios Herakleides. The question is whether either of them is responsible for the inscription in II-252. If so, this inscription is most probably from the time of Augustus. But this is not certain. If the father and the grandfather are both called Herakleides, it is possible that a son or grandson has the same name too and that brings us even further in time. II-252 cannot, therefore, be used to prove that, in Ephesus, Augustus was called θεός in Ephesus during his lifetime.

The second text (I-17 line 67) is quite different. In 42 AD, Claudius together with the Senate decided to allow Julia Augusta (= Livia, Augustus' wife) to have her apotheosis: "(since) the Senate and the God Sebastos thought that she ... was worthy of deification and deified her". Claudius is the subject of this sentence together with the Senate and, therefore, Theos Sebastos applies to him. Because the edict in which this is mentioned is from 44, there is a text which qualifies a reigning emperor as θεός during his life. I think that especially the title Sebastos is responsible for this 'promotion'.

This leads me to my second observation. A number of emperors are not called θεός even after their death: Tiberius (notwithstanding his temple in Smyrna!), Caligula, Nero, and Domitian. The last one is of more direct importance for the Ephesus of John. He has a very special aura around him. He is the first emperor who introduces the emperor-cult in Rome by erecting a temple for the house of the Flavii. Not only does he have a divine father (Vespasian) and brother (Titus), but he also creates the apotheosis for Julia, Titus' daughter—and his own second wife—and for his own son, for whom he has a coin minted which shows Domitia —his first wife—on one side and on the reverse side a child surrounded by seven stars, with the inscription Divus Caesar.[36] From Ephesus we also know of a coin where he presents himself on the reverse side as Zeus Olympios with the statue of Artemis in his hand.[37]

Domitian finds in a number of contemporary authors promoters of his divine aspirations:

—Statius in Silvae I.1.42-65 about his equestrian statue "led by the one star", almost flying "under the genius of Domitian"; in Silvae IV.1.1-5 in the panegyric on the fact that Domitian is consul for the 17th time: "he rises with the rising sun and the mighty constellations, himself more brilliant than they and outshining the early morning star"; in Silvae IV.2.35-39 about a meal in the presence of Domitian with his regal look;

—Martial dedicates his eighth book to Domitian with the words: "as part of my book—and the greater and better—is attached to the Majesty of your sacred name"; in 9.1.7 he can write: "the towering glory of the Flavian race shall endure, co-eternal with sun and star" and in 9.65 about the statue of Domitian as Hercules: "after that thou wearest the features fair of Caesar our god" ("pulchra dei Caesaris ora geris"); and, dependent on the dating of his various epigrams before or after the death of Domitian, he calls Domitian in an either positive or negative way "Dominus et Deus" (5.8.1; 7.34.8; 8.2.6; 10.72.3).

Later authors react to this negatively, but not without mentioning certain particulars,

—such as Suetonius who writes: "When he (=Domitian) became emperor, he did not hesitate to boast in the senate ... that 'he had recalled her (=his divorced wife) to his divine couch'. He delighted to hear the people in the amphitheatre shout on his feastday: 'Good Fortune attend our Lord and Mistress' (Domino et Dominae)... With no less arrogance he began as follows in issuing a circular letter in the name of his procurators, 'Our Master and our God bids that this be done' (Dominus et Deus noster hoc fieri iubet)." (Suet Domitian 13);

—and such as Cassius Dio who writes in 76.4.7 (Epitome): "He (=Domitian) insisted upon being regarded as a god and took vast

---

[36] Mattingly-Sydenham 1968, plate V.86.
[37] Karwiese RE Suppl 332; Friesen 1993, 119.

pride in being called 'master' and 'god' (δεσπότης καὶ θεός). These titles were used not merely in speech but also in written documents."[38]

Although Price justly remarks that the expression 'damnatio memoriae' is never used in the old sources,[39] Ephesus executes in its own peculiar way the decree which the Senate promulgated after the death of Domitian "that his inscriptions everywhere should be erased and all record of him be obliterated" (Suet Domitian 23). From all inscriptions the name of Domitian is either completely defaced or it is exchanged with the name of Vespasian; in most cases his title Germanicus has also been erased (but not in II-263A; 422B; VI-2047). If his personal name is not mentioned, nothing is changed (in II-508), a solution which also holds for the inscriptions after his death (VII-2-5102/03). As far as I can see, only one inscription escaped: the one for Tib. Cl. Clemens, freedman of the emperor (III-853).

Was Domitian ever called κύριος or θεός in Ephesus? As becomes clear from the Ephesian coin where he presents himself as Zeus Olympios, not all traces have disappeared, but the bad end to his life had a lot of influence. The title κύριος plays a not unimportant role with the emperors in this time. Titus is called that in II-412 and 415B—although it is an addition by the editors of IE. Trajan, certainly, gets this title in the foundation text of Vibius Salutaris in which it is said of Salutaris that he has "been honoured with military functions and procurations ἀπὸ τοῦ κυρίου ἡμῶν αὐτοκράτορος (I-27 line 16). The text is somewhat ambiguous. The expression κυριοῦ ἡμῶν refers to Trajan, but in fact Salutaris owed a number of his functions also to Domitian.[40] The religious connotations of this *kyrios*-function are clear from two inscriptions from Pergamum where Trajan is called "*Kyrios* of Earth and Sea" (I.Perg. 395 and 396). An accidental find in Priene proves that something must have happened to some texts. In a text where the

---

[38] Cf. Dio Cassius 67.13.4; see also Pliny Pan. 2,3: 'Dominus et Deus', and Dio Chrysostom Orat. 45,1: 'δεσπότης καὶ θεός'; Magie 1950, 576-78; Mattingly 1960, 146ff; Hannestad 1986, 139-141; Hemer 1989, passim.

[39] 1984, 194.

[40] See also line 25 and 150; in line 112 the expression 'our *kyrios* and emperor' is used in a more absolute sense.

evidence of defacing is still visible, for example in the title 'Germanicus', Domitian is honoured as θεός ἀνίκητος, κτίστης τῆς πόλεως, "God Invincible, Founder of the City" (I.Priene 229). We can take it for granted that Domitian played an important role in the city.

Perhaps, I may refer to the papyri in this case because they show how the use of the title *kyrios* develops historically. According to the dictionaries of Preisigke and Kießling, it starts with Nero (43 times), and it goes on in these numbers: Galba (3 times), Vespasian (58 times), Titus (18 times), Domitian (115 times), Nerva (17 times), Trajan (280 times), and Hadrian (492 times).[41]

Finally: the *kyrios*-title as an indication of the divine character of the emperor has a long future ahead. There are texts with this title preserved of almost all the succeeding emperors—whether they reigned for a long or a short period of time: Marcus Aurelius (III-665); Commodus (I-26; III-627; IV-1106A; VII-1-3056), Septimius Severus (II-296); Caracalla (II-299; VI-2026); Macrinus (III-616; 802); Elegabalus (III-723; 739); Alexander Severus (III-632; 557) and so on till the Domini Augusti of the time of Maximinus and Constantius. For the interference with the text of John, IE III-814 is especially interesting: an (anonymous) high priestess of Asia is seen in relation to the temple of *the kyrios* Hadrian, an absolute use of the term which is not unknown in Johannine circles.

There is something special with the title σωτήρ. In Greek and Hellenistic history it is a title which belongs to Zeus from time immemorial; which has been appropriated by the Ptolemies and the Seleucids; and which in Roman times is used for individual Roman commanding officers. In Ephesus there are inscriptions in honour of Zeus Soter as well as in honour of Roman commanders.

To begin with the latter: it is remarkable that precisely in the era which we are studying, the title does not appear. The inscriptions which are found, belong to the time of Julius Caesar and the beginning of the reign of Augustus and, then, to the time of Hadrian:

---

[41] Therefore, it seems as if the single use of the word δεσπότης in stead of κύριος in Dio Chrysostom, Or. 45,1 is ideologically influenced by the bad experiences Dio has suffered under Domitian.

—in II-251 Julius Caesar is honoured as σωτήρ τοῦ ἀνθρωπίνου βίου (and also as θεὸς ἀπὸ Ἄρεως καὶ Ἀφροδείτης);
—in III-800 a certain Gallus, son of Publius is called "saviour and benefactor" in the name of "the people from Italy who trade in Ephesus", an expression which suggests an early date;
—in VII-1-3435 the people of Metropolis honours Sextus Appuleius, a proconsul from the early time of Augustus (23-22 BC) as σωτήρ;
—and in III-713 the proconsul Q. Roscius Murena from the time of Hadrian (123/4) is honoured by the inhabitants of Neapolis in Samaria as "their benefactor and saviour", an important inscription because it makes clear that Samaritan interests are at stake in Ephesus.

It is remarkable that precisely the emperors of the first century do not carry this title: even more so because with Hadrian we find a multitude of inscriptions which do give him this title:
—σωτήρ πάσης τῆς οἰκουμένης (καὶ εὐεργέτης): II-271F;
—σωτήρ καὶ εὐεργέτης: V-1501; VII-1-3271;
—σωτήρ καὶ κτίστης: II-272; 274; VII-1-3410; SEG 1983, 943; 1989, 1212.

VII-1-3271 is very special (an inscription from nearby Larisa) in which, because of the sequence of the words, it is not so clear whether Zeus or Hadrian is addressed as σωτήρ: 'To Zeus Sotēr Olympios and Autokrator Kaisar', cf. the Zeus dedications in IV-1243: 'To Zeus Sotēr'. It is an implication which is really valid for all Hadrian-texts. He is venerated as Zeus (and his wife as Hera) and he is called *sotēr*, because he is a God who influences the life of the *polis* and the *oikos* in an active and salutary way.

2.2.3 *The titles of Artemis*
ἡ θεός/ἡ θεά; κυρία; σώτειρα

Artemis plays a role in first century Ephesus which is at least as important as that of the emperors. She has been linked with Ephesus from time immemorial and is still very much present in this era. The emperors link themselves with her; get involved with her (her right of asylum, the proceeds from her temple, the organization of her liturgies); they also serve her. Other aspects of this cult will be discussed in this study, but right now it is important to have a look at her titles. She has various names but also carries various titles which are semantically parallel to the titles which the emperors have appropriated to themselves and which in the Johannine Gospel are used for Jesus.

First of all we have the title 'God' which appears in abundance. It is remarkable that the title is used in two forms ἡ θεός and ἡ θεά and that they are used interchangeably. This is clearest in the text of the Salutaris dedication (I-27), where we see a continuous interchange without any apparent change in meaning:

ἡ θεός:
the statue of the goddess: line 271; 283; 353; 396; 462; 556;
the birthday of the goddess: line 275; 313; 494; 524; 535; 537; 539; 553;
the bearers of gold for the goddess: line 420; 456;
the sanctuary of the goddess: line 310;
devotion for the goddess: line 367.

ἡ θεά
the birthday of the goddess: line 224;
the adornment of the goddess: line 324;
in honour of the goddess: line 345; 385;
the sanctuary of the goddess: line 407;
a foundation for the goddess: line 453.

The other texts do not give a different vision in principle, even though there are fewer texts where ἡ θεά has been used.

ἡ θεός:
devotion for the goddess: III-690; 853; V-1538; VII-1-3041;
gifts for the goddess: II-274;
feast days for the goddess: III-987; 988;
income of the goddess: V-1522;
the holy herald of the goddess: III-708;
priestess of the goddess: III-992; SEG 1983, 936;
sacrifice for the goddess: III-859A;
the mysteria of the goddess: VII-1-3059;
altar for the goddess: SEG 1984, 1121.

ἡ θεά
the income of the goddess: I-8B, line 6; II-459;
the bearers of the golden adornments of the goddess: II-276.

It is interesting to note that in the case of the title ἡ θεά, more
than once (and never with the title ἡ θεός), an adjective is used :
μεγίστη[42] and μεγάλη.[43] It is an expression which we find also
in Acts concerning Ephesus: "the sanctuary of the great goddess
(μεγάλη θεά) Artemis" (19,27); "great (μεγάλη) is Artemis of the
Ephesians" (19,28.34.35). It is remarkable that even in this
relatively short text we find an interchange between ἡ θεά (in
19,27) and ἡ θεός (in 19,37) without a difference in meaning.

In a number of texts Artemis is called κυρία, never in an
absolute sense but always in addition to the name Artemis. Most of
these texts cannot very well be dated, but the use of the title in I-27
line 363 shows that the title is used from the time of Trajan. The
text is about a monetary penalty which is to be paid "for the
adornment of the kyria Artemis", if the stipulations of the
foundation are not followed. Perhaps, it is not by accident that this
text speaks about money which is to be paid to the treasury "of our
kyrios and emperor" (line 112). Artemis is the kyria of the
inhabitants of the city together with the emperor or, rather, the
emperor is kyrios together with Artemis.

That the title is used as a cult word is clear from the often
repeated formula εὐχαριστῶ σοι κυρία ᾿Άρτεμι in texts of neopoioi
(temple-officials) who express their gratitude for the fact that they
have been in service to Artemis (III-940; 943; 957; 958; V-1578B;
1586; 1588; 1590A). These texts cannot be dated precisely, but the
form of the names seems to point to a time between the first and
the third century. The formulas are traditional and prescribed, but
are still quite special, if seen against the total of all other texts in
which citizens only want to present themselves. The use of words is
linked directly to a number of New Testament texts.[44]

---

[42] In II-276, time of Hadrian.
[43] In I-27 line 224; 324; 407; 453, time of Trajan.
[44] See Horsley 1987, 127ff.

There is another expression which indicates something of a relationship which has been experienced. We have two texts in which there is mention of "our *kyria* Artemis":

—in IV-1078 which expresses the gratitude of a certain Eutuchēs for Hestia and the Gods "in the year in which our *kyria* Artemis was *prytanis*" i.e. when the expenses of this function were paid out of the income of the temple of Artemis. The text is about a religious festive meal in which his sister was *mantelaria*: 'a woman who brings towels or napkins to a banquet'[45] and at which he and someone else were the honorary host;

—in VII-1-3263 which speaks about a *neopoios* of "our *kyria* Artemis"; a text from which Christians later erased the word 'Artemis'[46] and so created the ambiguity whether maybe Mary became the successor of Artemis.

Finally, σώτειρα has twice been added to the name Artemis in a text of dedication to indicate that the goddess actively enters into the lives of people in a salutary manner (IV-1255; 1265). In IV-1255 an altar has been dedicated to Artemis Soteira and Agathos Demon; in IV-1265 the editors of IE question—because of the text of dedication: "to Artemis Soteira from the family of the Sebastos"—whether this cult was, maybe, erected at a time when one tried to prevent an attempt on the life of the emperor or a member of the imperial family (cf. II-296). The inscriptions cannot be dated precisely. In accordance with the use of *sotēr* for the emperors, a later date (later than the first century) cannot be excluded.

---

[45] LSJ Suppl.
[46] Horsley 1987, 128; 256.

2.3 *Jesus and the politico-religious authorities*

From what has been said so far, it should be clear that the various titles of Jesus do not all interfere in the same way with the history of the city. Jesus' kingship is interfering differently from the other titles, because different people and authority figures are involved.

2.3.1 *Jesus as king*

To understand Jesus' kingship as the Johannine text ascribes it to him, various aspects need to be considered. First of all, it is to be remembered that kings had played an important role in the history of the city and especially that this role had not yet ended in society as a whole. The revitalization of the foundation myth of king Androklos is a symbol of that. Ephesus was founded by a king and this is commemorated in coins, statues, and festivities. In addition, there are also kings in the present who want to make contact with the city and are being used by the city, if it seems advantageous. Kings belong to the authority figures; they are received with honours and they return honours. But since the time and the events surrounding king Mithridates, their political independence is fundamentally changed. Kings are kings only, because and in as far the Roman emperors allow them to be. Kingship is linked with the question on whose authority one is a king.

When Jesus is called 'king' in the Johannine Gospel, the readers in the city will link that to other kings who played and play a role in the city. Jesus is king next to other kings. The effect of this is reinforced, because his kingship is linked to the name of a country (Israel) or to the inhabitants of a country (king of the Jews), the same as other kings from far away regions: from Pontus, Armenia, the Commagene. Johannine history is about such a king from a far country.

More important still is the question of authority: from whom did he get his kingship? The background of Ephesus' history evokes this specific political implication of the Johannine text. Pilate acts as representative of Roman authority. Even if Jesus rejects this Roman pretence of authority—he (or the evangelist) states that his own regal and divine origin are more important for the truth—for the acceptance of Jesus' kingship in Ephesus it is extraordinarily relevant that Pilate recognizes Jesus as king of the Jews: that he presents him as such to the *Ioudaioi* and that he puts him on the cross with this title. This peculiar witness of Pilate is, actually, reinforced by the fact that the *Ioudaioi* and the high priests of the Jews do not accept this: instead of Jesus, the king of the Jews, they choose for Barabbas the bandit (18:40); they reproach Jesus that he has made himself king (19:12); instead of recognizing him as king, they want only the emperor as king (19:15); they protest to Pilate against the official title of Jesus on the cross (19:21). In contrast to the *Ioudaioi* and the high priests of the people, Pilate recognized, although in a negative way, that Jesus was king of the Jews in God's name.

2.3.2 *Jesus as son of God and as God*

The interference with the other titles is of a different order. It is mainly oppositional, because these other titles (son of God, God, Lord, Saviour) in as far as they deal with historical personages, are practically exclusively reserved for the emperors. Opposition exists, because in the Johannine text they are exclusively attributed to Jesus: not the emperor(s) but Jesus alone can lay claim to these titles, because he alone has proved in word and deed that he is from God. If we read this in the social context of Ephesus—but in this case it holds true for almost the whole of the Hellenistic area—we see, via these titles, a text which has a clear political meaning.

Let there be no misunderstanding. I am not interested here in the history of how the text came into being: that it will have been formulated under the influence of these emperor titles. My point of departure is, rather, that the origin of these texts should be found in the discussions with Jewish partners and against the background of Jewish traditions. But that is not to deny that, if the text is read by Hellenistic readers, semantic aspects will be evoked which were not originally foreseen: a monotheistic tradition which is confronted with a polytheistic culture.

Peculiar to Ephesus in the religious arena, is the combination and the association which the emperors make with Artemis, Zeus' famous daughter and the only divine protector of the city. We will return to this later. Looked at from the titles, this is about the homogeneity and parallelism in which the distinction between man or woman is unimportant. The divine qualities of Artemis reinforce the divine qualities of the imperial family. That is true also in reverse, because Artemis always follows the state policy.

One does well to note that, also in this regard, there is a difference between city politics and the 'policy' followed in the Johannine text. Even though Jesus' titles are rejected by the *Ioudaioi* and the high priests; even though they are placed in the context of the emperor's function; and even though Jesus is finally condemned to death, he does not lose his titles of honour. On the contrary, the disciples who see Jesus after Easter, reinforce the strength of the titles: Jn 20:28 is the only place where Jesus is called 'God' (and in the prologue by an author who is surveying the whole of the world's history); and only from Jn 20:2 do we see the title 'Lord' in rich abundance.

This opposition in the Johannine text to that which is witnessed and celebrated in the centre of city life—the opposition with the meaning of the emperor and the meaning and politics of Artemis—does not negate the similarities.

If we look carefully at the text, we notice the following things:
—The texts about the emperors, in which we hear of their divine origin and the divine character of their deceased forefather(s), accentuate more the fact that the emperor-*father* is God than the fact that the present emperor is the son of God. And that is true not only qualitatively. It has also a quantitative influence, because more people can appeal to that: not just the divine sons but also the people who have served the emperors in the administration and the army.

This is true also in the Johannine text. That Jesus' father is God, is said infinitely more often than that Jesus is 'the son of God'. This is a result of the way one thinks in antiquity about origin. Origin determines one's status and this is true for Jesus as well as for the emperor.

—The emperor-texts are very reserved, when it comes to call a living emperor 'God'. They take on divine attributes: divine partners such as Artemis and in the case of Domitian and Hadrian also Zeus; they take on divine names—as especially Hadrian, and incidentally also other emperors—but they do not call themselves 'God', although there are exceptions as we mentioned above. 'God' is a title which is given after their death and after the rite of deification on the field of Mars.

This also is true in the Johannine text. Jesus takes on many divine attributes: divine names and divine qualities, but only after his death is he taken up by God and called 'God' by the disciples:

Thomas in his final profession and the author of the prologue who places Jesus as *logos* in the context of creation and of history.

—In the texts of the Johannine Gospel, Jesus is presented as someone who in this cosmos stands up for the interests of the *oikos* of his father. He acts as representative of this *oikos*. In the texts which speak about 'the son' this is linked with the metaphor of 'envoyship'. Jesus is in this world as son of the *oikos* of the father-God, the envoy of his father. The father 'sent' Jesus to this world out of love (the technical words are πέμπω and ἀποστέλλω) to be his envoy in this world, a work that Jesus fulfils out of respect (the verb τιμάω is used), and that in essence consists in speaking the "words which he has heard from his father", and having finished the work he will return to his father.

In the history of the city of Ephesus, there is the memory of legations of various imperial sons who in the name of their father-emperor re-established and confirmed the absolute power of Rome in Asia: Agrippa, Gaius Caesar, Tiberius, and in this context especially Germanicus, the adopted son of Tiberius who in 17 AD in Colophon, near Ephesus, hears from Apollo Clarius that he will die soon—which is what in fact happens—and who was loved by all the people who came near him (cf. Tac. Ann. 2,54). Although I am somewhat hesitant about this 'parallel', the story of Jesus who, as son-envoy of an absent father must die for the sake of his father's affairs, is not without precedent for the inhabitants of Ephesus, whichever way one looks at it.

2.3.3 *Jesus as Lord*

The emperor texts show that the emperors in the second half of the century appropriate the title 'Lord' in its more special and religious meaning which links this title with the *kyrios*-name of God: Domitian who links the *kyrios* title with the title 'God': dominus et deus; Trajan who is called "Lord of Earth and Sea"; the parallel use of *kyria* for Artemis, at least from the time of Trajan; and the use of the *kyrios* title in later inscriptions, when the hierarchizing of society goes on and the emperors take an ever higher position.

The manner in which the *kyrios* title is used for Jesus in the Johannine text, is fairly well parallel to this. Jesus' *kyrios* title has its own religious connotations which apparently are valid only after his death and resurrection. That is shown in the multiple and unanticipated use of the title in chapters 20 and 21. That the title is

used also in Jn 6:23 and Jn 11:2 is not really an exception, because
these are sentences which are written distantly from the narration,
from a perspective which respects the Easter events. That Jesus is
kyrios, is part of the reality that God in Jesus' resurrection showed
that he is *kyrios* over life and death. Jesus' being *kyrios* is not
identifiable with the God-title, but it is not separate from it either.

This link is most clearly verbalized in Thomas' confession: my
Lord and my God (20:28). Mastin[47] believes that this confession
sentence originated under the influence of the emperor cult under
Domitian. I will return to this imperial cult later. For the moment
we can say that it is difficult to *prove* the origin, especially in this
case, because, so far as I can see, 'Dominus et Deus' from the
Suetonius and Martial tradition about Domitian is translated in the
Greek texts (in Dio Chrysostom and Dio Cassius) as δεσπότης καὶ
θεός but, on the other hand, there are the many papyri which show
that, from Nero on, the title *kyrios* is used increasingly (Nero 43
times; Vespasian 58 times; Domitian 115 times, Trajan 280 times,
Hadrian 492 times). Therefore, a (negative) reference of Jn 20:28
to Domitian's κύριος καὶ θεός is more than probable, although the
unambiguity of the reference cannot be proved. At the same time,
this means that the Thomas confession stands in opposition to every
emperor who calls himself κύριος and θεός.

2.3.4 *Jesus as Saviour*
This last title plays a very special role in the historical reception of
the Johannine Gospel. In the inscriptions of this era the title can
hardly be found. The title σωτήρ is no longer given to individual
persons or to members of the imperial family in the first century
and re-appears then explosively in the time of Hadrian. That means
that, for the inhabitants of Ephesus, this Jesus-title has little
meaning in relation to the emperors at the start, but that in a later
era—under Hadrian—the title becomes very important—again in a
negative way, now in combination with the enormous Zeus-
attributes which Hadrian appropriates for himself (and his wife). It
is interesting to note—after all, the title σωτήρ is given to Jesus by
Samaritans—that an important proconsul from this Hadrian era is
given the title σωτήρ also by Samaritans—the inhabitants of

---

[47] 1975/76, 46.

Neapolis in Samaria (III-713). So, in the Hadrian era, the text of Jn 4:42 receives, unexpectedly, a very real meaning.

CHAPTER THREE

EMBEDDING JOHN IN THE CITY LIFE
OF EPHESUS

The Johannine Gospel has few clues, if any, to put it in a social scheme. That is the reason that scientific exegesis paid attention only to the intellectual history of the text: mainly about the question whether and how there is a connection with the gnostic movements of the first century; how the Jewish scriptures influenced the text; about the question also how the history, internal to the text, can be reconstructed: the history of the text and the history of the groups with whom the texts originated. This study will not fill the gap but there is another possibility. From the point of view taken, we can try to show more precisely how the text of John interferes with the 'city life' of Ephesus. This study wants to begin this process through the study of some selected realities.

3.1 *City and country*

Connecting with what we found above under the prosopography, I want to start with a study of the interlinking categories πόλις and χώρα: the city and the area of the city as place where the citizens live and work. At first sight it seems that the story as told in John and the city of Ephesus speak about different realities geographically. Ephesus is one single, specific city, while the text of John relates a story of a journey which covers a whole country.

3.1.1 *City and country in John's text*

Wanting to draw a literary, geographical map of John's text, various observations have to be made:

—There is mention of a limited number of place-names, some of which are qualified as πόλις (Bethsaida 1:44; Sychar 4:5; Ephraim 11:54, and Jerusalem 19:20) or κώμη (Bethlehem 7:42 and Bethany 11:1). In opposition to Sychar which is qualified as 'city' many times (4:5,8,28,30,39), about Jerusalem this is said only in one single adverbial sentence: "the place where Jesus was crucified, was close to the city" (19:20). There is a distinction between the two Bethany's: one where John exercised his ministry "on the other side of the Jordan" (1:28 cf.10:40); and the one where Lazarus and his sisters live: "the village of Martha and Mary" (11:1); "close to Jerusalem, about two miles away" (11:18; 12:1). For the narrative setting Bethsaida, Nazareth and Bethlehem are unimportant, although the last two names play a not unimportant role in the discussion about Jesus' origins.

—Not without importance is the use of the word θάλασσα (6:1,16-19,22,25; 21:1,7). The question is whether in these texts one should think of the geographical meaning 'the lake' or the more usual Greek meaning 'the sea'. Jn 6:1 uses an unexplainable double genitive: "on the other side of the sea of Galilee, of Tiberias"; Jn 21:1 says it in the singular: "on the other side of the sea of Tiberias". In 6:17 the disciples go "to the other side of the sea, to Capernaum" and in 6:22 are the people who remained behind "on the other side of the sea", and boats come "from Tiberias, close to the place where they ate the bread". The people decide to take the boat to Capernaum to search for Jesus and they find him "on the other side of the sea" (6:25). That means that Capernaum as well as Tiberias are situated "on the other side of the sea", an expression which can be explained, if the sea looks like a bay.

In 11:54 the geographically significant term 'desert' is used. In exegesis not much significance is attached to this.

—That is different with the noun 'mountain' which plays an important role in various places, directly or indirectly. Near to the sea of Galilee lies, near Tiberias, the 'mountain' which Jesus climbs; where he sits down with the disciples; where the meal of the people occurs (6:3) and where Jesus retreats when the people want to crown him king (6:15): near the sea, the mountain. In the Samaria-story another mountain plays a role, the mountain near Sychar where the Samaritans adore God; different from the *Ioudaioi* who "go up" to Jerusalem (4:20 and the use of ἀναβαίνω for the journey to Jerusalem). This "going up" to Jerusalem is sometimes directly linked to the temple ("Jesus went up to the temple": 7:14), sometimes indirectly when ἀναβαίνω is combined with events which happen in the temple: "going up to sanctify themselves" (11:15); "going up to pray at the feast" (12:20). In fact, this evokes the image of a temple-mountain.

—The country is divided in three large areas: Judea, Samaria and Galilee, which have common boundaries (cf. 4:4). From the text it is nowhere clear that they lie on the (Mediterranean) sea. All three play a definite and different role; each is mentioned with at least one city; all three have a mountain which fulfils a religious function.

—More than this general geography, we see the characteristic that the Johannine Gospel is a travel story. Jesus alone, and Jesus in the company of his disciples, travels all over Israel and is also always on the road to Jerusalem. Typical for John is the fact that Israel is travelled in its distinct areas: Judea, Samaria, and Galilee, but also that Jesus and his disciples arrive in Jerusalem four times and experience all kind of happenings. Schematically it looks like this:

1:19-42: Bethany on the other side of the Jordan: the Bethany of John the Baptist (1:28)
1:43-2:12: journey to Galilee (1:43;); Cana (2:1-11; no. 1); Capernaum (2:12; no. 2)
2:13-3:21: Jerusalem (no. 3)
  3:22-36: Judea (no. 4)
  4:1-42: Samaria: the city of Sychar (no. 5)
  4:43-54: Galilee: Cana (no. 6)
5:1-47: Jerusalem (no. 7)
  6:1-7:9: Galilee: the other side of the sea of Galilee, of Tiberias (6:1; no. 8); the mountain (6:3); the other side of the sea, to Capernaum (6:16-59,60-71; no. 9); Galilee (7:1-9)
7:10-10:39: Jerusalem (no. 10)
  10:40-11:16: on the other side of the Jordan, the Bethany of John the Baptist cf. 1:28 (no. 11)
  11:17-53: Bethany of Lazarus, about 2 miles from Jerusalem (no. 12)
  11:54-57: the city of Ephraim, near the desert (no. 13)
  12:1-11: Bethany of Lazarus (no. 14)
12:12-20:31: Jerusalem (no. 15)
  21:1-23: Galilee: the sea of Tiberias (no. 16).

It is imaginable that the readers in Ephesus read this imaginary map in the following way:

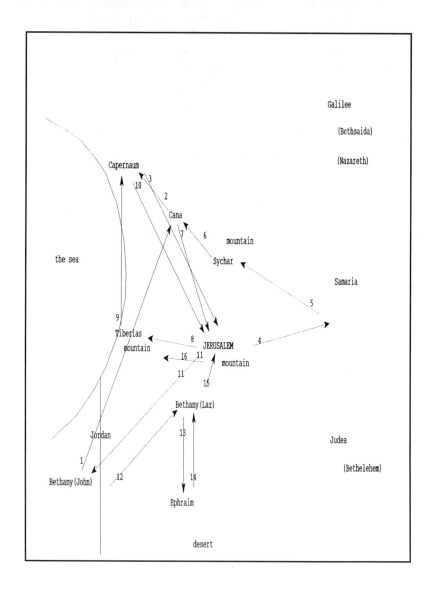

The main difference with the physical geography of Israel is the location of 'the sea' on the west side of the map and, probably, much larger than 'the lake of Galilee', to combine with the location of 'the mountain' of Tiberias near the sea. I have maintained more or less the north-south orientation. In itself there are no indications in the text for this.

Jerusalem plays the star role geographically. Quantitatively, two thirds of the action takes place there, still reinforced by what happens there. It is important to notice that narratively the journeys themselves do not take any time at all—apart from one exception about which I will speak soon. On the journeys themselves nothing happens, independently from the distance to be travelled. In the same way as it is said that Jesus goes from Cana to Capernaum, it is also said that he goes from Capernaum to Jerusalem. He leaves and right away he is there (2:11; 2:12 and 2:13). This is true also for the journey from Galilee to Jerusalem (4:54 and 5:1) and again his unexpected presence after this, near the sea of Galilee, of Tiberias (6:1; 21:1). For those who have no idea of distances, because they have no idea of the geography of Israel, all places are close together. The only real indication of distance is found about the village of Martha, Mary, and Lazarus: "fifteen stadia from Jerusalem" (11:18) which is quite close (under two miles); cf. the 25 or 30 stadia which the disciples were at sea before they saw Jesus (6:19). The just mentioned exception is the description of the journey through Samaria. Jesus arrives in the evening at six o'clock[1] in the city of Sychar; it is said that he is tired from the journey and that he remains there for two days (4:5,6,40). It is the only indication for the uninformed reader that there is quite a distance between Judea and Galilee.

All this makes it possible to read the Johannine Gospel as a city-story about Jerusalem which can be compared to Ephesus where people are aware that they live in a city with extended environs, near the sea with a bay, a beach, and a mountain, but where the city itself is seen as the most important reality.

Therefore, I want to have a closer look at Jerusalem to see where the possible interferences occur. There are only small indications which yet want to evoke a total vision:

---

[1] Probably, cf. Culpepper 1983, 219.

—the naming of one of the city gates—ἐπὶ τῇ προβατικῇ (5:2) which suggests that there are other gates;[2]

—the mention of two bath houses with the specific indication κολυμβήθρα:

—the bath house which is called in Hebrew Bethesda; which has a special miraculous power; and which is known because of its five galleries of columns—something which makes it at least into a richly decorated but maybe also quite large building, which anyway is clear from the mention further on of "the πλῆθος of visitors": a large crowd of visitors (5:1-7);

—and the bath house of Siloam where people can clean/wash themselves; which also has a special miraculous power and which the author identifies with Jesus (or Jesus identifies himself with it) by translating Siloam as "sent" (9:7);

—the mention of the χείμαρρος, the Kidron (18:1);

—the mention of two gardens (κῆπος):

—the garden on the other side of the river, the Kidron where Jesus gathered his disciples often, a habit known to Judas (18:1,2; see also 18:26);

—and the garden at the place where Jesus is crucified; where the unused tomb is situated which Joseph of Arimathea and Nicodemus use to bury Jesus quickly before the beginning of the passover (19:41-42; see also 20:15 where Mary Magdalene believes she sees a κηπουρός of this garden);

—the mention of the names of two places which play a special role in the passion story of Jesus: the place Lithostrotos, in Hebrew Gabbata (19:13) and the place of the skulls, in Hebrew Golgotha (19:17);

—the mention of two special buildings:

—the αὐλή of the high priest complete with a gate—with a guard and other personnel; where in the courtyard a fire can be lit by the servants;

—and the πραιτώριον where Pilate stays; there is an inner part and an outer part and people can pass from one to the other (18:28,33; 19:9).

---

[2] At least, if this is about a gate and is not meant as an adjective for κολυμβήθρα, see Duprez 1970, 133

—most important is obviously the description of the temple itself. Two different words are used: mostly the word ἱερόν,[3] but in the first temple-story, the temple is also called ναός.[4] I already mentioned above that the temple is presented as being situated on a mountain (a high place): Jesus "goes up" to the temple (7:14); the people "go up" to sanctify themselves and to adore (11:55; 12:20). The temple is a place of sanctification and worship. It is also a place for sacrifice. There are facilities for people to buy sacrificial animals and money for sacrifice (2:14,15). It is a large place: there is space to gather people around and teach them (7:14,28; 8:20; 18:20); people argue with each other (about who Jesus is or whether he will come (7:25; 11:56); and one can walk to and fro and then gather people in a circle, positively or negatively (10:23,24,31,39). Two sections of the temple are separately mentioned in John's text: the γαζοφυλακίον, the treasury of the temple which must be a large room because Jesus teaches *in* the treasury (8:20), and the stoa of Salomo where Jesus acts as a peripatetic teacher: he walks back and forth and attracts people (10:23). The importance of the temple comes to the fore mostly because of its ubiquity in the stories in John's text. For John, Jerusalem is the city of the temple. Every time Jesus comes to Jerusalem he goes to the temple:

—in 2:13ff to make sure that the temple will no longer be a market place;

—in 5:1ff to tell the person, cured from his lameness, who he is (5:15);

—in 7:14ff to preach his message: see 8:20 and 10:22;

—for 12:12-20,31, see 11:56; 12:20 and 18:20.

For the narrator of the story Jerusalem is a temple-city where the main character of his story often dwells.

3.1.2 *The interferences with the Ephesus context*

In a certain sense one could say that in first instance only the difference between John's text and the Ephesus context is important. The Johannine story plays in a strange country which

---

[3] Jn 2:14,15; 5:14; 7:14,28; 8:20,59; 10:23; 11:56; 18:20.
[4] Jn 2:19,20,21.

has only strange places: there are no Greek names at all. This is even reinforced when, in a number of cases, we find added in commenting sentences what the real name means in Hebrew (the bath house = Bethesda, Lithostrotos = Gabbata, Place of the skulls = Golgotha). On the other hand, the Hebrew name Siloam is translated into Greek. The literary effect in the context of Ephesus can thus be summarized as: somewhere else and different.

That is not denying the point that on a different, more general, level there are certain similarities. This is certainly true for the description of Jerusalem as a city. It is a city with city gates, with bath houses, with stoae, with a river in the environs, with several gardens, with neighbourhoods and places which have their own names, with special buildings, the most remarkable of which is Pilate's praetorium. However generally, Jerusalem is presented as a large city which presents characteristics one can find also in Ephesus. Archaeologically, most of it can be traced in Ephesus too: city gates, a large number of bath houses—which in the inscriptions never (or not yet) are called κολυμβήθρα;[5] there is surfeit of stoae; there are smaller and bigger rivers, there are many neighbourhoods with specific names and a large number of public buildings; there are gardens—as far as I know these are not archaeologically certain, but in VI-2328 an inscription on a tomb mentions a κηπουρός, a keeper of the garden; cf. also the description of the estate of Xenophon as a miniature of the temple and the temple area of the Ephesian Artemis:[6] "in the ground sacred to Artemis there are meadows and thickly wooded hills ...; round the temple itself there has been set a plantation of fruit trees which produce fruit to eat in all the appropriate seasons"; and finally, if Paul's letter to the Philippians was written in Ephesus, there is even a πραιτώριον (Phil 1:13).[7] For the Ephesians Jerusalem is a strange, but also a contemporary Hellenistic city.

---

[5] For the specific, almost Hellenistic function of the bath house Bethesda in Jerusalem, see esp. Duprez 1970.

[6] Anabasis 5.3.4-6.

[7] Cf. Schnackenburg 1991, 46 and Thiessen 1994, 118; epigraphically, the existence of a praetorium cannot be proved at the time of the first century; IV-1345 is early Byzantine; and III-737 speaks of a praetorium in Philippi!—but is also much later, from the time of Philip Arab (244-249 AD).

Most important is the similarity and the difference regarding the ubiquity of the respective temples in Jerusalem and Ephesus: Jerusalem and Ephesus as temple cities. Two lines show that this reality plays an extremely important role for the Ephesians.

1. The first line is the most direct but also the most limited. The temple of Jerusalem is for the Jewish inhabitants of Ephesus an actually existing reality of which they are reminded every year because of the temple tax. Josephus writes:

> But Agrippa himself also wrote on behalf of the Jews in the following manner: 'Agrippa to the magistrates, council and people of Ephesus, greeting. It is my will that the care and custody of the sacred monies belonging to the account of the temple in Jerusalem shall be given to the Jews in Asia in accordance with their ancestral customs. And if any men steal the sacred monies of the Jews and take refuge in places of asylum, it is my will that they be dragged away from them and turned over to the Jews under the same law by which temple-robbers are dragged away from asylum. I have also written to the praetor Silanus that no one shall compel the Jews to give bond (to appear in court) on the Sabbath'. (Ant. 16.168).

This decree is from the time of Augustus (14 BC) and clarifies a number of things. Relevant for our context is especially that Ephesus is apparently a collecting point for the Jewish temple tax which —because large sums of money are involved—attracts robbers against whom one must take measures. With the support of the Roman power this responsibility is placed completely under the control of the Jews.

In three places in his story, John makes it clear that he wrote his story after the destruction of the temple of Jerusalem: indirectly in 2:19ff where the demolition is mentioned; in 11:48 with Caiaphas' prophecy in the meeting of the Sanhedrin as the decision is taken to murder Jesus: "if we let him go on in this way, the Romans will come and destroy the temple and our whole nation"; and most directly in 4:21: "believe me, woman, the time will come when man will not worship the father either on this mountain or in Jerusalem": this hour (4:23) has now come. The past tense in the story as told is followed by the time, in which the contemporary readers and listeners live.

This reality is important too for the Jewish inhabitants of Ephesus. The temple tax is maintained also after the destruction of Jerusalem and the destruction of the temple: after 70 AD no longer as a freely accepted obligation but as a prescription of Roman authorities: the famous *fiscus judaicus* which must be paid to Jupiter Capitolinus.[8] For the Jewish inhabitants of the city the temple remains, therefore, an existing reality and every story about it must have had special meaning for them.

2. For the rest of the population of Ephesus, and this is obviously the largest group, there is another kind of interference. Ephesus itself is also a temple city. The Artemis temple colours all the activities in the city in a way which can very well be compared to the function of the temple in Jerusalem. That can be described in many ways but I will limit myself to two aspects: the double name of the temple and the practices of sacrifice and money. I do that because I suspect that—at least for this temple—there is a real interference with the temple story of John on the level of these two realities (2:13-22).

What is the case? Jn 2:13-22 is the only story where the temple of Jerusalem plays a narrative role. It is also the only story where the temple is given the double name ἱερόν and ναός and where a relation between temple and commerce is mentioned. Jesus comes into the temple, sees the business of the sellers of the sacrificial animals and the moneylenders. He cleans the temple of this commerce and says to the men selling pigeons: "Away with all this. Do not make my father's house a market place". This event causes a violent discussion between Jesus and the *Ioudaioi*: about the right which Jesus appropriates to himself; about the building activities in the temple and about the temple which is Jesus' body.

As I said, I take it for granted that these two aspects are important in creating a possible interference between this Ephesian reality and John's text:

---

[8] Cf. Jos. Bell. Jud. 7.218; Suetonius, Domitian 12.2; CPJ no. 160-229; Cassius Dio 66.7.2.; see Smallwood 1981/2 (1976), 375-8; Stern 1976-1984, II.129ff.

a. *The use of the words* ἱερόν *and* ναός
The temple of Artemis is indicated with this double name just as the temple in Jerusalem in John. For the period which we cover in this study, we have the following texts:

The temple is called τὸ ἱερὸν τῆς ᾿Αρτέμιδος:
—in the edict of Paullus Fabius Persicus (44 AD) which wants to stop the financial abuse and mismanagement of the temple of Artemis (I-18b line 2): "the *sanctuary* of Artemis, which is the jewel of the whole area by its size as well as by the ancient worship of the goddess and the munificence of the income—returned to the goddess by Augustus—is being robbed of its wealth..." (by the many abuses);
—in the foundation text of Salutaris (I-27 line 277: 104 AD) about money which is being paid to the *paidonomoi* (the supervisors of education) and to the children who are selected by lottery, because of the feast day of Artemis in the *sanctuary* of Artemis;[9]
—in the foundation text of Salutaris (I-34 line 23) on the base of the statue for the ephebes about money which is being paid on Artemis' birthday to the ephebes, temple-officials, the priestess, the bearer of the sceptre, and the singers of the *sanctuary* of Artemis;
—in a number of texts,[10] set up by *neopoioi* who appeal to the fact that they "took care of *the* sanctuary" (= the temple of Artemis) (III-947,969; V-1588);
—in the honorary inscription for Gn. Domitius Ahenobarbus —Nero's father—who in this inscription is called "*patronus* of the *sanctuary* of Artemis and of the city" (III-663, circa 30 AD);
—in the foundation of the sepulchre of M. Antonius Albus, erected by the city in honour of his merits for the city as "προστάτης of the *sanctuary* of Artemis and of the city" (III-614c: Tiberius era);
—in a text which speaks about restoration activities, probably in the temple of Artemis; the city council has met "in the *sanctuary* of Artemis" itself (IV-1384, circa 111/117 AD).

---

[9] In I-27 line 262, the ἱερόν is added by the editors of IE.
[10] Which, however, cannot be dated precisely; they are from the first till the third century AD.

The temple is called ὁ ναὸς τῆς Ἀρτέμιδος:

—in the foundation text of Salutaris (I-27, line 104), in a part of the text that exists only fragmentarily. Nevertheless, it means that the words ἱερόν and ναός appear in the same text (cf. supra);

—in the thanksgiving texts of the priestesses of Artemis, Vipsania Olympia and Vipsania Polla (III-987; 988, the middle of the first century) who have crowned with wreaths the *"naos* of Artemis"—perhaps meaning only a part of the building;

—in the text about restoration activities, probably of the temple of Artemis (IV-1384). Again both words are in the same text (cf. supra);

—in the inscription from the time of Augustus in which he glories in the fact that he has restored the *"naos* of Artemis" (V-1522; 6/5 BC);

—in the text of the foundation of the tomb of Peplos (VII-1-3214; Domitian-Trajan era), in the restoration of the editors of IE "for the adornment of the *naos* of Artemis"; in SEG 1983, 946, the text is restored into "for the adornment of the goddess Artemis".

The use of this double name, sometimes even in the same shorter or longer texts is, as far as I can see,[11] unique for Ephesus in the first century.

The emperor-temple of the Sebastoi (and later on that of Hadrian) is also called ναός, but not ἱερόν. The 'Domitian'-temple has the very special name ὁ ναὸς ὁ ἐν Ἐφέσῳ τῶν Σεβαστῶν κοινὸς τῆς Ἀσίας: in all texts of dedication at the erection of the temple[12] and in the Salutaris text (I-27 line 457). Sometimes τῶν Σεβαστῶν is not there, as in I-27 line 259 and in VI-2062; 2063. In later texts, the temple is called "naos of the God Vespasian"[13] or simply "naos", parallel with the name of the emperor temple in Pergamum,[14] and after the second neocorate implicitly in the plural—ναοὶ ἐν Ἐφέσῳ.[15] The emperor temples are never called ἱερόν, and that is remarkable to say the least.

---

[11] The word registers of IE are not completely reliable, but this is the only help available.

[12] II-232-235; 237-242; IV-1498 and VI-2048.

[13] III-719B; 710C; VI-1-3038.

[14] II-279 and IV-1393.

[15] As e.g. in III-810; VII-1-3017; 3080.

There are (a few) texts which call other temples ἱερόν:
—the temple of Zeus and Apollo (II-101-104; 5th century BC);
—the temple of Apollo (I-22 line 49; Antonius Pius era);
—the temple of Dionysus (II-106, found in the houses on the hills);
—(maybe) the temple of Asclepius (VII-2-4105; between 90 and 130 AD).[16]

There are also some texts which call other temples ναός:
—the naos of Demeter (IV-1210; circa 120 AD; I-10; 2nd/3rd century);
—the naos of Zeus, Dionysus and Sebastoi (VII-2-3757, undated);[17]

Except in one single text, the double name is never used for these temples. The exception is IV-1246: "following the prescription of the god he built a ἱερόν and a ναός and following a prescription of the god he dedicated (to the god) the sacred τεμενός". The editors of IE suggest to think of the god Sarapis. The succession of the words ἱερόν, ναός, and τεμενός shows that the words ἱερόν and ναός in this case do not refer to the same (part of the) building; furthermore, the probable date of this inscription is third century AD, so that this text cannot really be used as an intertext for John.

b. *The sacrificial and monetary practices in the temple of Artemis*
There is some interference even in content between the temple story in John 2 and the temple of Artemis. The text of John tells in a few short sentences that sacrificial animals are sold in the temple in Jerusalem and that there is an exchange of money. By telling the way Jesus acts, the story becomes very lively. It finds its first climax in Jesus' saying: do not make the house of my father an οἶκος ἐμπορίου. The usual translation is 'market place', but should it not rather be 'trading centre'? Against the Ephesus background of the temple of Artemis this cannot be excluded.

Artemis plays a dominant role in the inscriptions of the first century. That does not mean that there are no lacunae in our knowledge. For example, there is a clear difference between what

---

[16] The editors of IE suppose that this is about a temple of Asclepius, because the text mentions an aqueduct which leads 'to the temple'.

[17] The '*naos of Soteira*' in I-26 line 4.18 (Commodus era) indicates the temple of Artemis.

can be known about the sacrificial cult in the temple and monetary matters. The latter is massively represented, the first only in a general way.

The following data seem significant:

—From a (small) number of texts it appears that there was a sacrificial cult in the temple of Artemis:

—the thanksgiving texts of the priestesses of Artemis Vipsania Olympia and Vipsania Polla (III-987; 988, the middle of the first century) who each for herself had it recorded that "the mysteria and the *sacrifices* have been fulfilled in a dignified manner";

—a foundation text of a freed slave of Augustus who mentions a sacrifice for Artemis (and probably for Rome and Augustus) (III-859A, beginning of the first century);[18]

—in the beginning of the story *Ephesiaca* it is told, after the description of the processions to the temple of Artemis, how in the sacrifice (ἦλθον εἰς τὸ ἱερὸν θύσοντες), the boys and girls are in the temple together—where the two lovers Anthia and Habrocomes see each other for the first time and fall head over heels in love(I.3.1-3; see also I.8.1; I.10.5);

—very interesting too is the text of the Salutaris foundation, because it combines a sacrifice with a distribution of money. Different people receive money among other things in order to pay for the sacrifice. They must personally come to the temple of Artemis (I-27, lines 220ff and lines 485ff).[19] And if they do not do that, they have to pay a fine of 5 denarii for the adornment of Artemis (I-27 line 528ff).[20]

---

[18] If this sacrifice takes place in the temple of Artemis.

[19] Picard 1922, 86 thinks that this offer shows how serious the city's financial problem is; and he sees this getting worse in the following century. Modern archaeological research has proved that, at least as a generalisation, this is not true.

[20] This practice of mixing sacrifice and the distribution of money is not unique for Artemis, see III-690 (Trajan-Hadrian era) with a sacrifice for 'the gods'; see also I-26 (Commodus era) for sacrifices to Artemis and the emperor.

—I-10; IV-1210A[21] describes which rules the *prytanis* must keep when he/she offers a sacrifice. There must be 365 sacrifices for the year. The hierophant receives from every sacrificial animal the heart, the tongue, and the skin. The herald, the flute-player, the trumpeter, the overseer of the sacrifice (and other persons) also receive gifts. The mention of these cult ministers is interesting because they—next to their probable function with other gods—play a role in the Artemis cult.

It is a pity that the text does not specify which animals are involved. If is still valid in the first century what Xenophon said about it—he mentions pigs, goats, antelopes, and deer[22] as sacrificial animals—there seems to be a real difference with John's text.

The legal text of the sacrificial cult makes it clear that there is a real intermingling of interests. As can be expected this creates abuses, as appears from the decree of Paullus Fabius Persicus (I-17-19; 44 AD): priestly positions are publicly sold and everyone can make a bid; and priests of Artemis lend sanctified money to other people.[23]

From later texts it is clear that an organization has been set up to regulate these matters: the ἱερωτάτον συνέδριον τοῦ μισθωτηρίου, "the most sacred council of the society of hirers" which became well-known because of a number of inscriptions in honour of its own members in the second half of the 2nd/first half of the 3rd century.[24]

Anyway, it is clear that money plays an important role in the temple of Artemis. It is considered 'the bank of Asia'. What Dio Chrysostom wrote about it determines the image:

> You know about the Ephesians, of course, and that large sums of money are in their hands, some of it belonging to private citizens and deposited in the temple of Artemis, not alone money of the Ephesians but also of aliens and of persons from

---

[21] The text is from the end of the 2nd to the beginning of the 3rd century, but because it describes existing laws and rules, one can suppose that the content is valid for a much earlier time, cf. Knibbe 1981, 57-59.

[22] Anabasis V.3.

[23] Cf. Oster 1990, 1716/17.

[24] See V-1577; 1993; VI-2227; VII-1-3050; 3071; VII-2-4124.

all parts of the world, and in some cases of commonwealths
and kings, money which all deposit there in order that it may
be safe, since no one has ever yet dared to violate that place,
although countless wars have occurred in the past and the city
has often been captured. Well, that the money is deposited on
state property is indeed evident, but it is also evident, as the
lists show, that it is the custom of the Ephesians to have these
deposits officially recorded.(Or. 31.54)

The important position of the temple of Artemis is undoubtedly
connected with what Strabo writes about the city: "The city,
because of its advantageous situation in other respects (than the
harbour), grows daily, and it is the largest *emporium* in Asia this
side of the Taurus" (14.1.24)

From the inscriptions too, it appears directly several times that
the temple of Artemis functions as a bank. People bequeath
inheritance money with which the heirs erect monuments (see esp.
III-678; 692; 725 and 731) and even more directly in II-274, the
important text regarding the relation of the city with Hadrian. The
emperor is honoured in this text, because he regulated (anew) the
legislation "about the inheritances and deposits to the goddess".[25]
The temple possesses enormous sums of money which are used for
various ends depending on the origin of the money.

John 2:13-22 is an important text in the Johannine Gospel,
because it initiates the discussion between Jesus and the *Ioudaioi*
and because it gives a first description of the way Jesus relates to
the 'passover of the Jews'. From what is said above, it is clear how
the text interferes with the situation in Ephesus and how it gets a
specific meaning in this context: the double name for the temple;
the commerce in and around the temple; especially the relation
between the temple and the money transactions, in John's text re-
enforced by the relatively large number of commercial words (the
sellers; the money changers; small change; money changers of
small change; money tables) and by the sentence "do not make the
house of my father a trading centre", a sentence which is unique in

---

[25] Cf. the explanation in IE of οἱ βεβληκότες = depositores = 'Leute
die Geld im Tempel deponiert hatten'.

comparison with the Synoptics, and of which the exegetes do not know the historical origin.

Readers in Ephesus will understand the story from their knowledge of their own social context. They will, obviously, also see the differences. When Jesus, jealously proud of his God, is so enraged because of the commercial activity, which, compared to the temple of Artemis, is rather modest, how much more will that be when the commerce of the temple determines the social life of a city. And furthermore—and this is in a way the most important element in the Johannine story—Jesus says: "tear down this ναός and in three days I will make it rise again". And the *Ioudaioi* answer: "Forty-six years they have laboured for this ναός and you will make it rise again in three days?" But Jesus is speaking about the ναός of his body. From the very beginning of the book, it may be clear to the reader in Ephesus that the access to God, the temple as ναός, is not to be found in the temple as ναός of Artemis—or in whatever ναός—but only in the resurrected body of Jesus. That is the only ναός which will certainly make it possible to reach God.

3.2 *The social realities in John's text*

Apart from these more general similarities and differences there is also, on the level of city life, mention of more specific relations: social realities which from John's text interfere with what happens in the city. Again I will first mention the data from the Johannine Gospel.

3.2.1 *Work and ideas about work*

Work plays a minor role in the Johannine Gospel. Symptomatic is how there is silence about the way Jesus and his group take care of their daily needs. They are always on the move and one can suppose that they live from the money which people give them. Judas holds the purse, which is presented as communal—and the accounting does not seem to be above suspicion. Several times there is mention of the fact that the disciples go and "buy" food (4:8; 13:29; see also 6:5), but in the context of the story this "buying" is always subject to criticism: Jesus has other food (4:32); Judas does not go to buy food for the Passover but to betray Jesus (13:27); Jesus himself will give the people food (6:1ff). The care for the material things in life is always incorporated by the narrator of the story in his ideology about the more important reality of life: everything comes from God and first of all Jesus himself.[26]

That does not mean that John's text does not interfere in any way with this specific and obviously necessary part of the city life in Ephesus. There are some concrete work situations and functions and John's text uses images from this sector which link up with things which exist in Ephesus.

The indications of the functions and professions of people who play a role in the story
   —the men selling cattle, sheep, and doves in the temple of Jerusalem together with the money-changers, the κερματισταί and the κολλυβισταί in the first temple story (2:13-16)
   —Nicodemus as an ἄρχων of the *Ioudaioi* (3:1) who pretends to be a διδάσκαλος (3:10);
   —the βασιλικός in 4:46-54 who owns slaves;
   —the ἀρχιερεῖς who have an important position as the story unfolds and with whom the ἀρχιερεὺς τοῦ ἐνιαυτοῦ ἐκείνου (11:49,51; 18:13) plays the starring role;
   —the blind προσαίτης in chapter 9;
   —the χιλίαρχος and the στρατιῶται who appear in the story of Jesus' passion (18:12; 19:1-34);
   —the female θυρωρός to whom Peter is introduced by the disciple who is known to the high priest (18:15-17);
   —the κηπουρός whom Mary Magdalene believes to see at Jesus' tomb (20:15);

---

[26] It is interesting to see what, in fact, is being said about the group's food and drink. They drink wine (2:1-12); water (4:7-15; 7:37-39) and vinegar (19:29: the ὄξος which the soldiers have with them, when Jesus hangs on the cross; see Hagenow 1982, 122-125); there is mention of the eating of bread (barley loaves in 6:1-13; ἄρτος in 13:18; 21:9,13) and fish (ὀψάριον in 6:9,11; 21:9-13), a way of eating and drinking which for people around the Mediterranean is well known; in 6:52ff there is mention of sacrificial meat, in the well-known coarsely formulated sentences about the 'eating of the flesh of the son of man' and 'drinking of his blood'; for the combination of sacrificial meat and the daily diet in the classical period, see e.g. Jameson 1988, 105ff.

—Jesus himself is introduced as a διδάσκαλος. People address him this way (1:38; 3:2; 13:13; 20:16); or he is seen like that by people (11:28; 13:13); he sees himself in that role (7:16,17; 13:13,14; 18:20). Because on the level of the telling of the story there is also mention of 'the teaching of Jesus' (6:59; 7:14,28; 8:20) and because 'the teaching of Jesus' plays an important role in the trial before Pilate (18:19), the image of Jesus as teacher is reinforced considerably.

Work indications
—"undoing the bindings of Jesus' sandals", a work for which John (the Baptist) feels unworthy (1:27);
—2:20 says that "they worked for forty-six years to build the temple", which indicates an enormous activity;
—"drawing water" as the Samaritan woman does (4:7-15) which is told as not being easy work;
—5:10 speaks of "carrying one's bed" by the cripple who is healed, work which is forbidden on the Sabbath;
—in 9:5 Jesus "makes mud with spittle"; again an activity which is not allowed on the Sabbath;
—at the meals in Cana and Bethany, the service at table is proposed as '*diakonia*' (2:1-11; 12:12); at the last supper of Jesus and his disciples, Jesus washes their feet like a slave (13:1-20);
—in the passion story Pilate's way of acting is directly linked to his function. He acts as the highest Roman authority who must make decisions in a complicated juridical situation; who has soldiers and who, as judge, can take decisions about life and death and who can dispose of prisoners' bodies—Barabbas; Jesus and the two who are crucified with Jesus;
—does the embalming of Jesus' feet by Mary (11:2 and 12:3-4) belong in this series too? If so, then we should mention also the embalming and entombing of Jesus' body by Joseph of Arimathea and Nicodemus (19:38-42);
—in the last story of his apparition (21:1ff), the disciples who are present are presented as fishermen. A group of seven (or, if the beloved disciple is not part of the list of 21:2, a group of eight) is gathered at the sea of Tiberias. Peter says: I am going fishing. And the others answer: let us go with you. Because it is said that they were unsuccessful, it appears to be a 'professional'

trip. In the context of the ancient world only those people go fishing who are dependent on it: as professional fishermen or as a source of extra income.

The indirect indications

—Jn 4: The metaphor of the work in the field: sowing and harvesting (4:36,37,38) are presented as 'laborious' work: κοπιάω and κόπος are used, words which in Greek are used for manual labour as well as intellectual work. In fact, we find a mixture of images: on the one hand (in 4:36), the coincidence of sowing and harvesting as a eschatological-paradise-like situation; and on the other hand (in 4:37ff), the separation of sowing and harvesting as an apocalyptic event.[27]

—Jn 10: the image of the shepherd: he is a shepherd who together with other shepherds brings the sheep into the sheepfold. There is a (hired?) guard who is a gatekeeper. The (or every) shepherd takes his own sheep from the sheepfold. He calls them by their name and the sheep know his voice—it does not suggest a very large flock. There is a danger of stealing, and outside in the field a danger of wolves. The shepherd himself is not a hireling but he owns the sheep.

—Jn 15: the image of the vine and the gardener. The gardener does the work himself: he cuts off the loose branches and prunes the fruit. When the branches which are cut off are dried, there are people to set them alight.

—Finally, typical for John is the fact that the activities of the father as well as those of Jesus are seen as ἐργάζομαι (5:17; 9:4): a word which also originates in the agrarian culture. The real 'work' of Jesus (ἔργον is the word used) is to be *ben bait*: the son of the house who must reveal himself as the messenger of his father, as we explained in the last chapter. He has the obligation to "speak in the name of his father" and "to give an account of this to the father". Because he wants to do this "work", Jesus is crucified as

---

[27] The interpretation of these texts is not unanimous: see e.g. Brown 1966, I, 181ff and the commentary on this by Olsson 1974, 241ff who accentuates especially the Samaria connection; by Okure 1988, 132ff who does not see 'a coincidence of the time for sowing and the time for harvesting' and by Botha 1991, 168ff who interprets the apocalyptic reading of the 'separation of sowing and harvesting' in a positive way.

the 'king of the Jews', a title which he has not on his own merit but in the name of his father. As Lord over life and death only God is king and judge in the real sense of the word.[28]

In fact, we see a broad scale of functions which run socially from low to high: at the bottom of society: the slaves and the servants; in the category of people who must take care of earning their own living: sellers of sacrificial animals, money changers, and small change providers, gatekeepers and a gardener, labourers, fishermen, rural labourers, shepherds and workers in the vineyards, soldiers under the leadership of a *chiliarch*, teachers and a court official; and on the side of authority: a leader of the Jews, high priests, a high Roman functionary, an emissary, a king and a judge. It is a mirror image of the social order of the ancient society. Before we look at the context of Ephesus I want to elaborate on this for John's text.

3.2.2 *Free persons, servants, and slaves*

The ancient economy and social order is essentially determined by the system of inequality between free men and slaves—two classes of people which indicate two forms of status without intermediary. The slave can reach a very high social position, but he/she will always be lower than the simplest free citizen. Even riches cannot change that. This does not mean though that there is not some kind of sliding scale: slaves, servants, helpers, and manual labourers, male and female, belong to the lowest class in society. One uses them to make life more bearable and there is little attention to their situation.[29] The Johannine Gospel follows this social order and ideology.

The free persons
As has been said implicitly several times already, all personages, who are somehow important for the story, are presented as 'free persons': obviously Jesus himself, but also the disciples and the people he meets; also the antagonists, the high priests and the

---

[28] See 5:19,21,25,30; 6:39,40; 10:18.
[29] Cf. Finley 1975; Gagé 1971/2 (1964); Hirschfeld 1963/3 (1905/2); Macmullen 1974; Weaver 1972; White 1977.

Pharisees. The strongest proof of this is the fact that, if names are named, the father's name is also given. In Greek culture this is a sign that one belongs to an *oikos*, which is the basis of citizenship. This has been explained sufficiently in the foregoing.

Servants and slaves
The Johannine Gospel is characterized by a typical fact. If we trace who in the story as told owns slaves and servants, one arrives at a remarkable observation.

The slaves and servants can be localized precisely. Slaves (δοῦλοι) are owned only by the βασιλικός and the high priest Caiaphas. Servants (ὑπηρέται) are owned only by the high priests and the Pharisees. In his trial Jesus says that his 'servants' would have fought for him, if he had wanted them to, but that his 'kingdom' is not from this world and that is why it did not happen.

Slaves and servants also have a different narrative function. The servants are involved in the capture of Jesus (7:32,45; 18:3,12); they are present in the house of the high priest (18:12,22); they get actively involved in the trial (a servant slaps Jesus in the face, 18:22) and also in the crucifixion (together with the high priests they are the first to shout that Jesus be crucified, 19:6). It is a rather aggressive group which is presented more or less as a personal body-guard. That is true also for the 'servants' which Jesus could have appealed to: they would have fought for him (18:36: ἀγωνίζω). The narrative role of the slaves is much more limited. In the story of the court official we find house slaves who know precisely what happens in the house and who go to meet the master with a message of joy (4:51,52). Considering what happens to the slave Malchos, it is clear that slaves were present at the capture of Jesus, but during the trial they are outside, warming themselves at the fire; slaves and servants are clearly distinguished (18:18), but there is also a mutual relationship (18:26).

That is to say: the slaves and servants in John tell their own special story.

That this is not accidental, is clear from the stories about meals. While it would be the place by preference to let them appear, they do not make an appearance at all in these stories.

The people do what needs to be done themselves:
—at the meal of the people (6:11,12);

—at the last meal Jesus shares with the disciples where, astounding Peter, Jesus takes upon himself the work of the slave in washing their feet (13:4ff);

—at the meal with Lazarus after his resurrection, where Martha serves at table (12:2);

—in the Cana story, the marriage feast where Jesus changes water into wine, there is mention of 'staff', but they are called διάκονοι.

Those are all the factual data available. The other texts where 'slaves' are mentioned, are ideological:

—1:27: John (the Baptist) compares himself with Jesus and believes himself unworthy to undo his sandals. The work of a low house slave is used as a metaphor to indicate the order of importance between Jesus and John.

—8:34,35: the slave does not always remain at the house, the son does. The opposition presupposes the social opposition of the free man and the slave and whether one belongs to a house or not. A slave can be sold. The son of the father-*kyrios* has acquired rights.

—13:16; 15:20: the slave is not greater than his *kyrios*. The pronomen possessivum shows the difference of position between the slave and *his kyrios*. The slave belongs to the possessions of the *kyrios* and can, therefore, never become higher or acquire a different status. It is a position of dependence which remains, even if he were to be set free.

—15:15: I no longer call you slaves, but I call you friends, because the slave does not know what the master does. The opposition here is again in the context of the *oikos*-culture. Friends belong to the *oikos*, slaves belong to the possession of the *oikos*. οὐκέτι creates a problem. Did Jesus call his disciples slaves before this? Should we think of the story of the washing of the feet where he asks the disciples to act as slaves, and is that now no longer valid?

Ideologically, the position taken is always that of the *kyrios*-owner and never that of the slave. Slavery is natural and is not criticised. That is most apparent in the most explicit 'slave' story: when Jesus ties a towel around his waist and washes the feet of his disciples. Peter's reaction expresses the feelings of all: you will never, at any time, wash my feet. That Jesus acts as δοῦλος, throws all relations out of kilter. And probably that is significant for the real situation. To be a slave is a humiliating position which one can never strive for. If one asks a free man to act as a slave, this is shocking because a free person cannot abandon his rights.

If one looks at all this, it is apparent that there is a tripartite social division. The possession of slaves exists only among the 'higher' social strata: the royal official and the high priest Caiaphas. Jesus and his disciples participate in the social ideology about slavery, but they do not profit from it. Jesus himself uses the system to bring his message across 'prophetically': service is more important than power. The slaves themselves, finally, do not represent any interest group. They are—as 'staff' and as subjects for discussion—in the service of the narrator of the story.

3.2.3 Income, expenses, professional activity, and social contacts

What will later be called 'the middle group', is well represented in the text of the Johannine Gospel. These are people who are free citizens; they provide for their own family through their work and they have reached a certain financial and social position in this way; but ultimately they are not part of the power structures of society. We can describe certain things:

Indications of possessions and money
    Initially, there is no explicit mention of the financial position of the disciples, but as the story unfolds there are some data. On the occasion of the meal of the people, Philip says that 200 denarii would not be enough to give each person a piece of bread (6:7). And when Jesus is at table with Lazarus and Mary embalms his feet with a pound of precious nard, Judas says: "why was not this perfume sold for 300 denarii?" (12:5,6) Two hundred and three hundred denarii are apparently large sums of money. From the last story it is clear also that Judas holds the γλωσσόκομον: a money chest in which the alms received are kept and used to buy things for the group (13:29: to buy what is necessary for the pesach-meal), and also to be able to give to the poor (12:5,6; 13:30): alms go both ways. A last indication of the financial position of the disciples can be found in the closing story of the fishing in the night. Peter has 'naturally' a boat which he can use: a situation which is consistent with what happens after the people's meal. The disciples

and Jesus have the use of boats (6:16,22; 21:3ff), in the same way that boats and small boats are available for 'the people' (6:23,24).

In the first temple story, money also plays an important role as we saw already. In the description of the events precisely those elements are used in which the Jerusalem temple is similar to pagan temples: the sale of cattle, sheep and pigeons and the presence of many moneychangers: the temple as a retail centre and a money market. This impression is reinforced by the sentence which Jesus speaks to the sellers of pigeons: do not make my father's house into a trading centre. For the context the most remarkable thing is that, notwithstanding the 'enlargement', John still consistently speaks about κέρμα. He even coins his very own word for it which does not appear (so far) in Greek: κερματισταί: changers of small change. Against the background of Ephesus and Artemis it seems almost as if the sentence which Jesus speaks to the sellers of pigeons(!) is meant ironically.

The texts which use as metaphors the work on the land, the tending of sheep, and the work in the vineyard, are consistent with this. There is real understanding of the work done. It is laborious, it costs a lot of energy, and it is not particularly attractive. The only good thing is the harvest. In the metaphor of the shepherd, he is the owner of the flock; together with other shepherds there is a common sheepfold. The real danger is theft, against which they have hired a common gate-keeper. He knows his own sheep by name and takes them out every day. It is nothing spectacular. The metaphor of the vine is the most 'pastoral' of the similes: a single vine and a single worker, but here too all attention is on the fruits, and the work itself is not described 'pastorally'. Without belittling the metaphorical character of these texts, it is clear, nevertheless, that very specific choices have been made which evoke—together with other data—a special interference.

3.2.4 The people in authority

In John's text,[30] the centre of power is in Jerusalem. Every visit by Jesus brings him closer to this centre until in the last trial the

---

[30] Because I can refer to the preceding chapter for the metaphors which relate to Jesus' functioning regarding God (his kingship, his divine authority, his being emissary etc.), I will concentrate here on the power relationships as they are exercised narratively in the story as told.

decision about his death is made and executed. The high priests and Pilate are ultimately responsible because, with the help of soldiers, servants, and slaves, they pass sentence on Jesus. It is a peculiar case which shows what the real power relationships are: the power of the high priests regarding the people and regarding Pilate; Pilate's own power and the way the power relations of Pilate and the high priests are interwoven with the emperor. On the first two aspects I want to dwell a little more.

The high priests

We have seen already that the high priests are presented as belonging to the top social layer of the population. They own slaves and have servants and make use of them. There is among them a kind of hierarchical order. Caiaphas is 'the high priest of the year', a function which indicates his leadership. Mutual family relations play a role. The only other high priest mentioned by name is Annas, Caiaphas' father-in-law, in whose house the trial of Jesus takes place.

Typical for the Johannine Gospel is that the plan to murder Jesus takes place in two phases.

The first time is in 7:45-52 at the occasion of the Feast of Tabernacles. Jesus has taken over the theology of the feast (I am the light, I am the water of Siloam, I am) and, therefore, Pharisees-high priests send out their servants to capture him (7:32). That plan misfires but it brings them to plan together. The Pharisees condemn Jesus, but Nicodemus comes to his defence.

The second time happens as a result of the successful resurrection of Lazarus (in 11:47-53) and matters are far more serious. There is mention of a συνέδριον and again two factions face each other: the Pharisees-high priests on one side who do not know what they should do, and Caiaphas, the high priest of the year, on the other side who accepts the political analysis of his co-conspirators but who also is willing to draw the consequences: instead of the whole people this one man must die.

It is a plan which, from that moment on, is executed with the help of the people and of Judas and which, after the festive meal of Jesus and Lazarus, is expanded with the intention to also kill Lazarus (12:10).

It is in this context that the most 'political' words are spoken. The story relates how the high priests meet (συνάγω συνέδριον: in

11:47); sitting in council to discuss together (βουλεύομαι: 11:53; 12:10; συμβουλεύομαι: 18:14) whether and how Jesus (and Lazarus) could be killed. These are meetings in which the decision is taken about the lives of people. The people are given the command that "whoever knows where he is must report this" (11:57): μήνυσις as the protection of the state against religious subversion.[31] It is also remarkable that only in this context the word ἔθνος is used in John's text (11:48,50,51,52; and in 18:35 where Pilate says: "Your *people* and the high priests have handed you over to me"), suggesting that this συνέδριον of high priests and Pharisees represents the people; that in any case this meeting takes decisions in the name of the people.

Pilate

The story makes it clear that, for the execution of this plan, they depend on external Roman authority. Pilate represents this authority. He has the use of a whole cohort of soldiers—which apparently could be lent (18:3) and which is under the command of a tribune (18:12). The praetorium is its dwelling, a large space with an inner and outer space; Pilate moves from one to the other. There are again soldiers who can be called on, and on the forefront there is a βῆμα, sitting on which final judgment is rendered.

The story of the trial is a complicated text with many layers of meaning. Relevant for the context in which we now find it, is the way in which the high priests exercise influence on the factual way things are going in the condemnation of Jesus. They intervene at the crucial moments:

—the high priests and their servants are the first to begin shouting that Jesus should be crucified (19:6);

—the high priests say that they have no other king but Caesar (19:15), a sentence which shows how much the high priests put their interests in the service of the interests of the emperor and which, narratively, forces Pilate to condemn Jesus to be crucified.

—the high priests protest officially against the *titlos* on the cross. Pilate should have written: "He has said that he is the king of the Jews" (19:21), a protest which Pilate does not listen to.

---

[31] Cf. Pauly-Wissowa s.v.

The story relates how Pilate tries his best to keep the trial juridically correct: how he is frustrated in that and how he in the end does not sanction the law but an injustice. It is a way to present the fact how laboriously the various group-interests are kept in balance. In Pilate's consideration a good understanding with the local powers prevails over the protection of the Jesus' interests. That has to do with the larger picture of the politics of state which on this general level is important also in a city like Ephesus.

3.3 *The interferences with the Ephesus context*

This social tripartite division[32] responds to a similar tripartite division in Ephesus. Because, in this case, the similarities are very direct, it effects a special interference.

3.3.1 *The presence of slaves*
Ephesus is a city where slaves play a rather conspicuous role. We can make some distinctions. There are direct indications: the mention of slaves of private citizens and a rather long list of names of (probable) city-slaves who occupy an important position in the cult of Artemis and of the *prytaneum*. And there are indirect indications: the list of names of the freed slaves, again to be distinguished as those emancipated from private citizens and those from the *familia Caesaris*. I will limit myself to texts from the first century:

Slaves of private citizens
—Furbus and Secundus in the list of participants of the fishery-toll-house (I-20A.2, line 32 and 34) who are both παραφύλαξ (at the toll-house?) and they both contribute 1000 stones;
—in the same list it is said that Gn. Kornelios Eunous together with his παιδίον pays 15 denarii (I-20A.2 line 43); it is fairly

---

[32] For Ephesus see esp. Pleket 1990 who sees the social stratification of this city as a dichotomy between the urban elite (the *bouleutic* order) and the rest of the demos (the *demotai*). As we will see, the slaves play a not unimportant role in Ephesus and there is a special place of authority for the Roman administration.

certain that this does not indicate his son, because the sons in these texts are always called υἱός;[33]

—Symphoriōn with his wife Trophimia and child in an inscription on their tomb from the first century (VII-2-4353);

—the association "qui in statario negotiantur", the Latin association of the traders on the slave market, is mentioned twice: in VII-1-3025 for their *patronus*, the proconsul G. Sallustius Crispus Passienus Equi[ ], 42/43 AD, and in III-646 for Tib. Cl. Secundus (Trajan era)—of whom also freedmen are known.

City-slaves

—In the lists of the *kouretes*[34] people are mentioned with a single name who each have their own function at the sacrifices for Artemis and the other gods: dancers, flute players, trumpeters, incense bearers, heralds, inspectors of the victims, bearers of the sacred objects.[35] At a given moment and with certain people (Aristōn and Moundikios are in later texts indicated with the *tria nomina*, a sign of Roman citizenship), it is no longer clear whether these could be freedmen or adopted men or whether the function allowed only one single name, even though it would not indicate the status of slave. This complication does not take away the slave-status in the case of such people as Trophimos, Onesimos, Markos, Olympikos and others.

—In the edict of Vibius Salutaris, Mousaios and Hermias must take care of the welfare of the statues (I-27 line 201ff). They are called ἱερός of Artemis, temple-slave of Artemis;

—in the decree of Paullus Fabius Persicus (I-17-19, 44 AD), it is indicated how financial abuse can happen with the slaves of Artemis: "freemen do the work of public slaves, thereby burdening the treasury of Artemis with excessive expenses; and they allow the public to purchase infants cheaply and to consecrate them to

---

[33] See Horsley, *New Documents* 5, 1989, 109 who, with some doubt, believes that more people have the status of slaves. Epaphras (A1 line 47) is not a slave, not only because he appears together with a son, but also because his father is named. Horsley sees the παιδίον in A2 line 43 as 'child' and not as 'slave'.

[34] For our period IV-1001-1033.

[35] See Knibbe 1981,79ff; and IE IV p. 56ff.

Artemis in order that they might be reared as slaves at the goddess's expense".[36]

Slaves freed by private citizens
Slaves can sometimes achieve (great) wealth. That is shown to some extent already in the foregoing lists. If they are members of a rich *oikos*, their chances improve. In fact, there are a number of inscriptions preserved of freedmen who achieve high positions; who finance large edifices or who in any case honour their *patronus* with a statue. In historical order we see the following:
—in the era of Tiberius, two freedmen are mentioned in the long list of contributors (to the temple of the emperor in Smyrna?): "[ ]aios Preimos with freedman" and "Skribonios Hilaros with the freedman Valens". They donate 50 denarii (SEG 1989,1176 and V-1687).
—in the era of Nero, C. Stertinius Orpex, a freedman of Stertinius Maximus (consul AD 23) who officiates at important liturgies:
    —II-441: a building-inscription about restoration work and expansion of the stadium, devoted to Artemis and Nero, together with his daughter Stertinia Marina, priestess of Artemis;
    —III-720: homage by council and people (was he perhaps a member of the council ?);
    —VI-2113 and VII-2-4123: inscription on a tomb with a foundation: a yearly sum of money for the members of the council and the gerousia (was he perhaps a member of the gerousia also?); and the erection of statues. In VII-2-4123 Stertinia Quieta (his wife?) is also indicated as *liberta*.
—an inscription on the tomb of Gaius Stertinius Achillas and Stertinia Irene (VII-2-3906), probably freedmen of either G. Stertinius Maximus, the consul, or of Stertinius Orpex;
—the freedmen (two man and a woman) of L. Cusinius Messalinus who himself has been a tribune and procurator of the god Nerva: III-660C; VI-2246A; VII-3335;
—Cl. Strymon, the freedman of Tib. Cl. Aristion, high priest and asiarchēs (VII-1-3046). The three sons of Cl. Strymon erect a statue for the Roman benefactor L. Vibius Lentulus;

---

[36] Formulation, cf. Oster 1990, 1716/17.

—Philadelphos, a freedman of the high priest Ti. Fl. Montanus erects a statue for his benefactor (VI-2063, Trajan era);

—Tib. Cl. Hermes, the freedman of Tib. Cl. Secundus erects, together with his son, Hermias statues for his *patronus* (V-1545) and for Athamas (III-857). The son reaches the post of *grammateus* of the city (VII-1-3056). Tib. Cl. Secundus plays an important role himself in the slave trade of the city (III-646; Trajan era).

Freedmen of the emperor

A special group is formed by the *liberti Augusti*, the freedmen of the imperial family who obtain very high functions in the administration; who sometimes achieve great wealth and who then influence the welfare of the city. It is a group of people who are socially directed to the higher classes and functions and who are helped in this, and used, by private citizens and by the city. Even though they are not without importance in the reconstruction of the functioning of the slaves in the city, they are, owing to their high positions, of less importance for the interference with John's text. In historical order these are the following people in Ephesus:

> —Mithradates and Mazaios, the freedmen of Agrippa, the son-in-law of Augustus, erect a large triumphal arch in honour of Augustus and his family (VII-1-3006; III-851);
>
> —G.J. Neikoforos promises to be *prytanis* for life (III-859, Augustus era) and erects the *Romaia* in honour of Roma, Augustus, and Artemis (III-859a, maybe also VI-2272b);
>
> —Pelago, who in Nero's time has an important position, was stationed in Ephesus (III-862);
>
> —Eutaktos is procurator of Asia and Lycia under Vespasian and Titus (II-262);
>
> —Tib. Cl. Clemens is honoured by the council and the people because of his merits for the city and for Artemis. He has probably been involved in the new determination of the temple goods under Domitian (III-853; V-1812);
>
> —M. Ulpius Chresimus (III-856, fragmentary; in SEG 1988, 1183 a discussion about dating and restoration of the time: from the time of Domitian or of Trajan);
>
> —M. Ulpius Glyptus (III-854, Trajan era) in contact with T.Fl. Soter, the father of the later high priest T. Fl. Montanus;
>
> —Tib. Cl. Classicus honoured by the people and the council (III-852, Trajan era);

—Tib. Fl. Epagathos dedicates a group of statues to Artemis, Trajan, and the people of Ephesus (III-858, Trajan era);
—M. Ulpius Repentinus erects a statue for Ti. Julius Alexander Capito, a tribune (III-684b, Trajan era);
—Hermes who had all kinds of functions and who acts in Ephesus as *adiutor* of Valerius Eudaimon (III-666, Hadrian era).[37]

It is clear that the slaves determine the way a city functions in very different ways: as domestic slaves, as workers, as people who know how to become rich, as participants in city politics, and as agents for imperial interests. The rights of possession of a *kyrios*, the sale-ability but also the possibility to free slaves are contemporary practices of which every citizen is aware. The narrative role of slaves in the Johannine Gospel—which links up with the 'lower' domestic slaves and finds its culmination in the washing of the feet of the disciples by Jesus—and the Johannine ideology about slaves regarding the dependence of the slave on the interests of the family of the *kyrios*, regarding the right to sell and regarding the status, all this must have been well understood in Ephesus and have been seen as normal.

3.3.2 *The working population*

The mass of data forces us to make a stringent selection. Ephesus is a working city where the harbour, the expansion of the city and the beautification of the city in the first two centuries AD, brought enormous activity. It is a trading city which attracts lots of businessmen. By virtue of the Artemis-temple it is a banking centre with a real aura. In the Roman authority structure, it is the administrative centre of the province where the proconsul resides with all the activity this brings with it. It is a city where specialised studies can be undertaken—especially medicine and rhetorica grow to great heights in the second century. It is also a large city which needs a lot of internal care regarding food and drink, clothing and cultus and festivities. It is against this more general background that

---

[37] As far as I can establish, the names of Mithradates, Mazaios, G.J. Neikoforos, Pelago, Tib.Cl. Clemens, Tib. Cl. Classicus, and Tib. Fl. Epagathos are new in comparison with Weaver's *Familia Caesaris* 1972.

we can see the interference with John's text. To specify this a little more I will look at the list I have made up from John's text.

—the sellers of sacrificial animals (Jn 2:14ff) do not appear as such in (existing) inscriptions. The presentation of facts, however, is in line with a phenomenon which is in use in antiquity in many cities: wide-ranging specializations of the sellers. In the various inscriptions in Ephesus we find the following sellers: ὀψαριοπωλεῖται (I-20: fishmongers); the πυρηνᾶδες (VI-2079, 'sellers of nuts' according to the editors of IE); the εἱματιοπωλοί (VII-1-3063: clothes-dealers); and the ἐριοπωλοί (II-454: dealers in wool). The sellers of cattle, sheep, and pigeons from John's text belong in this series.

—the moneychangers and the changers for small change (Jn 2:15) are not far removed from this. As we said already, this is about the small jobs which take only a minor place in the context of the city of Ephesus where in certain circles large sums of money can be used. Very concretely, one can think of the τραπεζεῖται who rented three places in the public lavatories, next to the booth-keepers of the stoa of Servilius, the dealers in wool, the towel-weavers, the basket-weavers etc. (II-454).[38] Maybe one can think of the *nummelarius* Calyx who checked a sum of money for his *patronus* Autronius (II-562; 4 BC). The words used in John's text are not found in the Ephesian inscriptions but the functions and the status are well-known.

—in a way this is true also for the even more modest functions of 'porter' (Jn 10:3; 18:16) and 'gardener' (Jn 20:15). In the

---

[38] It is a text which mentions a number of συνεργασίαι of manual labourers; for a more complete list see Knibbe RE, Suppl, sv Ephesus, 288 who appeals to Poland 1967/1908, 1361. In fact, the lavatory-list of II-454 is completed with the inscriptions of M. Fulvius Publicianus Nicephorus from the time of Alexander Severus (II-444; 445; 679; VI-2076/78/79/80/81). Notwithstanding Knibbe's assertion, Poland's list is no longer complete. Two tomb-inscriptions have been discovered in which new συνεργασίαι are mentioned: the συνεργασία τῶν κλεινοπιγῶν (or κλεινοπισῶν) = makers of couches (VI-2213) en de συνεργασία τῶν λινύφων = flax-weavers (VI-2446).

Johannine Gospel they play a very minor role. In Ephesus there is
one inscription in which a κηπουρός is mentioned (VI-2328); a
θυρωρός never made it into the inscriptions.

—the construction workers of the temple, who are implied in Jn
2:20, obviously, play a much more important role in Ephesus
where, in this period, there is a lot of building activity. They have
united in a kind of guild (see VII-1-3075 where the ναουργοί
τέκτονες erect a statue for their benefactor P. Vedius Antoninus,
middle of the second century; and II-295 where Septimius Severus
restores the earlier rights of the ναϊκὴ ἐργασία). The 'builders of
the temple' (meant is the temple of Artemis) have their own
interests. They put these against all other construction workers who
directly—as τέκτονες—and indirectly—in all building-texts where
someone presents himself as ἐργεπιστάτης—appear abundantly in
the texts from the first century. In this case we can speak of a
rather direct interference.

—the fishermen have organized themselves into a guild also (see Jn
21:1ff) cf. the famous inscription from Nero's time where a toll
house is mentioned which is financed by the members of a cartel (I-
20, 54-59 AD, and V-1503, middle of the second century). Horsley
wrote an extensive and good commentary[39] on the text, the
following elements of which are relevant for the possible
interference with John's text:
   the text is about a group of people who, under several aspects,
are a mixture: the group is composed of people with the *tria
nomina* (50%), with the Greek name-system (46%) and with slave-
names (at least two names, according to Horsley maybe more);
   the individual contributions to the toll house run from very high
(4 columns or 2 columns and altars) to fairly low (5 denarii);
   in the two well-preserved lists of names, the contributions in
money—apart from the contributions in kind: columns, pavement,
stones—reach a total of 938 denarii. That means an average of

---

[39] *New Documents* 5, 1989, 95-114.

24/25 denarii per family. The highest amount is 50 denarii, the lowest in this list 15.[40]

That means that it will not have been seen as strange in Ephesus that the disciples-fishermen in John come in contact with rich to very rich people through Jesus; but one will have understood very well too that the disciples-fishermen see 200 and 300 denarii as a large sum of money.

—for obvious reasons there are no inscriptions preserved of farmers, vineyard workers, and shepherds (cf. Jn 4; 10; 15). Those activities happen outside of the city and they are not considered 'highly placed' in the culture of the time; there is little 'honour' in them. That does not mean that their activities have not left traces. The discovery of all kinds of boundary stones made it possible to chart approximately the area of the city and of Artemis (see esp. VII-2-3501ff). It was in use as farmland, as grasslands, and maybe also as vineyards.

The care for grain has had the most attention. The προμέτραι are known from two inscriptions: they are the people who weigh the grain for tax purposes at the sale, the distribution, and the transport (VI-2299; VII-1-3216). In another text a decree of Hadrian is mentioned in favour of grain from Egypt (II-274).[41] On feast days there are people who distribute grain (III-712B) or who sell it at a lower price (III-815). Grain is the staple food of the people and is, therefore, under the care of the authorities. The farmer himself and farming are not explicitly mentioned.

That is true even more for the winegrowers and the shepherds. Because of a special event—the decree of Domitian to allow wine growing only in Italy—the story of Scopelianus is preserved: he was a rhetor who, in a delegation to Rome, is the spokesman of the province favouring the existing wine growing in Asia.[42] Because

---

[40] Horsley says that 'the total surviving monetary value indicated is just short of 1000 den.; and ... the full sum cannot have been much more' (p.107).

[41] See also II-211 about grain from Egypt from an unknown emperor.

[42] See Suetonius, Domitian 7,2 and Philostratos, Vita Soph. 1.21.520; see also Deininger 1965, 57 and especially Magie 1950 I, 580; II, 1443 with all other references.

the wine from the region of Ephesus[43] is well known, Ephesus
will have been represented in this delegation. For the shepherds
there is not even such a direct indication. One single time a νομή is
mentioned in the sense of 'grasslands' in a foundation which
permits the use of a νομή καὶ καρπεία ἀγρός to a settlement of a
neighbourhood of which the name has not been preserved (VII-1-
3245, found in Apateira, a village in the area of Ephesus). As far
as I can see this is the only indirect indication in the existing
inscriptions.

This seems to be a rather negative result but, in a way, it is the
same in John's text. Farming work, shepherds, and wine growing
exist there also only as 'metaphors', as part of the larger religious
discourse of the text. In this sense also John's text is a city-text.
The work is known, but the people who do the work are much less
well known.

It should be clear that also in Ephesus the professions are part of
the religious context. One can think of the veneration of the gods
who have a special link to these realities of life: in fact, the
veneration of Demeter (agriculture) and Dionysus(winegrowing).[44]
Both have taken their own place within the cult of the city.

Demeter is the most modest.[45] She is venerated as καρποφόρος
(I-10; II-213; IV-1210; VII-2-4337). One can imagine that "the

---

[43] Cf. Strabo 14.1.15.

[44] According to Turner (in Beutler-Fortna 1991,35ff), we must think
of Hermes and Apollo in connection with the shepherds. In Ephesus,
Apollo as Apollo Clarius has especially mantic functions: the Apollo
μαντεῖος in the *prytaneum* (IV-1024 line 24 and 29); Apollo Clarius (IV-
1060; 1072; 1077) and Apollo Pythios (I-9b). The god Hermes is even
less well known in Ephesus. In IV-1012 he is connected with the
gymnasium; the same in IV-1101 via a dedication to King Eumenes which
gives the link to Pergamum—where Hermes plays a much more important
role (see Ohlemutz 1968, 234ff). In Metropolis, there are two stoae
dedicated to 'Tiberios Kaisar Hermes' (VII-1-3420); an identification
which does not exist in Ephesus.

[45] For the cult of Demeter and Dionysus, see esp. Knibbe 1978 and
Oster 1990,167ff.

priest of the fruitful earth" is a priest of Demeter.[46] The veneration of Demeter is deeply rooted in the history of the city. In our period there is mention of a special cult-association—"the demetriasts before the gate"—who take all kinds of initiatives: they start a priesthood for the Sebasta (=Livia, the wife of Augustus) as Demeter Karpoforos (VII-2-4337, between 19 and 23 AD); they approach the proconsul L. Mestrius Florus to ask for financial help for the yearly *mysteria* and sacrifices (II-213, 88/89 AD); and a priest of Demeter erects for her a *naos* (IV-1210, 120 AD). The texts seem to me to suggest[47] that, in a later period, Demeter associates with other gods: with Dionysus (V-1595), with Hestia and the Eternal Fire (I-10) and with many others.[48] I do not think there is a direct interference with John's text.

Dionysus is more exuberantly present. His person is tied to the history of the city. In the Ephesian tradition it is told that Dionysus, at the time of the Amazons, made a visit to the city to make peace with the Amazons—as the mission from Ephesus tells the Senate in Rome in the plea to obtain the emperor temple for Tiberius (Tac. Ann. 3.61); and as is shown on the freeze of the temple for Hadrian.[49]

Ephesus is a city of Dionysus,
—where Dionysia are held yearly (I-9, Augustus era); this feast is well known in the Christian tradition cf. the *Vita Timothei* in which it is told that Timothy has been murdered 'in festivitatem Catagogiorum';
—where a βαχχεῖον stands on the agora (II-434, undated);
—where Dionysus is venerated under the well-known dionysian names: ὄρειος, βάκχιος (IV-1267), βασσαρεύς and βρόμιος (V-1600), but also under the less well-known φλεύς (III-902; IV-1257; 1270; V-1595) and ποιμάντριος (III-902);

---

[46] III-902, Augustus era; can it not be imagined in SEG 1986, 1034 (early imperial era) that the dedication has been directed Γῆ Καρποφόρῳ. That makes the addition [Διο]κλῆς more probable.

[47] But many texts are not easy to date.

[48] In the thanksgiving inscriptions of later *prytaneis*: IV-1058/60/76/70a/71/72.

[49] Museum in Selçuk inv. no. 715.

—which has been the home city for an association of the play-
actors and musicians under the protection of Dionysus and the
emperor (Strabo 14.1.29 and I-22 line 36);[50]
—where the personal commitment and veneration of people is
evident from the many statues of Dionysus, Selenus, Pan, and
satyrs,[51] a fresco of Dionysus,[52] the dedication to Dionysus of the
house of G. Flavius Furius, the grandson of T. Flavius Python, the
famous high priest from the time of Trajan (IV-1267); the
dedication of θυρσοί to Dionysus by Moundikios, who is also
known as a slave of Artemis(IV-1210);
—and which knows the cult association of "the initiated of
Dionysus before the city", presented in long lists of participants and
all kinds of cult officials (V-1601, Trajan era; 1602, undated; 1600,
Commodus era) and which apparently linked up with the devotees
of Demeter (V-1995).[53] It is an association which makes the
emperor, at Hadrian's first visit to the city (124 AD), σύνθρονος τῷ
Διονύσῳ, an honour which in the history of the city has been given
only once: to Anthony and Cleopatra when they visit Ephesus in 39
BC (Plut. Vita Ant. 24.3) and which will happen again with
Commodus (II-293). If there is a chance, Dionysus knows how to
manifest himself politically.

This marked presence of Dionysus in the city is not unimportant
for a possible interpretation of the story in John where wine is
flowing freely. In Johannine research there is a continuing small
group of interpreters who link Jn 2:1-12 to Dionysus,[54] to those

---

[50] But see SEG 1990, 1003 where there is a discussion about the
historical reliability of the data about the place of the association.

[51] See Aurenhammer 1990 nos. 31-48; and in the inscriptions in II-
506; 507; SEG 1985, 1116; the mosaics published in Jobst 1977, nos.
112-117 and 180-183 are dated 4th/5th century.

[52] Museum Selçuk, inv. no. 10.5.77.

[53] The link-up is seen by the editors of IE as very typical for Ephesus.

[54] Always with an appeal to Bultmann—cf. Broer 1983—to be found
by such diverse authors as S. Schulz 1972, E. Linnemann 1973/74, M.
Smith 1974/75 and J. Becker 1979, 111; see also more recently yet,
Davies 1992, 88 and Stibbe 1992, 139ff. The last mentioned author
develops a parallel between the Bacchae, the Dionysus tragedy of
Euripides, and Jn 18-19. I suppose that the worshippers of Dionysus from
the G. Fl. Furius house would have found this parallel marvellous.

stories about Dionysus in which it is related that water was changed into wine at his feast day. The wine-miracle at Cana cannot be explained completely religious-historically from the Jewish tradition —which in the miracle stories of Elijah and Elisha does speak about multiplication and which predicts an abundance of wine and good wine for the end of time—but which nowhere speaks about the motive of the change of water into wine. In the opinion of these historically oriented exegetes, certain Dionysus-stories have essentially influenced the origin of the Cana-story. That is not easy to prove because the place as well as the dating of these stories must be brought in contact with the place of origin and the dating of the Cana-story[55] and yet it is an open question whether there is direct influence.

In the method of reading which is used in this study, it is not the question of the origin which is discussed, but the question whether the text in Ephesus can be read from this background information. Considering the strong presence of the Dionysus-cult in Ephesus, this is not only possible but it seems self-evident. Add to this that precisely the most significant Dionysus-stories—the stories in which it is related that water is changed into wine—are situated in an Ephesus-related place: in Andros but also in Teos, a place near Ephesus, and a place with which Ephesus has a fight in relation to Dionysus.

The relevant texts from this Dionysus-tradition are:[56]
—Pliny, Nat. Hist. 2. 231: "It is accredited by the Mucianus, who was three times consul, that the water flowing from a spring in the temple of Father Liber (= Dionysus) on the island of Andros always has the flavour of wine on January 5th. The day is called God's Gift Day (Θεοδοσία)";
—Pausanias 6.26.2: "The Andrians too assert that every other year at their feast of Dionysus wine flows of its own accord from the sanctuary";
—Diodorus Siculus 3.66 & 2: "The Teans advance as proof that the god was born among them the fact that, ever to this day, at

---

[55] Cf. Broer 1983, 120ff.

[56] Cf. Broer 1983, 114ff who shows, supported by arguments, that the texts are about a temporary change into wine from an existing well; see also Loos 1968, 603ff.

fixed times in their city a fountain of wine, of unusually sweet fragrance, flows of its own accord from the earth".

For the relation between Teos and Ephesus in relation to Dionysus, a text of Strabo about the domiciles of "the association of the artists of Dionysus" is relevant: "They formerly lived in Teos, the city of the Ionians that comes next after Colophon, but when the sedition broke out they fled for refuge to Ephesus" (14.1.29). The Dionysus devotees must have been aware of this struggle. From the fact that the mission from Ephesus to Rome under Tiberius relates the visit of Dionysus to Ephesus in the description of the history of the city, and that this visit is to be seen in the freeze of the emperor-temple of Hadrian (cf. supra), it is clear that at least the authorities of the city were interested in the link between Dionysus and the city. A 'Dionysus-reading' of the Cana story—the epiphany of Jesus similar to that of Dionysus, as σύνθρονος τῷ Διονύσῳ, as νεός Διονυσός—can certainly not be excluded.

—The cohort of soldiers (a σπεῖρα) from John's text fulfils a police role (the capture, scourging and crucifixion of Jesus); it is there for the use of the high priests as well as Pilate and it is led by a χιλίαρχος (Jn 18 and 19). Such a military police assistance does not exist in Ephesus. The police is under the authority of the citizens. If this aspect of city life is organised as it is in Pergamum, the στρατηγός is responsible for a civilian guard which takes care of the maintenance of some rules (cf. the document on the city guard in AthMitt 17, 1902, no.71 regarding the maintenance of streets, wells, drainage etc. where the punishment is given by a πράκτωρ). Soldiers play no role in this in Ephesus or in the whole province during this period.

That does not mean that there are no soldiers in the city. There is a fairly large number of inscriptions of Roman noblemen who made a military career and who have some relation to the city. In their *cursus honorum* they make clear where and on what level they held military positions. Limiting myself to the nouns σπεῖρα and χιλίαρχος, it is remarkable that the combination of these two is practically non-existent. A σπεῖρα is led by an ἔπαρχος, resulting into the title ἔπαρχος σπείρης + name and a χιλίαρχος is the commander of a λεγεών, resulting into the title χιλίαρχος λεγεώνος + name. Only in VI-2069 and VII-2-4112 is there mention, in accord with John's text, of a 'chiliarch of a cohort'. In VI-2069 Gn. Pompeius Hermippus is called χειλίαρχος σπείρης Σπανῆς and in VII-2-4112 Flavius Iuncus is called "trib. cohortis V gemellae civium Romanorum". Whatever the precise details, for these people this is about functions in faraway places (the whole of the Roman Empire makes an appearance) and these people do not bring soldiers with them.

Ephesus is not a garrison city. Soldiers are mentioned only exceptionally. There are two tomb-inscriptions which cannot be dated (VI-2274C and VII-1-3291A) and, quite remarkably, there is the dedication on a statue of M. Gavius Bassus, who took part in the war against the Dacians and was honoured for that by Trajan with a crown, a lance, and a standard (III-680). The statue has been erected by eight 'lower' soldiers who have the titles of strator (=equerry), cornicularius (=helper), optio (=elected deputy) and tesserarius (=who hands on the password). In the Greek version of this *cursus honorum*, Gavius Bassus is called: χειλίαρχος στρατιωτῶν λεγ. [α'] βοηθοῦ.

For the interference with John's text, this means a kind of alienation. The behaviour of the soldiers is linked to the power which the Roman noblemen exercised in other countries but with which the citizens of Ephesus did not much have to do directly.

—διδάσκαλος is a very specific word for elementary education but also a general term for everyone who teaches anything. In the Johannine Gospel, Jesus is a teacher who appears parallel to the Jewish rabbi as a teacher of law and wisdom. In Ephesus, the office of teacher is part of an extensive educational system headed by teaching in philosophy, jurisprudence, and medicine. For now I only want to show the texts which speak about a διδάσκαλος. There are not many and only one or two are certainly first century:

    —III-611 (late second century): Lucius Fifius Severus, the διδάσκαλος, honours Manius Acilius Glabrio as the inspector of the city accounts (because he has been appointed by him?);
    —VI-2026: in an edict of Caracalla, Aelius Antipatros is addressed as friend, *teacher*, and expert in Greek letters;
    —VII-2-4340 (undated): Caelius Marcellus erects a statue for his *"teacher*, the Platonic philosopher [ ] Secundus Trallianus". The text can be brought in relation with VII-2-3901 (cf. SEG 1984, 1088; 1988, 1176) which may date from

the era of Domitian[57] and where Ofelius Laetus is called a
"Platonic philosopher";
—III-683A + B (in a time after the second neocorate): in a
tomb-inscription, Heraclides Didymus is honoured διὰ τὴν ἐν
τῷ μαθήματι δύναμιν καὶ πίστιν.

How Jesus presented himself as teacher and which interferences
with the Ephesus context have exercised their influence, will be
dealt with in more detail in the next chapter.

—the βασιλικός in Jn 4:46ff, finally, is a rich man with slaves
who—in the most probable interpretation[58]—is connected with
some court. In fact, there are two possibilities: he may have been
involved with the government or with the court proper. A regal
court and a regal government do not exist any more in Ephesus as
we have seen but the imperial court and the imperial administration
are very well known. How the imperial court functions, appears
especially in the *cursus honorum* of the members of the *familia
Caesaris*, the freedmen of the emperor.[59] As an example I give the
cursus of Tib. Cl. Classicus, libertus Augusti, which can be seen as
the most instructive in Ephesus. In a double-language inscription he
is called: "divi Titi a cubiculo et procurator castrensis" (i.e., he
was responsible for the personnel of the bedroom of the divine
Titus and for the personnel of the whole palace), "divi Nervae
procurator a voluptatibus" (responsible for the games of the divine
Nerva), "Imperatoris Traiani procurator a voluptatibus et ad ludum
matutinum" (responsible for the games of emperor Trajan and for
the morning games), "et procurator Alexandreae" (responsible for
the Roman administration in Alexandria) (III-852). As we said, it is
also possible that the βασιλικός had a more administrative function.
In Ephesus, one can then point to the imperial or civil
administration, to all the functionaries who have a function *a
rationibus* (concerning all money matters) or *ab epistulis* (regarding
all juridical questions), and everything that is subject to this. The

---

[57] See Runia 1988, 242 and Horsley, *New Documents* 4,1987,70ff.
[58] Cf. Bauer s.v.
[59] See esp. Hirschfeld 1963/3 (1905/2) 288ff; 300ff; about the *cursus
honorum* of Tib. Cl. Classicus, see also SEG 1990, 1004.

βασιλικός, probably, did not live in such a complex community. The readers from Ephesus may have associated him vaguely with that.

The most important effect of this research is that it shows how much the interference on this level is pulverized into an almost limitless number of small data. In fact, this means that on almost every page of John's text there are interferences to be discovered, some small and some more important. In an indirect way these data offer a commentary on all the authors who read John's text as a report about a group which is closed in upon itself and is more or less sectarian. The proven interferences show that the book knows also another movement, which points in a carefree way to the external world, to innumerable social realities which have their own interest in giving meaning to the texts.

3.3.3 The high priests

In elaborating the data, the discussion about the people on the highest level of authority is still lacking, people who at the same time represent the rich upper class: in the first instance the high priests and their economic and political function in the city. In the analysis of John's text, we have seen that the high priests are the rich ones who have possessions and slaves and who, in their own manner, participate in political power. In the context of Ephesus the picture is as follows:

1. In the history of Ephesus, the position of the high priest(s) changes fundamentally at the moment that the city has its own imperial temple. The local high priests then become the mediators between the city and the emperor. In a way they (he or she, because women can also be 'high priest of Asia', as we will see) represent the presence of the emperor in the city in the name of the citizens. So, if citizens of the city become high priest in their own city, the history of the city changes. That is the case with Tib. Kl. Aristion who, for the first time, in 88 obtains the function of high priest for the temple of the Sebastoi in Ephesus.

In the inscriptions of Ephesus a number of names of high priests from before this time have also been preserved.

They were connected with the temple of Pergamum:

—G. Joulios Pardalas, "high priest and president of the games
for life of the Goddess Roma and the Emperor Sebastos, son of
God" (VII-2-3825);

—G. Joulios Anaxagoras, "high priest of Asia and president of
the games for life of the Goddess Roma and the God Sebastos"
(if this is about Augustus, VII-2-3801.2);

or, probably, with the temple of Smyrna:

—Gaios Joulios [ ], "high priest" (I-17 line 68, 44AD);

—G. Joulios Kleon, the master of the mint from Eumeneia and
chiliarch of the VI Ferrata, "high priest of Asia" (III-688);

—Pomp. Demeas Kaikilianos,[60] the maternal grandson of
Flavius Aristias, "high priest of Asia" (III-708);

—an anonymous ἀρχιερεὺς τοῦ Σεβαστοῦ Τιβερίου Καίσαρος
(SEG 1987, 883; 1989, 1176).

These people have had their influence in the city, especially in
relation to the continuation of the imperial cult: that the Sebastoi
are still venerated after their death:

in relation to Augustus on the initiative of an anonymous high
priest (IV-1393);

to Tiberius on the initiative of Anaxagoras (VII-2-3801.2);

and in a long list of contributors,[61] which list possibly has some
relation to the temple of Tiberius and Livia in Smyrna, under the
high priest Gaios Joulios [ ] (I-17 line 68).

But whether there are other initiatives or liturgies is not known.

That changes when Tib. Kl. Aristion becomes high priest in
Ephesus. He is the first high priest of the imperial temple in
Ephesus. He is present when people from Keretapa, Teos,
Klazomenai, Hyrkanis, and Kyme (probably) come to celebrate (II-
234/9/5; V-1498; II-240). He also takes the initiative for a number
of constructions and provisions in the city: the construction of the
palaestra near the harbour under Domitian, of the nymphaeum of
Trajan, of an aqueduct and the canalizing of several streams, of the
library in the name of the heirs of Celsus.[62] His wife Julia Lydia
Laterane is involved several times. It cannot be completely ruled
out that she was "high priestess of Asia". On the dedication of the

---

[60] As far as I can see, he is not mentioned in Friesen, 1993, 172ff.

[61] V-1687 and SEG 1987, 883; 1989, 1176.

[62] II-424/5; 461; III-638; VII-1-3217; VII-2-4105; 5101; 5112.

nymphaeum of Trajan she is called "daughter of Asia, high priestess and *prytanis*" (II-424) and on the dedication on the spot where the water comes out, she is called "high priestess and daughter of Asia" (II-424A). The text is not completely clear. The expression certainly means that she has been high priestess of a particular deity. Because of various parallel texts from this time, Artemis would then be first choice.[63]

Whatever the precise situation, the high priestships of Tib. Kl. Aristion and Julia Lydia Laterane make it clear that they are the most important couple in the city at the end of the first century and the beginning of the second.

This husband-and-wife link is not so strange, especially in this period. It appears at least two more times:

—Tib. Kl. Pheseinos, the successor of Tib. Kl. Aristion, who is present as high priest at the dedication of Kyme (maybe), Aizanoi, Aphrodisias, Silandros and Stratonikeia (II-240; 232/2a/3/8/7), is married to Stratonike from Teos who is called "high priestess of Asia of the temple in Ephesus" (IGR IV-1571). Their daughter will also become high priestess of Asia.

—and somewhat later (between 85 and 130) Ti. Fl. Kalvesianos Hermokrates "high priest of Asia of the temple in Ephesus" (IGR IV-1323) is married to Flavia Ammion Aristion "high priestess of Asia in the temple of Ephesus" (IGR IV-1325).

One other woman is known as "high priestess of Asia", Vedia Marcia who combined the function with that of being the priestess for Artemis and being *prytanis* (IV-1017). She belongs to the Vedii who play a leading role in the second century in the history of the city, especially in the building history of the city. Again she too represents the financial elite of the society.

The same is true—and it can proven to be so—for the other high priests in this period:

---

[63] One has to ask oneself whether the fact that the most important priestesses (of Artemis) are called ἀρχιερεία, originates in this period. Anyway, it is remarkable that only in the time of Trajan-Hadrian the title appears in the plural: III-980, Julia Polla (Trajan); III-980, Mindia Potentilla (Trajan/Hadrian); III-643C, Klaudia Tertulla (Hadrian, her husband is probably not a high priest); IV-1030, Julia Peisonis (Hadrian); while before this time, we find only ἱερεία (and variations).

—Ti. Fl. Montanus who called himself after the proconsul of the year 95/96,[64] restored the harbour and gave lots of festivities: from gladiatorial games to a popular banquet and who, in the year of his function as high priest, renovated the theatre (VI-2037; 2061/2/3). He also calls himself "sebastophantes", a function which is parallel to a hierophant: he who in the cult (processions, at sacrifices etc.) shows the holy (here the Sebastos), some attribute or image which brings the Sebastos into the cult situation.[65]

—Ti. Fl. Pythion who under Domitian did not yet have Roman citizenship (see V-1578A) but who, through his friendship with the famous G. Antius Aulus Quadratus and his sister Julia Polla for whom he erected statues (VII-1-3033/4 ?), reaches the highest functions and founds an important *oikos* (see III-674; V-1500);

—Tib. Kl. Menandros from the time of Trajan who functions in the municipal politics in a slightly minor position, sets up a foundation from which every citizen receives money (III-644A; 926A);

—for the Jouliani (III-674) and the Pompeii (III-708; IV-2069);

—Tib. Kl. Piso Diophantes (II-428) who is actively involved with the construction of the temple for Hadrian, was probably the first high priest of this temple;

—an exception is Tib. Ioulios Damas Klaudianos, the successor of Tib. Kl. Pheseinos of whom we know only that he is the third high priest in the series of high priests of Ephesus and that, in his time, there was one last dedication to the temple of the Sebastoi by the city of Tmolos (II-241).

2. The high priests belong to the rich upper class of the population. One can imagine them to have been owners of slaves. That can be proved from two inscriptions which mention an emancipation:

—the three sons of Kl. Strymon, the *freedman* of Tib. Kl. Aristion erect a statue for their benefactor L. Vibius Lentulus (VII-1-3046). The latter had good relations with the high priest Ti. Flavius Montanus (VI-2061);

—Philadelphus, a *freedman* of Ti. Flavius Montanus erects a statue for him as his *patronus* (VI-2063).

---

[64] T. Junius Montanus, cf. Kreiler 1975, 63.
[65] Cf. I. Smyrna 591 notes.

Even though only in a limited way, these texts give an insight in the web of mutual social relations and obligations.

3. Without doubt the high priests took part in the exercise of power as it was exercised in Ephesus via the institutions of "the council and the people". However, we are not too well informed about these institutions and especially not about the mutual relations: about the internal relations with the βουλευτικόν συνέδριον (I-27 line 17) and the γερουσία and about the precise position of the πρύτανις, the γραμματεὺς τῆς βουλῆς and the γραμματεὺς τοῦ δήμου.[66]

It is remarkable that none of the high priests calls himself βουλευτής, a title which is added honourably to their name by many others. Does this mean that the high priests find their membership of the council so natural that there is no need to mention it? In fact, some of them exercise the highest political and social functions, which, supposedly, were 'given' by decisions of those who were in power:

—πρύτανις has been Tib. Kl. Aristion (II-425; 427; III-638); Julia Laterane (II-424; V-1600E) and Vedia Marcia (IV-1017);

—γραμματεὺς (τοῦ δήμου): Tib. Kl. Aristion (II-425) and Ti. Fl. Pythion (III-858), as also the son of Tib. Kl. Montanus (III-644A; 828)[67] and the son of Ti. Fl. Pythion (V-1500);

—the council and the people are actively involved in the erection of statues for Tib. Kl. Menandros (III-644A) and Tib. Kl. Piso Diophantes (II-428);

—they approve that Ti. Fl. Montanus erects a statue for L. Vibius Lentulus (VI-2061) and Ti. Fl. Pythion for Trajan (V-1500);

—the most relevant and most direct expression of power participation is found in VI-2061.2 where it is said of Ti. Fl. Montanus τῇ τε βουλῇ καὶ τῇ γερουσίᾳ πληρώσαντα τὰ δίκαια πάντα: "he did everything which was fitting in favour of the council and the council of the elders".

Because of their functions as high priest of the imperial temple(s), the high priests of Ephesus are those who, among all the

---

[66] Cf. Knibbe RE, Suppl s.v. Ephesus, 271ff.

[67] In IV-1023, in a list of *kouretes*, he is called also βουλευτής.

people, lean most closely to imperial power and government. This needs to be developed further. For now it may be clear that an intensive interference takes place between the Ephesian and the Johannine high priests. In a way it is about the same people, about the same sort of people: as the Ephesian high priests the Johannine high priests belong to the top ten; they are rich and they have servants and slaves (in the plural) at their disposal; they exercise influence on what happens in the city in a special way; they assemble to take decisions on the lives of civilians; they are in contact with the Roman administration and influence its decisions.

Most important is the title given to Caiaphas, ὁ ἀρχιερεὺς τοῦ ἐνιαυτοῦ ἐκείνου, 'the high priest of that year' (Jn 11:49,51; 18:13). This expression has caused exegetes a lot of trouble. The Jewish system of high priests does not know of high priests for just one year. Principally, high priests are nominated for life. And although, during the time of Roman dominion in Palestine, the Roman administration makes this impossible—it is a politically too important function not to be touched by Roman influence—several Jewish high priests, and among these Caiaphas, occupy the function for more than just a single year. In Schürer[68] we find the following list: Ismael (c. AD 15-16); Eleazar (c. AD 16-17); Simon (c. AD 17-18); Caiaphas (c. AD 18-36); Jonathan (AD 36-37); Theophilus (AD 37-?); Simon Cantheras (AD 41-?); ...Ismael (c. AD 59-61); Joseph Cabi (AD 61-62); Ananus (AD 62 for three months); Jesus son of Damnaeus (c. AD 62-63); Jesus son of Gamaliel (c. AD 63-64); Matthias (AD 65-?). Exegetes are aware of these data and find it difficult to understand the expression ἀρχιερεὺς τοῦ ἐνιαυτοῦ ἐκείνου. Is it imaginable that the author of John did not know the Jewish system? Did he rule out Caiaphas's remaining in office for several more years? Bultmann states that "der Evangelist also falsch orientiert (sei) über die jüdischen Rechtsverhältnisse".[69] Other exegetes defend the author and

---

[68] Schürer 1973-1987, Vol II,230: starting from the time of procurator Valerius Gratus and only mentioning the names of the high priests who are given a time-index in this list.

[69] *Johannesevangelium* 1968, 314.

translate the expression as "the high priest in that fateful year"; "the high priest of that memorable year".[70]

In the readers' attitude which is the supposition of this study, this much discussed expression is simple enough. For Ephesian readers it refers to their own system of high priests who remain in function for a single year and whose names determine the calling of that year: "in the year that Caiaphas was high priest".

The acting high priest of the year and the high priests in the plural who appear in the Johannine Gospel are functionally linked to the temple in Jerusalem, but they wear, so to speak, the clothes of the high priests in Ephesus.

3.3.4 *The relation between the proconsul and the citizens of Ephesus*

In John's text, the city authorities are under the aegis of the authority of Pilate. The high priests and the *Ioudaioi* enter into a discussion with Pilate about what should be done about Jesus. The authority structure runs parallel with that in Ephesus. The proconsul is at the top of the pyramid and determines which decisions the city takes. Because the mutual responsibilities are not precisely determined, there is a certain space for manoeuvre where dialogue, discussion and arguments influence concrete decisions. The proconsul guarantees the interests of the emperor, the senate, and the empire; the local authorities stand for the local interests of the city and its inhabitants. These interests are not always on a parallel course. Most often the highest authority (i.e. the proconsul as head of the Roman administration) determines what is to happen, but the local authorities are not completely helpless; certainly not if they can prove that the interests of the emperor are damaged, for whatever reason.

It is important to notice that, in the Johannine Gospel, the threat of conflict by the high priests—implicitly there is an appeal to the emperor—runs parallel to a number of conflicts and threats of conflicts in Ephesus.

---

[70] Schnackenburg 1975, 449; Carson 1991, 421; Brown 1994, Vol 1, 411. It is an interpretation which is "as old as Origen" according to Brown 1970, 441.

The most famous happens in the era of Tiberius. The province has managed to get the proconsul C. Iunius Silanus convicted because of his rapacity, in the words of Tacitus a *crimen maiestatis* because it damages the *numen Augusti* (Tac. Ann. 3,66; 20/21 AD). When the province in the next year manages to get Lucilius Capito, the *procurator res privatae* of Tiberius, convicted because he authorized a military intervention on his own authority (Tac. Ann. 4,15), the province decides, out of gratitude, to erect an emperor-temple for Tiberius which, finally, was built in Smyrna.

Other real convictions by the emperor are not known to have happened in Asia and maybe they did not happen. There is further mention of smaller and bigger interventions by Rome.

Because of court politics a number of proconsuls die prematurely. Messalina, the wife of Claudius, has Marcus Vinicius killed in 46 AD (proconsul in Ephesus 38/39, VII-1-3024); Agrippina, the future wife of Claudius, does the same to G. Sallustius Crispus in 48 AD (proconsul in Ephesus 42/43, III-716). Under the more 'dictatorial' emperors Nero and Domitian, two are even murdered while in office as proconsul: under Nero, Iunius Silanus (Tac. Ann. 13,1) and under Domitian, C. Vettelenus (87/88, Suet. Domitian 10,2; Tac. Agr. 42, 1).

In the era of Trajan, the proconsul Aulus Vicirius Martialis (113/114) intervenes in a conflict about water provision in the city (VII-1-3217A + B). Some years later (in 120/121, under proconsul Subrius Dexter), this decision is re-confirmed. The question is an interesting one because, in both texts, Tib. Kl. Aristion is mentioned as the person primarily responsible for this aqueduct. Perhaps this story can be linked with a trial which this Aristion has to conduct before Trajan. Pliny writes: "There were several different types of cases which tested Trajan's judicial powers in various ways. The first one was that of Claudius Aristion, the leading citizen of Ephesus, popular for his generosity and politically harmless; but he had roused the envy of people of a vastly different character who had suborned an informer against him. He was cleared of the charge and acquitted" (Epistles 6.31.3). From a Roman point of view it is all very simple.

Some years later, under Hadrian, there is a case of fraud about inheritances and debts. By means of an emissary from Ephesus, the proconsul brought the matter before the emperor, who took a decision in favour of the *gerousia*. The next proconsul, Subrius

Dexter (120/121) is charged to execute this decision and the city is asked to pay for the mission unless the envoy has said beforehand that he would pay himself. The emperor, the proconsul, and the citizens of the city maintain intricate relations.

It is clear from all this that the Johannine story about the relation between the high priests and Pilate is a political one, something which is not unknown in Ephesus. Maybe it is not unimportant to mention that the biggest victory of the province comes in the era of Tiberius, a story which has been very important for Ephesus because of the emperor-temple: the memory of it carries on till the erection of their own emperor-temple under Domitian. Under Tiberius an appeal to the emperor brought real results. The continuous line of imperial interventions in city politics made sure that the awareness remained vivid that the 'higher power' of Rome can be manipulated; and it is precisely this awareness which the high priests in John's text use effectively. In the last chapter it will be made clear how this is explicitly linked to the imperial cult.

CHAPTER FOUR

GROUP FORMATIONS IN JOHN AND IN EPHESUS

Jesus' activity in the Gospel of John can be described in a variety
of ways. Not all aspects of his activity interfere with city life in
Ephesus in as far as we can trace that historically. A number do.
As was clear in the preceding text, that is true for some important
christological titles: Jesus as king, as lord, as saviour, as son of
God, as God. These titles express on a narrative-reflexive level the
meaning of Jesus' actions. In John's text they are combined with
the more down-to-earth reality of Jesus as 'teacher in and of Israel'.
Jesus acts in this way and is seen in this way by the people he
meets and by the writer of the book. I use this important narrative
embedding as a framework to show how the text of John interferes,
in yet another different way, with the existing city-culture in
Ephesus.

4.1.1 *The scope of Jesus' teaching activity*

As we said above, the Johannine Gospel is a travelogue in which
the main personage, Jesus, travels widely. Because he acts as a
teacher in all the places he visits, we get the image of a 'travelling
teacher' who does not stay in any one place for a long time.
Jerusalem is the central point of reference: Jesus goes back there
each time. At the beginning of the story we hear that "the house of
his father is there" (2:16), but, because the conflicts about his
doctrine and action come to the boiling point there too, it cannot
become Jesus' home. On the contrary, in the final analysis, through
his elevation on the cross in Jerusalem, Jesus will show that his real
home is "with his father in heaven".

From the story about Jesus' trial, it is clear how important Jesus' teaching activity is for the leaders of the people. The only thing which the high priest wants to know is about Jesus' disciples and his doctrine (18:19). As so often in the Johannine text, Jesus' answer can be understood in different ways: "I have always spoken publicly to everyone; all my teaching was done in a synagogue and in the temple, where all the Jews come together. I have never said anything in secret" (18:20). Not only in the synagogue but also in the temple, Jesus always acted as teacher. Everywhere he went, Jesus always acted openly and publicly (πάντοτε, παρρησίᾳ) as the teacher of Israel:

—indiscriminately in Galilee, Samaria, Judea, and Jerusalem; indiscriminately also among Jews from Israel and Greeks from the diaspora: 7:35; 12:20-36.[1]
—in the temple: 7:14,28; 8:20,59; 10:23.
—in a synagogue: 6:59 in Capernaum, Galilee.
—in the open air in the country: 1:35; 3:22; 4:1ff; 4:46-54; 11:1-44; 13:1ff?
—on the beach: 21:1-23.
—publicly in the city: 5:19-47?; 9:35-10:21; 12:20-36; 12:44-50;
—in a house: 12:1-11; 13:1ff?; 18:28-19:16.
—during the day: passim; in the evening: 4:1-44 and in the night: 3:1-21; 13:1; 17:26.
—with various emotions and in different circumstances: tired from the journey: 4:6; sad and angry: 11:35,38; in confusion: 12:27; full of love: 13:1,2; under threat of death: 8:59; 10:39; and publicly before his judges: 18-19.

Jesus' teaching activity is all-encompassing. We can say that, in a different way, Jesus addresses individuals, small groups, apparently innumerably large groups. Narratively this brings about certain layers: a small group of people who are called "disciples",

---

[1] From the formulation of Jn 12:20 it is clear that this is about 'Jewish' Greeks: "they had come to Jerusalem to pay homage on the feast"; Davies 1992, 158; 227; 328 implies wrongly that these are 'pagans'.

embedded in an ever larger group some of whom react positively but most of them negatively.

The Johannine Gospel is, therefore, a special travelogue. It is the story of a travelling teacher who finds acceptance and resistance among the various peoples and cities which he visits; who sometimes attracts disciples and sometimes loses them. The story begins as a success story: Jesus finds his first disciples in Galilee. In Jerusalem he comes into contact with Nicodemus, a Jewish leader. In Samaria he can spend two nights because of the insistence of the Samaritan woman, and, back in Galilee, he wins over the whole family of the official at court. Then comes the set-back: a real conflict in Jerusalem because of the healing of the cripple on the Sabbath, which runs into the crisis-story in Galilee. The *Ioudaioi* start a fight; many disciples leave and only twelve remain, among them is Judas who will betray him. From then on the conflicts increase, but Jesus goes on to act as a teacher. In 8:31 there is still mention of "*Ioudaioi* who believe in Jesus", but real success comes only with the man born blind. Led by the leaders of the people, the *Ioudaioi* have turned their backs on Jesus. They force him to retreat to lonely places. Lazarus' family is his last refuge. When Jesus again takes up the preaching of his doctrine—and expands it to the Greeks from the diaspora—the end is near. It becomes impossible for Jesus to manifest himself beyond the small group of his disciples. The doctrine which is discussed during the final meal of Jesus and the disciples, makes it clear that, as far as the content of the message is concerned, and the way it is communicated, Jesus has not lost his impact: apart from individual persons, larger groups are addressed: the listeners-disciples who are present and those who are foreseen in the future are placed over against the reality of the cosmos as the agglomeration of people who resist and will resist him.[2]

It is, finally, important that as διδάσκαλος Jesus never rejects anyone. He does not make any distinction between man or woman, between rich and poor, between Jew and non-Jew. It is remarkable

---

[2] In the interpretation of Davies 1992, 342ff, the story of ch. 21 tells in a symbolic way the story of the success of this mission among the 'pagans'.

that Jesus takes the initiative only rarely. I give the events in the sequence in which John's story tells them with the more relevant data:

1:35-51: The first people seek contact with Jesus. They take the initiative. They know one another because they are related or because they come from the same city or village. Their social position will become clear later on in the story. Mostly (Andrew, Peter, and Nathanael; cf. 21:2) they are fishermen, people who must earn their living by manual labour. Andrew and Philip are, later on in the story, connected with each other (see 6:7-9; 12:21-22).

3:1-21: Nicodemus, an ἄρχων of the Jews comes to Jesus in the night for a discussion. As appears in the rest of the story he is present in the consultation between the high priests and the Pharisees about Jesus' fate (7:50-52), where he defends Jesus. At Jesus' burial he appears publicly with 100 pounds of myrrh and aloes (19:39) and now as someone who gives a lot of money for a royal burial of Jesus.

4:1-42: The meeting of Jesus and the Samaritan woman who comes to draw water from the well: a woman as disciple, as preacher and as the one who takes the initiative to restore the contact between Jews and Samaritans.

4:46-54: At the request and on the initiative of the official at court—who, as has been said, owns slaves himself—Jesus heals his son, and the effect is that the man's whole family expresses their trust in Jesus.

5:1-17: Jesus looks for a cripple in the corridors of the bath Bethsaida: a crowd of blind and lame and sick people gather there: it makes the cripple declare solemnly (ἀναγγέλλω: 5:15) that it was Jesus who healed him.

9:1-39: Jesus takes the initiative to heal a blind beggar. The resistance of the leaders of the people makes the man profess Jesus all the more fervently. On a new initiative by Jesus, the two meet again (9:35) and the healed blind man becomes the first adherent following the crisis in Galilee.

11:1-12:11: Lazarus' family is a small house community of people who do not have a partner, or parents or children: Jesus is their counsellor and friend. Jesus raises Lazarus from the dead, a man who comes from a village and who, when he invites people for a meal, lets his sister Martha serve at table. The sisters Martha and

Mary see Jesus as their teacher and in a way they are the perfect disciples.

12:42-43: Not all ἄρχοντες follow Nicodemus' example. Many believe, but they do not openly profess Jesus because they fear that the Pharisees will evict them from the synagogue.

18:15-18: The famous ἄλλος μαθητής is presented as an acquaintance of the high priest. He can enter the aula together with Jesus. Peter can also enter because of him but he is not allowed beyond the gate where the servants are. The man's influence does not reach beyond that.

19:25; 20:1-8: Apart from Jesus' mother and his aunt, two other women are present at the cross. Mary Magdalene is the more important of the two. She is a disciple who, after the burial, will play a leading role as the one who discovers the empty tomb; as the one who guides Peter and the other disciple whom Jesus loved; as the first person who is allowed to see Jesus, and as evangelist of the resurrection for the other disciples.

19:38: Joseph of Arimathea, together with Nicodemus, buries Jesus in a royal manner. He is in a position to approach Pilate personally, and he is given permission to bury Jesus.

Even if Jesus does not deal with everyone in the same way, he is in touch with all levels of the population. If need be he takes the initiative. Otherwise the initiative lies with 'the other'. But even when others take the initiative, Jesus is open for anyone and does not reject anyone. A group evolves composed of people, men and women, who sometimes are related to each other; who know each other because they come from the same place or do the same work; who develop mutual relationships but who, for the rest, represent a cross-section of the population of Palestine: men and women, people from Judea, Samaria and Galilee, rich and poor. The change in composition of the group is remarkable:

—in 1:35-51 there is mention of Andrew, Peter, Philip, Nathanael and one anonymous person.
—in 6:1-71 we find Andrew, Philip, Peter, and Judas.
—in 11:1-44: Mary, Martha, Thomas and Lazarus.
—in 13:1-17:26 we find Peter, the beloved disciple, Judas, Thomas, Philip and the other Judas.
—in 20:1-31: Mary Magdalene, Peter, the beloved disciple, and Thomas.

—in 21:1-23: Peter, Thomas, Nathanael, the sons of Zebedee, two other disciples and the beloved disciple.

Sometimes other disciples are considered to be present, but sometimes not. That means that the group of disciples has some kind of structure, but is, at the same time, an open group where people can come when they please.

4.1.2 *Some special characteristics of Jesus' teaching activity*

4.1.2.1 *The dialogue character of the text*

The Johannine Gospel is a text remarkable for its immense discursive magnitude. Often this happens at the expense of the narrativity of the text itself. When Jesus speaks—and that happens continually—the story comes to a standstill. C.H. Dodd once said that the narrator learned his trade as narrator in the writing of the story. Originally, in chapters 3,4,5,6 the relation between the story and the spoken word is much more out of proportion than further on, in chapters 9,11,12,18,19,20.[3]

However that may be, the text of John is filled with words spoken by Jesus. One must be aware that these words are seldom real monologues but almost always take the form of a dialogue: with the antagonists of the sub-story, with the disciples, with the opponents. Such a dialogue form may seem peculiar to the modern reader, but one cannot doubt the intention of the writer. Jesus is a teacher who enters into dialogue with people and who, via misunderstandings and irony, brings them to insight and to awareness, or fails to do so.

It is a teaching method which many exegetes have seen as exponential of what happened in the Johannine community itself: misunderstanding as a characteristic of an inner and an outer group;[4] the irony as a means to distinguish between the good and the bad listener; the polemical undertones and overtones with the

---

[3] Dodd 1968/8, 352.363.423, even though one should forget for a moment that chs. 13-17 are also part of the narrative whole.

[4] Cf. esp. Leroy 1968 and the broad reception of this book in the Johannine research; see also Martyn 1968 and Brown 1979.

Judaeans as the expression of a contemporary polemic between Christians and (absent?) Jews.[5]

Exegetes who have a better ear for the narrative character of John's text usually do not make the step to historical practices. They look at the dialogue technique used by John and by Jesus as a kind of reader framework. It challenges the readers of the text to enter into a similar learning process: the gradual introduction by phases into the Jesus confessions by the characters of the story should be read as a description of the journey which the believer must make;[6] by solving the misunderstandings the reader is brought to a better understanding of the narrator's ideological point of view.[7] In this study we must limit ourselves to the question whether any form of relationship is provable with the 'teachers' in and from Ephesus.

4.1.2.2 *Jesus' miracles as signs*

Johannine research has always had a great deal of interest for another characteristic of Jesus' activity. His words are linked with a number of extraordinary activities: the change of water into wine in Cana (2:11); the healing of the son of the official at court (4:48. 54); the people's meal (6:14,26); the healing of the man born blind (9:16), and the resurrection of Lazarus (12:18,37): the famous σημεῖα of which one has heard also in Jerusalem (2:23; 3:2; 7:31); which are discussed even in the Sanhedrin (11:47); which indicate the distinction between Jesus and John the Baptist (10:41) and which—at the first closing of the book—are seen by the author as the most important events from Jesus' life: "Jesus did many other

---

[5] Cf. Ashton 1991, 417ff.

[6] It is a reading model which has been developed esp. by de la Potterie in his *La vérité dans saint Jean.*

[7] Culpepper 1983, 164: "The misunderstandings lead the readers to feel a judgmental distance between themselves as 'insiders' who understand the elusive implication of Jesus' revelatory discourses and those who have rejected Jesus"; cf. also Botha 1991, 190ff with his application of the theory of implicature; and Painter 1991 with his stress on 'the quest' which is similar for characters in the text and the readers of the text.

mighty works ... but these have been recorded that you may believe that Jesus is the Christ, the Son of God". (20:30-31).

The giving of this name, calling these miracles of Jesus σημεῖα, is a most interesting aspect. With one word an intertext is created with the deuteronomistic-prophetic literature about the miracles of God for his people,[8] as well as with the non-religious Greek meaning of the word where σημεῖον indicates 'the meaning which a good listener can give to an event': the physical symptoms which a doctor uses as σημεῖον to determine an illness; the flight of a bird which a priest uses as σημεῖον to predict the future; a dream which a dream-interpreter uses as σημεῖον for what will happen in the future.[9] That is to say: by using the word, the narrator of the story links Jesus' deeds with the deeds of the prophets of Israel. And by the connotation with 'understanding', there is a link between these deeds of Jesus and his words. By calling Jesus' miracles σημεῖα, they are brought into the teaching activity of Jesus. These deeds are to be understood as signs of Jesus' origin. They confirm what Jesus says about himself.

4.1.2.3 *The many meals*

Johannine research had not paid so much attention to another reality: Jesus' teaching activity often occurs in the narrative and/or discursive context of a meal: the marriage feast in Cana where Jesus is present with his disciples and his relatives as the conclusion of the first group-formation around him (2:1-12); the events in Samaria where Jesus talks with the woman about drinking water and with his disciples about eating food against the background of the fact that the disciples must go into the city to buy food (4:1-42); the meal which Jesus offers the people in Galilee near the sea and the mountain where 5000 men get bread and fish, followed by a discussion about manna for the people and bread from heaven, which ends with the sayings of Jesus about himself as a sacrificial animal: about the need to "eat his flesh" and "drink his blood" (6:1-71); the thanksgiving meal in Lazarus' house six days before Jesus' last Pascha, a meal in which there is a foreboding of Jesus'

---

[8] Cf. Bittner 1987 passim.
[9] Cf. Nicol 1972, 115ff; Bittner 1987, 19ff.

burial (12:1-11); the meal of Jesus and his disciples on the evening before his passion and death, the longest scene of the book which is arranged dramatically for the narrative readers (13:1-17:26); the final scene of the book, again a meal, now on the beach of the sea of Tiberias, a breakfast with bread and fish where Jesus asks the disciples for fish (21:5) which he already has (21:9).

Maybe it is not without interest to note that all these meals have a public function: they are about public interest; they happen publicly. At the one meal where it is expressly stated that it took place in a house—the meal in Bethany, after the resurrection of Lazarus: "the house was filled with the sweet smell of the perfume" (12:3)—there "is a large crowd of *Ioudaioi*" who want to see not only Jesus but also Lazarus. At the marriage in Cana one can suppose that the celebrations took place indoors, and for the last meal of Jesus and the disciples (ch.13-17), this has always been supposed from the viewpoint of the Synoptics, but it is not clear whether this must necessarily be so in John's text. The only indication is the use of the word ἐξῆλθον of Judas in 13:30,31 and of Jesus and the disciples in 18:1—but the same word is used for Jesus in 18:4, which certainly does not speak about him "leaving a building". The other meals, in any case, are open-air affairs; near to the sea at the mountain in chapter 6 and on the beach in chapter 21.

4.1.3 The special characteristics of the group of the disciples

The image of Jesus as teacher is mirrored in the activities of the disciples. Some of them interfere, in their own way, with events in the city of Ephesus.

4.1.3.1 The group of disciples as a group of friends

In the Johannine Gospel there is mention of a kind of combination of the titles rabbi and teacher (διδασκαλός). Significant is the use of the double title in the first sentence which the disciples speak to Jesus. The disciples call Jesus "rabbi"—i.e. the narrator of the story lets the disciples address Jesus as "rabbi"—but the implicit author adds "that means translated 'master' (διδάσκαλε)" (1:38). This difference in narrative communication is true for the whole of the Gospel. Jesus is never directly called διδάσκαλος; he is called

rabbi several times (in 1:49 by Nathanael; in 4:31; 9:2; 11:18 by
the disciples; in 6:26 by the people; in 20:16 rabbouni by Mary
Magdalene), but διδάσκαλος only indirectly (in 3:2 by Nicodemus;
in 11:28 by Martha speaking to Mary; in 13:13 by Jesus about how
his disciples call him, and in 13:14 by Jesus about himself).

This is to say that a double model is being used:

—on the one hand, there is this historicizing model of a rabbi who
gathers disciples:
  —whom he takes into his own life: see esp. the mysterious 1:35-
  40, but also the presence of the disciples in Cana, 2:1-12; during
  the journey through Judea and in Samaria 3:22-4:44; and the
  longer presence of the disciples with Jesus from 10:40 to 18:11;
  —but he leaves his disciples free also: cf. the non-presence of
  the disciples in Jerusalem in 2:13-3:21 (probably); in 5:1-47;
  7:1-9:1; and in 10:22-39;
  —although afterwards the disciples seem to be present with
  Jesus: 6:3; 9:2; 11:7;
  —or, conversely, Jesus joins his disciples: 20:19,26; 21:4;[10]
  —a rabbi who introduces his disciples in words and deeds to the
  heavenly realities from where he says that he comes;
  —and who prepares them for the mission which they will have to
  fulfil in his name: to make other disciples in order to create the
  unity of the children of God.
      The disciples are called τεκνία by Jesus (13:33), because Jesus
  is a wisdom teacher who relates as a father-teacher to his
  children-disciples.

—on the other hand, there is the hellenistically oriented image of a
teacher who forms an 'oikos of friends' through his teaching
activity: Jesus who no longer calls his disciples slaves, but friends
(15:14,15). Jn 15:11-17 is very important in this context because it
is based, more than other texts, on an alternative imaginary world.
Jesus is seen as the son of a mighty father. He has free access to

---

[10] See Davies 1992, 321, who is not too clear about it and, therefore,
somewhat summarily says: "Jesus' disciples almost always accompany him
... Curiously, the disciples are not said to accompany Jesus to Jerusalem
in ch. 7 ... Again, they are not mentioned in connection with Jesus'
withdrawal across the Jordan (10,40)".

his father. He chooses his own friends. He lets them know what he has heard from his father and he assures them that, when they ask something in his name, he will give it to them. And precisely as the son of a king he can tell them that they are his friends, if they do what he tells them to do. He appoints them to go out and to be fruitful, an order which is given content by the commandment of mutual love, on the basis of the love which the son has given them.

It is a metaphor which fits perfectly with what is said about the relation between Jesus and his father. Jesus introduces his friends into the *oikos* of his father, a promise which, in the mind of the author, is given material form if one is prepared to participate in this community of friends where mutual love and spirit-experience offer a safe haven against the hatred and the deceit of the surrounding cosmos.

4.1.3.2 *The special position of the beloved disciple*

In the group of disciples there is one who is given a special position: the disciple ὃν ἠγάπα ὁ Ἰησοῦς. He appears in the story —narratively unprepared—at the last supper, in fact after Jesus has spent a considerable time with the disciples in Bethany on the other side of the Jordan (10:40) and in the area close to the desert, in the city of Ephraim (11:54). The disciple is presented as someone
—who has access to the intimacy of Jesus (on his lap and in his bosom 13:23,25);
—to whom Jesus confides secrets which he does not share with others (13:21ff);
—whom Jesus takes on as his son; in a (quasi-) adoptive formula Jesus makes him, as son, responsible for his own mother, a task of which the execution is mentioned (19:26,27);
—who is witness to Jesus' death and to the meaning of that death (19:35);
—who is the first confessor of faith in the risen Jesus (20:8);
—who is the witness par excellence for the disciples—and, therefore, for the readers of the book (19:35; 21:24);
—who, finally, is the explicit author of the book, trustworthy and authoritative: model and paradigm for all disciples-readers (21:24).

In my book *Imaginative Love in John*,[11] I believe I have proved that these narrative realities are a typical selection of what in the Hellenistic culture is seen as a teacher's love for his favourite disciple: the active love of the teacher and the, initially passive, reception of the disciple—which, after the death of the teacher, develops into an active witness about the love received; the access to physical intimacy; the adoption as son; the meaning of the presence at the death of the teacher; the involvement with the last will and testament of the teacher and with the writing of a biography or the editing of writings. I believe I have also shown that certain platonic traditions play an important role in this reception. There is no need to repeat all that here. Now I want to show how this has existed in a city like Ephesus as cultural reality, and how certain links interact with this.

4.1.3.3 *The position of women in the group around Jesus*

In Johannine research, it has often been remarked that women play a special role in the story as told. That is so, not only with regard to their actual appearance but especially with regard to the meaning which these partial stories have for the main story:

—the revelation of the glory of Jesus and the faith of the disciples in the Cana story;
—the winning over of a city in Samaria for the Jesus movement;
—the resurrection of Lazarus as the proof that Jesus can make the dead listen to him;
—the awareness of the meaning of Jesus' death;
—the first witness of the risen Jesus and the covenant connotations which are expressed there,

and the central role which women play here:

—Jesus' mother makes him change water into wine;
—the Samaritan woman personally makes the inhabitants of the city come to Jesus and believe in him. She is in word and deed

---

[11] 1993, 59ff; also some other aspects in this chapter about Jesus' teaching activity refer to this book.

an evangelist of the coming of Jesus as the Messiah, a reality which, for the (male) disciples, is as yet no more than something to be discussed (see the opposition between word and deed in 4:28-30 and 4:31-38); the woman does what Jesus is only talking about to his disciples;

—the sisters, Mary and Martha, make Jesus come to Lazarus (11:3); and the death and resurrection of Lazarus make many Judaeans, who came to Mary to console her, believe in Jesus (11:45);

—Mary Magdalene makes sure that Peter and the other disciple go to the tomb: she receives the task to say the 'words of covenant' of the risen Jesus to "the brothers"; she is appointed by Jesus as his only evangelist of the resurrection (20:17) and she fulfils this mission immediately.

There are a number of indications in the text which suggest that some of these women are part of the group of disciples. Concerning the Samaritan woman it is said that "many believed in Jesus because of the *word of this woman who gave witness*" (4:39), a witness which is surpassed only by the word of Jesus himself. In the story about Lazarus, Martha tells her sister Mary: "the teacher is here and calls you", a combination of words which is typical for the classical 'school'-situation where 'the teacher' is supposed to call his disciples-followers. In the story about Mary Magdalene something similar happens. Jesus calls her by name and she answers with the title 'rabbouni', translated as 'master' (20:16). It is a teacher-disciple relationship supported by her previous way of acting toward the male disciples Peter and the 'other' one, and by the way in which she acts afterwards when she is sent by Jesus as the first and only messenger of his resurrection.

Important in this presentation is the fact that these women act rather independently from the men. That does not fit the usual pattern of behaviour of this time. Women are always linked to men: the father, the guardian, brothers, husband, or their own male off-spring. Therefore, it is very remarkable that a number of women in the Johannine Gospel behave without any form of *tutela mulieris* (=the male protection for the woman).

The activities of these women are partly linked to the factual role division between men and women: the Samaritan woman goes to draw water; Martha and Mary fulfil the prescribed death ceremonies at home; Martha serves at the table during the festive meal after the resurrection of Lazarus; the group of four women standing under the cross (although they had to travel to get there); Mary Magdalene takes care of the body of Jesus after his death. But these women also do a number of things beyond their role: the Samaritan woman successfully proclaims the good news in the city; Mary embalms Jesus' feet with precious nard against the objection of Judas; Mary Magdalene, a woman from Magdala, recognizes her responsibility for what has happened in Jerusalem. The public nature and the naturalness of their actions are striking. In John's imaginary presentation of things, the women fulfil a public function which is very important for the progress of the story as told.

The women in the Johannine Gospel are the active people who carry Jesus' message further; they form community; they profess faith in words which are similar to the intention of the writer, and the high point is the profession by Martha (11:27), which literally runs parallel with the reason why John wrote his book (20:31): "I believe that you are the Christ, the son of God who has come into the world." Historical memories of the important role of women in the Jesus-movement and the actual writer's intentions meet in the character of Martha, the ideal model of the intended reader.

In my study *Imaginative Love in John* I think to have shown that, notwithstanding all these positive aspects, the narrative relationship between Jesus and the women remains ambiguous. The beginning and the end of the various stories show quite a difference. In the beginning of the various stories Jesus is inviting and open; he opens the conversations and listens to them; he helps the conversation to progress. He also receives a lot, because the women make it possible for him to express himself in a way which in other situations is not given to him or not yet given. But each time there is a phase in the story where this openness is closed off: the active Samaritan woman is made anonymous; the theological Martha is accused of not having faith; the affective Mary hears an interpretation which is surprising; the radiant Mary Magdalene with her message that she has seen the Lord is rated lower than the beloved disciple who does not see him and yet believes. It is a part of John's story which makes it less woman-friendly than some exegetes would wish it to be. It is clear that, epigraphically, there are no means to amplify this aspect of the Johannine ideology.

4.2 *The interferences with the Ephesus context*

The interferences play a role on many levels, although I cannot always fit each part to another. The texts from Ephesus sometimes make different selections and combinations which are not always exactly parallel. The interferences, therefore, occur in a more general way via analogous practices, customs and situations.

The presence and the activity of teachers in Ephesus

In the previous chapter, I pointed out already that the title διδασκαλός does not appear often in Ephesus; in the first century AD maybe only once, indirectly via an inscription for Ofellius Laetus, who is called a "platonic philosopher" (VII-2-3901), a title which in VII-2-4340 is linked with the title διδασκαλός. Yet, Ephesus is a 'study' city, a city in which on various levels teachers and disciples make their appearance. This is so from the lowest level—as appears from the inscription of an alphabet (II-584)—through the higher school forms (cf. the appearance of γραμματικοί, παιδονόμοι, παιδοτρίβαι, and παιδεῦται), to the gymnasium with its ἐφήβαρχος, to the higher level where philosophy, rhetoric, the law, and medicine were taught. On this higher level education is firmly determined by the individual and it depends on the individual charisma of the teacher how the 'school' formation will be given. In Ephesus the παιδεῦται, σοφισταί, and ἰατροί (cf. VII-2-4101 = SEG 1981, 952) enjoyed special legal protection from the beginning of the era of Augustus-Antonius till the time of Trajan (when this edict was published): they were free from certain taxes. The city, probably, hoped that, in competition with other cities, it would attract the better people in this way.

4.2.1 *The travelling teachers*

For the first century AD, it is entirely natural that all kinds of teachers go from city to city to offer their services, to proclaim their special message, to earn a living. Many forms are possible. Sometimes the teacher takes on a job for a longer period of time in one city or he returns to a particular city time and again. Sometimes it is an ongoing travel from one place to another.

On the basis of the existing literature (inscriptions and writings), it is possible to form a fairly clear idea about the situation in Ephesus. And, even though a lot could be said about the historical accuracy of this literature, because the 'travelling teacher' can be found anywhere, it is clear that, in general, the information given is historically correct. Following the style of this research I will give the data more or less chronologically:

—Potamōn (Diogenes Laërtius I.21; IE III-789; SEG 1988, 1177; beginning of the first century); the anonymous φιλόσοφος ἐγκλεκτικός in IE III-789, a philosopher from Alexandria who made an impression in Ephesus with his combination of teachings from different schools, is, probably, the same man as Potamōn, the ἐγκλεκτικός from the Laërtius-text.[12] Relevant in this context is the fact that this teacher came from Alexandria and held conferences in Ephesus.

—Apollos (Acts 18:24-19:1; 1 Cor 1:12; 3:5-23; 4:6; 16:12) is a similar figure. He also comes from Alexandria, he teaches in Ephesus and he travels to Achaia and Corinth.[13]

—Paul (Acts 18:19-21; 19:1ff; 20:16; 1 Cor 15:32; 16:8) is a travelling teacher par excellence. For our study it is relevant that he stays in Ephesus for a longer period of time. With Paul we see this combination of staying for a longer period and travelling. He teaches for three months in the synagogue in Ephesus. When there is a conflict with the Jews, he gives daily addresses in "the school of Tyrannos" for two years.[14] According to the Western text of Acts, Paul speaks "from the fifth to the tenth hour" (= from 11 a.m. till 4 p.m., during the midday rest period).

In the Pauline tradition names of other people are known who appear as disciple and later teacher in Ephesus: Onesiphorus? (2 Tim 2:18); Tychicus (Acts 20:4; Eph 6:21f; Col 4:7f; 2 Tim 4:12;

---

[12] All this cf. Runia 1988, 241ff.

[13] See especially Thiessen 1994, 43ff.

[14] It is a name which appears more often in Ephesus: as a proper name in the Greek form in VII-1-3417 (first century BC); I-20B (Nero's time); V-1600 (Commodus' time); and as *cognomen* in the Latin form in IV-1001 (time of Augustus); I-20B (Nero's time); IV-1012 = IV-1029 (time of Trajan/ Hadrian); III-704 (time of Marcus Aurelius); I-47 (time of Commodus); VI-2299B (undated).

Titus 3:12) and especially Timothy (1 Tim 1:3 and the *Vita Timothei* in which his death as a martyr in Ephesus in the time of Domitian is related).[15]

In the Letters of Ignatius too 'travelling teachers' are mentioned for Ephesus: "I have learnt, however, that some from elsewhere have stayed with you (παροδεύσαντας τινας ἐκεῖθεν) who have evil doctrine; but you did not suffer them to sow it among you, and stopped your ears, so that you might not receive what they sow...You are all fellow travellers (σύνοδοι, θεοφόροι, ναοφόροι, χριστοφόροι—)...etc." (Ign. Eph. 9:1).[16]

—Apollonius (*Vita Apollonii*) is the famous philosopher/wisdom-teacher who, according to this *Vita*, travelled all over the then known world. On these journeys he stayed also in Ephesus in the time of Domitian/Nerva and he gave addresses "from the platform of their temple" (4:2); "under the trees which grow by the sanctuaries" (4:3); "amidst the crowd and before all" (7:6); and "in the groves of the colonnade" (8:26); therefore, publicly and, because of what he said, not without danger for his life.

—Ofellius Laetus (VII-2-3901; IG II², 3816 in Athens; SEG 1984, 1088; 1988, 1176; Plut., Aetia Physica) belongs, probably, also in the time of Domitian. The double inscription, one version in Ephesus and one in Athens, proves that this Ofellius must have been a travelling philosopher too. He is called πλατωνικός φιλόσοφος; and in the Athens-inscription also θεολόγος, in the interesting dystichs:

Hearing the sublime hymn of Laetus, the theologian,
I saw heaven open for people.
If according to Pythagoras a soul changes into something else,
Plato has come alive again in you, Laetus.

In the tradition of the Johannine Gospel, the word θεολόγος plays an important role, because the evangelist John is reckoned as θεολόγος among the New Testament writers, probably because of the prologue. Cf. the classical meaning of the word = "one who makes hymns of the gods". In Ephesus, the word appears quite

---

[15] For more details see Ollrog 1979, 20.36ff and Thiessen 1994, 248ff.

[16] Cf. Meinhold 1979, 20.

often as the title for people from classical antiquity and as a Christian title for the evangelist.

For the Christian use see I-45, IV-1279; 1356; VII-2-4133/34/44, 4311/14/15/18.

For the use in the classical period:

- I-27 line 146; 262; 295: in the edict of Vibius Salutaris, where the theologians are mentioned next to the singers of hymns.
- IV-1023 (time of Trajan), where one of the *kouretes* is called "theologian";
- I-22 (time of Antoninus Pius), where we find the mention of a "theologian of the temples in Pergamum who composed songs for God Hadrian";
- from a later era I-47 (Commodus); VII-1-3015 (approximately 220 AD); VII-2-4336 (AD 241-244); III-645 (AD 244-249), where there is mention of a "*synedrion* of singers of hymns and theologians and givers of oracles"; VII-1-3074 (undated).

—T. Claudius Flavianus Dionysius (II-426; VII-1-3047; Philostr. Vita Soph. 1.22; 522):[17] born in Miletus, buried in the *agora* in Ephesus in the time of Hadrian. He is a disciple of Isaios and had disciples of his own. In the words of Philostratus, "he visited very many cities and lived among many peoples, yet he never incurred the charge of licentious or insolent conduct, being most temperate" (1.22; 524); "the actual tomb of Dionysius is in the most conspicuous part of Ephesus, ... though during the earlier part of his career he had taught in Lesbos" (1.22; 526). As places which Dionysius visited Alexandria, Miletus, Ephesus, Sardeis, Smyrna, and Lesbos are mentioned.

—Favorinus (Philostr. Vita Soph. 1.8; 489) was an important figure for Ephesus. He was born in Arelate, Gallia; he was a disciple of Dio Chrysostom and taught in Greek in Rome, later on in the East, especially in Athens and Ephesus. He is elected by the city to plead with Hadrian, in the name of the city, for the new emperor-temple. He was to compete with Polemon who spoke in the name of Smyrna. Polemon is given preference by Hadrian and Smyrna gets the temple.

—Adrian of Tyre (V-1539; Philostr. Vita Soph. 2.10; 585) taught in Athens and Rome, but from an inscription in Ephesus, it appears

---

[17] Cf. Keil 1953.

that he taught there too, cf. Vita Soph. 2.23; 605, where it is said that Damianus was a pupil of Adrian when the latter was in Ephesus. His prime is in a time after the era with which this study is concerned.

—T. Flavius Damianus (III-672, and many other inscriptions in Ephesus; Philostr. Vita Soph. 2.23; 605) is the most famous and the richest sophist of Ephesus. According to the *Vita* he was away from Ephesus only while he was studying. He settles in Ephesus and remains there for the rest of his life; he marries into the Vedii family and participates in a royal way in the construction of the city in the middle of the second century; from a statue (kept in the Museum of Izmir)[18] it appears that he was also "high priest of Asia". Therefore, he is not really a travelling teacher, but because of the fact that he has a central position of power in the life of the city, it is not inappropriate to close this list of names with him, not because there are no others who are known but because these are later in time.

Most of these people were known to a certain extent in the city. People resisted them in the city as was the case:

—with Paul: besides the story of the popular resistance in Ephesus in Acts 19 see also 1 Cor 15:32: "what have I gained if, simply from human motives—ἐθηριομάχησα—in Ephesus"; because we cannot really imagine Paul as a gladiator, this is usually weakened to "fighting to the death" instead of "fighting with wild animals";[19] and Phil 1:13, when this text speaks of the imprisonment of Paul in Ephesus;

—with Apollonius who, in his trial in Rome, is accused because of his activities in Ephesus (Vita Apoll. 8.7.8);

—with Timothy who, according to his *Vita* was murdered because he resisted against the feast of Dionysus;

or one made common cause with them politically like:

—Dionysius who gets an official burial place on the *agora*;

—Favorinus who was to act in the name of the city;

—Damianus who, as we said above, is at the centre of the political life of the city.

---

[18] Inan 1966, 128 no. 151.

[19] See recently Thiessen 1994, 111ff

The Jesus-story in John runs mostly parallel with the first series of teachers: Jesus who travels time and again to the most important city in the country; Jesus who finds conflict with the authorities of the city and who ultimately is condemned to death because of his teaching. It is also a story with runs counter to the main events of the second series of teachers. Jesus does not belong to the guild of those sophists who know to comport themselves and to avoid the conflict with the politically important leaders of the city. Jesus is a travelling teacher who is not prepared to compromise the content of his teaching.

4.2.2 *The doctrine, the miracles, the meals*
The text of John links the teaching activity of Jesus with a number of special characteristics: the special way his teaching is given form; the relation with the special deeds of Jesus, and the attention to the various ways of having a meal. In different ways and in varying measure these are realities which exist also in Ephesus.

4.2.2.1 *The attention for the form and the content of the doctrine*

The teachers are in some way in competition with each other: one has to prove oneself over against the others. Maybe this can explain the concern in antiquity to express, directly or indirectly, one's belonging to a certain direction, the attention paid to the αἱρέσεις —not only in philosophy, but also in medicine and law. In the list of teachers who visited Ephesus, as given above, one can point to the following:

—Potamōn is called ἐγκλεκτικός, a special term which indicates that he relates in a special way to the various philosophical currents;
—Apollos is called ἀνὴρ λόγιος by Luke (Acts 18,24), someone who is "strong in the Scriptures", and who can find "proofs" and "counter-proofs" in them (Acts 18:28);
—Paul on the other hand is given the attribute διαλεγόμενος, a term which, in the philosophical discourse, indicates that someone practises dialectic, elicits conclusions by discussion (Acts 19:8,9);
—Apollonius: διαλέγομαι is a term which is used also for Apollonius, combined with the more specific διάλεξις, discourse (Vita Apoll. 4.2; 4.3; 4.4; 8.26). More precise is the description

given in 4.2, "The first discourse then which he delivered was to the Ephesians from the platform of their temple, *and its tone was not that of the Socratic school*; for he dissuaded and discouraged them from other pursuits, and urged them to devote themselves to philosophy alone, and to fill Ephesus with real study rather than with idleness and revelry such as he found around him there";

—Ofellius Laetus is precisely characterized as is Potamōn. In two inscriptions he is called πλατωνικός φιλόσοφος;

—In his *Vitae*, Philostratus several times offers a description of the doctrine of the various people.

—About Dionysius who is called ῥήτωρ in IE II-426 and ῥήτωρ καὶ σοφιστής in IE VII-1-3047, Philostratus writes: "He was a pupil of Isaeus, that is of one who, as I have said, employed a natural style, and of this style he successfully took the impress, and the orderly arrangement of his thoughts besides...And though he presented his ideas with honeyed sweetness, he was...economical with them" (1.22; 522);

—About Favorinus he says: "His style of eloquence was careless in construction, but it was both learned and pleasing. It is said that he improvised with ease and fluency" (1.8; 491). And Philostratus concludes these *Vitae* with the more general sentences: "This is all I have to say about the men, who though they pursued philosophy, had the reputation of sophists" (1.8; 492);

—About Adrian, who reputedly could imitate the styles of all kinds of sophists and orators, it is said: "This sophist had a copious flow of ideas and handled them brilliantly, and also in the disposition of his themes he showed the utmost variety, which he had acquired from his study of tragedy. He did not observe the conventional arrangement or follow the rules of art, but he furnished himself with the diction of the ancient sophists and clothed his style therewith as with a garment, with sonorousness rather than striking effects" (2.10; 590);

—About Damianus: "His style was more sophistic than is usual in a legal orator, and more judicial than is usual in a sophist" (2.23; 606).

If one refers this to the possible readers of John's text in Ephesus, one can expect that they will have tried to place Jesus as teacher into a framework within the usual 'streams'. Because the text does not give an account of that and does not reflexively indicate what the author or Jesus himself thinks about this, there are only indirect indications, much the same as we find in the author of the Acts.

As we have said already, it is relevant that Jesus is continually in dialogue. There are only few longer discourses (ch. 5 and 15). All other speaking parts are in the form of a dialogue. Symptomatic is a certain preference for the words ἐρωτάω (27x) and especially ἀποκρίνομαι (78x). The base-words are λέγω (206x), εἰπεῖν (204x) and λαλέω (60x). There are a couple of special constructions such as the introduction-sentence ἀμὴν ἀμὴν λέγω ὑμῖν (σοι) (20x + 5x) and the ubiquitous ἀπεκρίθη ('Ιησοῦς) καὶ εἶπεν (33x). Apart from this there are not too many other verba dicendi and these are used relatively seldom: διδάσκω (9x); ἐντέλλομαι (3x) and κράζω (4x).[20] The reduction in the vocabulary makes it clear that the dialogue structure is used in its most simple but also its most lucid form: he spoke—he asked—he answered—he said. Important is the fact that, in a number of cases in the dialogue, there is a kind of internal reflection, i.e. that in a number of cases there is a reference in the dialogue to other discussions—"as the Father spoke to me, so I speak to you"; "I told you before"—or there is a reference to the dialogue-character of the actual dialogue: "amen, amen, I say to you" (the present tense); "the word which I spoke to you" (the perfect tense); "I will not speak to you any more" (the future tense). The expressions reinforce the dialogical character of the text.

If readers in Ephesus wanted to place John's text in a framework and looked for possible links to some form of teaching, they will have compared this text with the representatives of the different schools that were present in Ephesus: platonists, eclectists, practitioners of dialectics and, possibly, cynics. Doing this for them, it is not to be excluded that some people will have seen some

---

[20] In this list belongs also μαρτυρέω. It is used 33 times (plus also the noun and other forms; cf. the literature about this word in Beutler 1972), usually indirectly as reference to other realities—'my father gives witness about me' etc.—but sometimes as introduction to a speech-act of Jesus or another person (see 3:11; 4:44; 8:14,18; 13:21; 18:37). There are some other verbs from this juridical sphere: ἀρνέομαι, ὁμολογέω, ἀντιλέγω, ἐξετάζω but these are not used in the dialogue structure of Jesus' teaching activity.

relationship with the platonists and that they, maybe, imagined Jesus as a teacher in the manner of Socrates, the unrivalled model of this dialogical teaching.

4.2.2.2 *The combination with the miracles*

John's text links the words of Jesus a number of times to miracles which are seen as σημεῖα—as proving signs for the truth of what Jesus says: Jesus as a genuine miracle-worker. For Ephesus the following data are relevant:

—In the text of the Acts, Paul is described in Ephesus as someone with magical powers. People place the sweatbands and the aprons which have been in touch with his body on the sick, and the sickness leaves them and the evil spirits depart (Acts 19:11,12). Paul receives a power which belongs to Jesus (in the Gospel) and to Peter (Acts 5:15: concerning the healing power of Peter's shadow). The story about Paul is followed in Acts by the story about the seven sons of the high priest Skeuas who, as travelling exorcists, succumb to a demon, an event which leads to the burning of expensive magic books (Acts 19:13-20). That means that with Paul's arrival in Ephesus there is not only the teaching of a doctrine. The doctrine is supported by the miraculous charisma of Paul which ties the demons to Jesus and to his person. It prevents other people from acting as exorcists. The magic books become dangerous and superfluous.[21]

---

[21] See also Arnold 1989, a book which studies the relationship between the 'magical' Ephesus and the letter to the Ephesians. The author is, probably, somewhat too much convinced of the magnitude of the presence of magical ideas and practices in Ephesus in the first century. Historical facts do not evolve because one *says* that Egyptian magical papyri exist also in Ephesus or that the second and third century documents contain first century material. His basic thesis about the relation between the letter to the Ephesians and magical thinking, however, does not, therefore, fall completely.

As a result of this study it has become clear to me how close the relationship is between the letter to the Ephesians and the Johannine text. A number of the central ideas from Ephesians are also central to the Jn-text:

—Apollonius is also seen as a miracle worker. He performs miracles, also during his stay in Ephesus. He predicts a plague for Ephesus for which prediction he must defend himself in his Roman trial, because he is being accused of being a γόης—i.e. someone with evil magical powers (Vita Apoll. 4.4; 8.7.9). He resists Domitian in Ephesus and at the moment that Domitian is murdered he sees what is happening in Rome: "he was delivering an address, just at the moment when it all happened in the palace at Rome; and first he dropped his voice, as if he were terrified, and then, though with less vigour than was usual with him, he continued his exposition, like one who between his words caught glimpses of something foreign to his subject, and at last he lapsed into silence, like one who has been interrupted in his discourse. And with an awful glance at the ground...he cried: 'Smite the tyrant, smite him'" (Vita Apoll. 8.26). It is a vision, the truth of which becomes known a couple of days later: it places Apollonius in the series of seers and prophets.

—In the book *Ephesiaca*, one can read how this commerce with the magical side of the world is given imaginary form. The heroes of the story are extremely ill because they are in love with each

---

- the figure of 'lord of the cosmos' as anti-power: Jn 12:31; 14:30; 16:11 and Eph 2:2;
- the transition from the time-scheme (the past in opposition to the here and now) to the spatial scheme (above in opposition to below): 'rise up' vs 'go down': Jn passim; Eph 4:8-10; 'heavenly things': Jn 3:12; Eph 1:3,20; 2:6; 3:10; 6:12.
- the darkness of former life and the light now: Jn 1:5; 6:17; 8:12; 12:35,46 and Eph 5:8,11; 6:12;
- the transition from the powers as transition from death to life and participation in the resurrection: Jn 5:24; 11:26; Eph 2:4-10;
- Jesus who speaks about 'the temple of his body' which will be pulled down and will be rebuilt in Jn 2:21 and the metaphor of 'the head and the body which needs to be built up' in Eph 1:22,23; 4:15-16; 5:23.

Is it possible that the letter to the Ephesians is a first attempt in Christian theology to combine the thoughts of Paul and John? If we suppose that Jn has been read in Ephesus, sooner or later one will run into the problem of the long and intensive presence of Paul in Ephesus and into the question how the quite different theologies of Paul and John have reacted to one another. Could the letter to the Ephesians be a specimen of that?

other but they are not yet sure of each other. No one understands what is going on. The parents of Anthia, the girl in the story, "let diviners (μάντεις) and priests come to heal her. They come, kill sacrificial animals, perform libations, speak barbarian words over them in order to put some demons in a favourable frame of mind, as they say." (1.5.6) The parents of Habrocomes, the boy in the story, do the same, but nothing helps. The children are in danger of death. The two fathers then decide that Apollo must be consulted in Colophon. From the answer they come to the conclusion that the two must marry. And immediately the mortal illness disappears.

—The matter finds discussion even among the Sophists who, obviously, do not present themselves as miracle workers. In the *Vita* of Dionysius, Philostratus touches on the relation between rhetoric and magic. It is said of Dionysius that he trained the memory of his disciples "by the help of Chaldean art". Philostratus thinks this is nonsense: "who that is enrolled among the wise would be so foolishly careless of his own reputation as to use magic arts with his pupils" (γοητεύων) (Vita Soph. 1.22; 523).

—In the *Vita* of Adrian, the same connection is made: "He (=Adrian) was about eighty when he died, and had attained to such high honour that many actually believed him to be a magician. But in my account of Dionysius I have said enough to show that a well-educated man would never be led astray into the practice of magic arts" (Vita Soph. 2.10; 590).

The slanderous accusations of the possible use of magical powers show how close the relation between teaching activity and miracle practice is seen to be. The background information quoted shows that this was true in Ephesus too and that the Jesus-story of John was in Ephesus understood against the background of miracle-working teachers. The accusation that Jesus is possessed by a demon takes on special meaning against this background, especially if we see that the accusation is about what Jesus says (7:20; 8:48-52) as well as about what he does (10:21,22).

The only thing which does not play a role in Ephesus is the lexicalization of the miracles under the word σημεῖον. In general this is true for all the literature about Greek 'miracle-workers',[22]

---

[22] Cf. Kuhn 1988; Rengstorf TWNT s.v. σημεῖον.

but especially for the people who have made their appearance, more or less provable, in Ephesus, and for the use of this word in the inscriptions. This last remark may seem strange but is not. In Magnesia, the neighbouring city of Ephesus (one of the gates in Ephesus is called the Magnesia gate) mention is made of a σημεῖον in the inscriptions (I. Magn. 215): in a plane-tree, split by the wind, an image of Dionysus was found. The event is seen by the people as a σημεῖον; a mission has been sent to Apollo in Delphi and a cult and a place for cult has been erected for Dionysus.[23] Probably it means that even the σημεῖον-character of Jesus' miracles in the Johannine Gospel is not completely separate from the Ephesus-context.

4.2.2.3 *The intense attention for the meals*

In the narrative of the Johannine Gospel, much attention given to meals: meal-scenes and discussions about eating and drinking. In this we see a clear parallel with the situation in Ephesus: there too we find a real interest in special, communal meals. If we take the study by H.J. Klauck about religious meals in the Hellenistic culture as our point of departure,[24] we find his ordering of these various meals to be almost completely in line with texts from Ephesus. With some preference for the first century setting and for possible links with John's text I may point to the following:

a. *The meals of the people*

—Like every Hellenistic city Ephesus is familiar with meals where, if not the whole populace, at any rate large groups of people participate. One must imagine them to be as large as possible. These are popular feasts which do not easily fade away. In Ephesus the institutionally most important meal is given on the yearly feast of Artemis on the mountain Solmissus (see I-27-34 about the foundation of Vibius Salutaris and Strabo 14.1.20).

---

[23] The middle of the first century AD, but maybe it is a restoration of a much earlier inscription.

[24] *Herrenmahl und hellenistischer Kult. Eine religionsgeschichtliche Untersuchung zum ersten Korintherbrief*, 1982.

Strabo writes:

> On the coast, slightly above the sea, is Ortygia, which is a magnificent grove of all kinds of trees, of the cypress most of all...Above the grove lies Mount Solmissus, where, it is said, the Curetes stationed themselves, and with the din of their arms frightened Hera out of her wits—protecting so Artemis and Apollo—...A general festival is held there annually; and by a certain custom the youths vie for honour, particularly in the splendour of their banquets there. At that time, also, a special college of the Curetes holds symposiums and performs certain mystic sacrifices.

Therefore, there is a distinction between what οἱ νέοι and τὸ ἀρχεῖον τῶν κουρήτων do. The younger people hold εὐωχίαι and the *kouretes* συμπόσια καὶ μύστικαι θυσίαι, a difference which probably does not mean much more than that the *kouretes* are responsible for the explicitly religious setting of the feast. In John's text we find, as a parallel, the story about the people's meal in chapter 6—which only in John takes place on the mountain (and near the sea), a mountain which for the readers in Ephesus represents a special reality, because on that mountain Artemis and Apollo, the children of Zeus are born of Leto with the help of the *kouretes* from Ephesus and against the machinations of the jealous wife Hera.
—Apart from this yearly city feast, there are many other yearly meals. The texts of several foundations have been preserved which prescribe a yearly meal for certain or all persons in authority and for the citizens:
—The freedman C. Stertinius Orpex (time of Nero) determined that every year the one hundred members of the γερουσία would be given a small sum of money, if they came to the festive meal (VII-2-4123);
—T. Flavius Montanus (Domitian-Trajan era), who organized gladiatorial games and hunting parties for the city, once also prepared an ἄριστον for all citizens while everyone furthermore received 3 denarii (VI-2061B);
—C. Licinius Maximus Julianus (Trajan-Hadrian era) is a benefactor of the city in a similar way, with large edifices near the harbour and the gymnasia, with the organization of games, and,

during the time that he was the *prytanis* of the city, he offered the
citizens κατὰ φυλήν a festive meal (VII-1-3066);

—Even if we cannot date them precisely, it is probably worthwhile
pointing to the following texts:

—III-951: Aurelius Varanus took care that during 11 days the city
would be lit up on the occasion of an evening meal of the βουλή
and all συνέδρια, 40,000 citizens plus the association of the temple
officials and the gold-carriers. The inscription reminds one of the
meal in Jn 6 where the number of participants is also mentioned
with such prominence ("there were about 5000 men" Jn 6:10) and
of the events in Jn 8 where the illumination of the city during the
feast of Tabernacles makes Jesus say that he is the light of the
world (Jn 8:12);

—VII-2-4330: in a much restored text, there is mention of a
benefactor of the city who offered a festive meal to "all συνέδρια",
apart from the reception and care of the 'foreigners', people who
represented a certain interest for the city;

—VII-1-3245: all the inhabitants of the village of Apateira are
asked to celebrate the birthday of the emperor together in an εὐωχία
for which money was set aside in a testamentary deposition.

b. *The meals of individual organizations*

Somewhat more modest are the meals which individual
organizations pay for, organize, and present. The difference is not
great but there are fewer people present. The kind of meal is much
the same. The texts which are preserved, are mostly texts from
tombs which as a rule cannot be dated so precisely; they are
generally 1st to 3rd century AD:

—"The singers of hymns of the temple in Pergamum" celebrate
Tiberius' birthday; sacrifices and a festive meal play an important
role in the celebration. It is an aristocratic organization but that too
does not make much difference as far as the style of the meal is
concerned (VII-2-3801B; time of Claudius);

—Aurelia Nike, Aurelius Zopyrus and their son determine that
"the organization of the woodcutters" must have a festive οἰνοποσία
using the interest of their capital for it (VI-2115);

—Pompeius Euprosdektos wants to use the interest on his capital
for a yearly οἰνοποσία and an εὐωχία for the organization of "the

workers before the gate near the statue of Poseidon" where wax images and wreaths should play a role (VII-1-3216);

—The "most sacred council of the society of hirers" (which oversees the priesthoods and the moneys of Artemis; second half of the 2nd century) ensures that the festivities are preceded by a procession in which the sacrificial animals for Artemis are shown in a δειπνοφοριακή πομπή (V-1577A; 1577B; I-26).

c. *The sacrificial meals and the libations*

Sacrifices, meat sacrifices and libations, are good for the gods, but they are also good for the ones who bring the sacrifice. In a division determined by tradition, the important and/or less important parts of the sacrificial animals are returned to the ones giving them. They organize a festive meal out of these parts where meat is the main ingredient. Where 'sacrifices' are mentioned in the inscriptions, one can suppose that a meal will have taken place.

—The sacrificial texts of the Artemis cult were mentioned in the previous chapter. They deal with a reality which affects all the citizens. The highest authorities are involved because they are concerned that the cult in this temple should function well.
—Apart from this there is a small number of texts which speak about other cults:
    —sacrifices for the god Augustus (and Roma): IV-1393;
    —sacrifices for Demeter and the Sebastoi: II-213 (time of Domitian);
    —sacrifices for Asclepius and the Sebastoi: III-719 (time of Trajan);
    —sacrifices for Asclepius in preparation for a contest of the doctors: IV-1162 (time of Hadrian or later);
    —sacrifices for Isis and Sarapis: IV-1213 (time of Hadrian);
    —sacrifices for Dionysus: V-1601/1602 (from the time of Trajan and later).
Probably, a meal is connected with the sacrifice in all these cults.
—For a good part these texts run parallel with the texts which place these sacrificial meals in the context of μυστήρια. In Ephesus in this period, there are celebrations of the *mysteria* of:
    —Artemis: III-702; 987; 988; 989; VII-1-3059; 3072
    —Demeter: II-213; V-1595; VII-1-3252

—Dionysus: II-275; 293; V-1595
—Sebastoi: II-213; 275; 293; V-1506
—Aphrodite: IV-1202
—Men: VII-1-3252

Even though not much is known about the rites, the supposition is that the celebration of the *mysteria* implies a (closing) meal. In some texts lists of names are given, an indication that large sums of money are involved and that it is, therefore, worthwhile to mention it in stone.[25]

—Sacrifices for the gods represent also an economic value. The texts about the "holy place of slaughter" which is part of the *agora* and where the meat, dedicated to the divinity, is sold, indicate in yet another way that there are 'sacred meals' in Ephesus: see V-1840; VI-2226; VII-1-3015; VII-1-3271 (in Tepe).

—Sometimes the sacrificial meals are linked to libations. The Artemis cult knows a σπονδαύλης as a ritual official. He is mentioned already in the oldest lists and his function remains till the latest times (IV-1001-1029; 1031-1044).

The combination of meat sacrifices and libations occurs also on other occasions and for other deities:

—at the cult for Augustus and Roma: IV-1393;
—at the thanksgiving meal which *neopoioi* offer to the people: III-965; V-1578b; 1579b; 1589b;
—at the start of great games: I-22 (time of Antoninus Pius).

d. *The meals at the tomb*

In Ephesus too,[26] it is made clear, directly and indirectly, that at the grave of a dead person communal meals are celebrated at set times: directly in the texts of sepulchral foundations in which the remaining capital is to be used for the yearly meal: the οἰνοποισία for "the association of the woodcutters" (VI-2115) and the

---

[25] In the letter to the Ephesians, *mysteria* are mentioned a couple of times; according to Caragounis 1977 this has no relation with what we know about the *mysteria* of Eleusis and other *mysteria*; there is, therefore, no relation with the mention of these *mysteria* in the Ephesian inscriptions.

[26] See Klauck 1982, 76ff.

οἰνοποιοία and εὐωχία for "the workers before the gate near the statue of Poseidon" (VII-1-3216), cf. the texts mentioned above; and indirectly in sepulchral inscriptions which prove that the tomb itself is built as a τρίκλινος: see especially VII-2-3312 and 3834 where the three *klinai* are mentioned, somewhat more simply also in VII-1-3254; 3292; 3453; 3456; 3460; 3469.

People are associated with each other and every association offers opportunities to meet. Communal meals are often the result. The multitude of inscriptions clarifies something of the frequency of the occurrence but also of its public character. With larger groups the communal meal will normally have taken place in the open air, in various places inside and outside of the city: the impact will have been different dependent on the way the group was constituted and how much was invested in the food. Also (or precisely) in a city culture, eating together is a constant reality. The readers of John in Ephesus, therefore, will have filled in the meal stories of John with personal and public experiences they have in such an abundance: the matrimonial celebration of Jn 2; the teaching about drink and food and the reception of strangers in Jn 4; the people's meal on the mountain near the sea in Jn 6; the sacrificial meal of Jesus' flesh and blood in Jn 6; the meal after the dead and the coming to life of Lazarus foreshadowing the death of Jesus in Jn 12; the symposium-like event of the teacher with his disciples as a gathering of friends during which the teacher's departure and return is discussed in Jn 13-17; and the breakfast of bread and fish on the beach of the sea in Jn 21. John's text inserts itself in a very special way and with very specific interferences into the Ephesian context.

4.2.3 *The group of the disciples*

The group of the disciples in the Johannine Gospel is a group of pupils/friends; it is a group which is open to varying new members, where not everyone is a permanent member, a group which minimalizes the distinction between the sexes, which is financially dependent on alms and which puts the financial management in the hands of some individuals. It is clear that this group, next to the realities already discussed, presents itself (also) as a 'religious association', as such comparable to, and by the readers compared to, groups (and practices) which exist in Ephesus.

4.2.3.1 *The religious groups and associations in Ephesus*

The inscriptions in Ephesus give much information about this sort of groups and practices. Based on a positive as well as a negative selection the mutual interferences can be indicated or at least can be presumed.

I speak also about a negative selection because, in my opinion, a number of situations which exist in Ephesus are not good material for comparison. I want to exclude everything connected with the exercise of the proper city religion: the adoration of Artemis, Hestia, and the God-emperor. Obviously, these are most often mentioned in the inscriptions. Via the lists of the *prytanies* and the *kouretes*, via the mention of the names of μολποί, λευκοφοροῦντες, χρυσοφοροῦντες, ὑμνῳδοί, νεοποίοι; via the descriptions of the foundations such as those of C. Julius, Stertinius Orpex and Vibius Salutaris, and via the decrees of Paullus Fabius Persicus and Claudius, this happens so explicitly that one cannot miss it. But for a comparison with the Jesus-group in John, these texts are not truly relevant, because, even disregarding looking at the content, these cults are almost in opposition with what is said in John about Jesus' disciples, organizationally, financially, and administratively. They are the object of continuing concern for the state. They are financed by the city; they have a staff of personnel, numerous cult-prescriptions, imposing processions and places for the cult. One could think of even more points of opposition but it is clear that all this is of no interest to the Jesus-group in John.

Closest in organization are those religious groups and associations which present themselves as existing groups on the basis of a private initiative:
  —οἱ Δημητριασταί (VII-2-4337, Tiberius era);
  —οἱ πρὸ πόλεως Διονύσου Φλέω μύσται (II-275; IV-1257; V-1600; 1601, Hadrian era);
  —οἱ πρὸ πόλεως Δημητριασταί καὶ Διονύσου Φλέω μύσται (V-1595);
  —the group for the veneration of Dionysus and the Eleusian Deities (= Demeter, Persephone and Kore) (IV-1270, time of Domitian);

—οἱ ἐργάται προπυλεῖται πρὸς τῷ Ποσειδῶνι (VII-1-3216, tomb-foundation of Pompeius Euprosdectus).

—the group of the "decuriones et tabellarii et equites qui sunt ad Lares Domnicos" (VII-2-4112, Trajan era).

The groups have to do mostly with the veneration of Demeter and Dionysus. I spoke about this in the preceding chapter. These are groups with benefactors, but the group itself remains primarily responsible. The lists of names which are known indicate that the inner-circle is rather limited and that it is organized according to various functions. One can presume that sometimes by way of exception women also participate—I will come back to this. Together with Latin names there are quite a few Greek names and there are probably some slaves. The founder is also the leader who apparently takes care that the people keep meeting to offer sacrifices and celebrate the communal meals. The most interesting texts in this regard are V-1600/1 (and 1602 from a later date). The yearly feast of Dionysus is probably commemorated. Because there is a series of inscriptions from different years, one gets a glimpse of some development. While a number of names remain the same through the years, new names are mentioned, more or less parallel to the way we find several combinations of disciples in the Johannine Gospel: in Jn 1: Andrew, Peter, Philip, Nathanael, and an anonymous person and in Jn 6, some time later: Andrew, Philip, Peter, and Judas etc. The leader of the group ensures that the group meets regularly.

Perhaps this is an appropriate point to refer to the group of names from Ephesus (and the surrounding cities) which are mentioned in the *Epistles of Ignatius*. When Ignatius arrives at Smyrna, he is visited by delegations from different cities: from Ephesus, by Onesimos, the *episkopos*; Burrhus, a *diakonos* who accompanies Ignatius at least as far as Troas (cf. Ign. Philad. 11:2; Ign. Smyrna 12:1); Krokos, Euplous and Fronto (Ign. Eph. 1:3; 2:1); from Magnesia, by Damas, the *episkopos*, Bassus and Apollonios, *presbyteroi*, and Zotion, a *diakonos* (Ign. Magn. 2:1); and from Tralles by Polybios, the *episkopos* (Ign. Trall. 1:1). In Smyrna itself a greater group is mentioned: Polycarp, the *episkopos*, Tavia, Alke, Daphnos, Euteknos, the wife of Epitropos and Attalos (Ign. Smyrna 13:1-2 and Ign. Polycarp 8:2-3).

A few remarks may be added. The names used are mostly of low status. The genre itself (the writing of letters) probably prescribes that only *praenomina* are to be used—but notice the use of the Latin form of the name Pontius Pilate. Nevertheless, there are differences between the names of, for example, Onesimos—which is often the name of a slave—and Fronto—which can belong to people of higher circles as with Lucius Peducaeus Fronto, the procurator of Claudius (III-703/703A) or with Aelius Fronto, a freedman of the emperor who has emancipated his own slave Aelius Hermias (VI-2202A); and between the purely Greek names and the Roman names Burrhus and Bassus; Polycarp must have been rather rich —when the authorities look for him, he can flee to a farm not too distant from the city to remain there with a few friends, and afterwards to another one to be betrayed under torture by one of his own slaves (Martyrdom of Polycarp 5 and 6); Burrhus functions as the personal secretary of Ignatius (Ign. Smyrna 13:1; Ign. Philad. 11:2); with Alke, Daphnus and Attalos, Ignatius has developed personal and emotional ties. The delegations (from Ephesus, Magnesia and Tralles) consist of men only, different from the description of the group in Smyrna which contains several names of rather independent women: the house of Tavia "who may be confirmed in her love both of the flesh and spirit" (Ign. Smyrna 13:2), the house of the wife of Epitropos, and Alke, twice mentioned "a name most dear to me" (Ign. Smyrna 13:2; Ign. Polycarp 8:3).[27] All in all, these data are rather similar to what we know, epigraphically, of the (other) religious groups in Ephesus.

All this demands a further addition. The text of John lives from the positive and negative relation with Jewish custom and Jewish philosophy and life. One must start from the idea that a number of readers lives in an emotional—even if not spatial—proximity to Jews. Concrete readers will read the text in this way. That is the reason that a number of exegetes place the origin of the Johannine Gospel closer to Palestine than to Ephesus: in Samaria, South-Syria or Antioch.[28]

---

[27] Cf. Bauer-Paulsen 1985 in loco; Meinhold 1979, 19-36.
[28] See a.o. Meeks 1972, Cullmann 1975, Wengst 1983/2.

In this study we concentrate on the question whether, in Ephesus, there was enough awareness of Jewishness to understand the Johannine Gospel under this aspect. The epigraphic data for Ephesus are not as abundant as for example one would expect from the Ephesus-story in Acts. Because the material has been recently discussed,[29] I give only the following summary for the sake of completeness:

1. In the first place we can refer to Josephus-texts in which the edict of Agrippa about the Jews in Ephesus is of great importance (Ant. 16.168).[30] Three questions are discussed in this text:
a. the Jews in Asia take care and accept responsibility for the safeguarding of the temple tax which has been collected;
b. thieves of this money are forbidden asylum and if caught the Jews may judge these people themselves;
c. no one is allowed to force a Jew to reach agreement on the Sabbath on the basis of securities.
This decree is in line with other decrees about Jews in Asia from about the same time: the letter of Augustus to Norbanus Flaccus about the right of the Jews to collect money for the temple in Jerusalem and to send it over;[31] the letter of Julius Antonius, the proconsul to Ephesus as confirmation of the Agrippa-letter[32] and the letter of Augustus to the proconsul Gaius Marcius Censorinus with a similar content which has to be published in Ancyra.[33]

2. Then there is the famous scene about Paul's presence in Ephesus as told in Acts 18:24-19:40 with its many precise terms, names, and concepts which in a special way give a touch of local colour

---

[29] See esp. Fergus Millar in the English edition of Schürer, 1973-1987, vol. 3,1 p.22f and Horsley 1992, 121ff.

[30] See ch.3, p. 67.

[31] Jos. Ant. 16.166; Philo, Leg. ad Gaium 311 (14 BC).

[32] Jos. Ant. 16.172; Julius Antonius is probably proconsul in 4 BC: he is condemned to death in 2 BC.

[33] Jos. Ant. 16.162ff; Censorinus is proconsul in 2 AD; the letter is mostly identical with the Agrippa-letter; added is "and if anyone is caught stealing their sacred books or their sacred monies from a synagogue or an ark (ἀαρῶν or ἀνδρῶν), he shall be regarded as sacrilegious, and his property shall be confiscated to the public treasury of the Romans".

and which have always impressed because of their vivacity. For our context it is important that the Jews are presented as such a well-known group that everyone in the city knows about them; that religious oppositions reach even the people's assemblies and are experienced as a Jewish-Greek conflict; that notwithstanding Paul's breach with the synagogue the Greek silversmiths see the Jews and the Christians as one party.

3. Important in the total *status quaestionis*, in relation especially to the question whether Jn 4 can have been understood in Ephesus (the story which speaks so much from the viewpoint of Samaritan interests), is IE III-713, in which the council and the people of Flavia Neapolis in Samaria honour proconsul Quintus Roscius Murena Coelius Pompeius Falco (123/4) as saviour and benefactor via their legates Fl. Iuncus and Ulpius Proculus. Because of its importance I give the text as it is edited in IE:

Κόιντον ῾Ρώσκιον Μου-   διατελέσαντα, ᾽Ασίας ἀνθύ-
ρήνα Κουέλλον Πομ-   πατον, ἐτείμησεν Φλαουι-
πήιον Φάλκωνα, πρεσ-   έων Νεαπολειτῶν Σαμαρέ-
βευτὴν Σεβαστοῦ καὶ ἀν-   ων ἡ βουλὴ καὶ ὁ δῆμος τὸν
τιστράτηγον Λυκίας καὶ   σωτῆρα καὶ εὐεργέτην
Παμφυλίας καὶ ᾽Ιουδαίας καὶ   διὰ πρεσβευτῶν καὶ ἐπι-
Μυσίας καὶ Βρεταννίας   μελητῶν Φλαουίου ᾽Ιούνκου
καὶ πολλὰς ἄλλας ἡγεμονίας   καὶ Οὐλπίου Πρόκλου.

> Through the ambassadors and managers Flavius Iuncus and Ulpius Proculus, the council and the people of Flavia Neapolis in Samaria honoured as saviour and benefactor Quintus Roscius Murena Coelius Pompeius Falco, ambassador of Augustus and governor of Lycia, Pamphylia, Judea, Mysia and Britannia; and having accomplished many other public functions, proconsul of Asia.

It is a text which can have been written in a meaningful way only if Samaritan interests had to be taken care of even in Ephesus. Pompeius Falco is proconsul in a year which is very important for Ephesus. Hadrian is in Asia for the first time and visits Ephesus. He has already given Smyrna an emperor-temple and Ephesus hopes to receive a similar favour. It cannot be excluded that the legation from far-away Samaria belongs in this framework, as support for the demand of Ephesus. Although fragmentary, there is another inscription in honour of Pompeius Falco (III-713a). That could be another province.

For a slightly later time, there is another indication of a connection between Samaria and Ephesus. It concerns Justin Martyr who was born in 100/110 in Flavia Neapolis in Samaria and who, in his book *Dialogue with Trypho*, says that he was in discussion with the Jew Trypho in Ephesus. That discussion would have happened in 135 AD and Justin reports on it around 155/61 when living in Rome.[34] The book is, in any case, a demonstration of the distance which has developed between Christians and Jews in the writer's perspective.

4. We can add the following epigraphic data. As appears from the list, they are few in number and maybe none dates from the first century AD. It is said and estimated that these are inscriptions from the 2nd and 3rd century:

—IV-1251: τῶν ἀρχισυναγωγῶν καὶ τῶν πρεσβυ[τέρων] πολλὰ τὰ ἔτη (a fragmentary inscription: "of the rulers of a synagogue and the elders the many years").

—V-1676: τὸ μνημεῖόν ἐστι Μαρ. Μουσσίου ἰαιρέος· ζῆ· κήδονται οἱ Ἰουδαῖοι (probably, "the memorial belongs to M[arcus] Au[relius] Mussius, a priest; may he live; the Jews took care of it").

—V-1677: [τὸ μνημεῖόν ἐστιν] Ἰο[υλίου] [...] ἀρχιατροῦ [καὶ] [τῆς γυναικ]ὸς αὐτοῦ Ἰουλίας [...]ης καὶ τέκνων αὐτῶν. [ζῶ]σιν· [ταύτης τῆ]ς σοροῦ κήδον[ται οἱ ἐν Ἐφέ]σῳ Ἰουδεοι ("[the memorial belongs to] Ju[lius...], a chief doctor [and his w]ife Julia [...] and their children; [may they l]ive; the Jews in Ephesus took care of this coffin").

—VII-2-3822: Ἰουδαίων νεωτέρων (from Hypaipa, probably about the Suzanne-story, "of the younger Jews");

—VII-2-4130: τὸ θυσιαστήριον (with a drawing of a menorah, from a synagogue ?);

—SEG 1989, 1222: [τοῦτο τὸ ἡμι][μόριόν ἐστι]ν [...]ίου [....] Ἐφε[σίου Ἰουδ]έου [...μό]ριον.

---

[34] Cf. Winden 1971, 5ff; Lampe 1987, 231.

τοῦτο τ[ὸ ἡμι]μόριόν ἐ[στιν] Αὐρ. Σαμ[βαθίου]
Ἰούδα Ἐφ[εσίου] Ἰουδέου ἐκοι[νωνη...].
   ("[this half belongs to ....]ius[...]Ephesian Jew...";
   ("this half belongs to Aurelius Sam[bathius] Juda, an
   Eph[esian] Jew; it is shared...").

A few minor points can be added:
—VII-1-3448b: Ἀννᾶς Μνασικράτου: a tomb-inscription in
Metropolis; although it is always complicated to argue only from a
name, it seems in this case that it is a Jewish name.
—VII-1-3032: a honorary inscription for Tib. Claudius Priscus
who was *chiliarch* of the leg. X Fretensis from the era of
Vespasian. This is not a Jew but a Roman soldier who served in a
rather important position in Vespasian's army which took part in
the Jewish war. It is scarcely well possible that he never spoke
about these Jewish affairs.
—VII-2-4112: a honorary inscription for Flavius Iuncus, who was
tribune in the leg. X Fretensis (in Judea, therefore) probably a little
later than Claudius Priscus; he was also tribune of the cohort V
Gemella which was stationed in Syria Palestine. The inscription was
erected by officials of the imperial administration in Ephesus where
Flavius Iuncus made a real career. The man is probably mentioned
in III-713 as one of the legates of Flavia Neapolis in Samaria who,
in the name of the people and the council of Neapolis (Samaria),
was sent to Ephesus to erect a statue for the proconsul Pompeius
Falco, the saviour and benefactor of Samaria. It seems that the man
is an expert in 'judaica'. And, although it cannot be shown how this
influenced his career, it is clear that it did not do any damage.
   The Johannine story is played out in a completely Jewish setting.
A group gathers around Jesus; they have general interests but strive
also for their own particular interests in knowledge, in mutual
relationships, and in honouring God. From the history of the Jews
in Ephesus we know nothing of internal group-formations apart
from the activity of Paul as told in Acts. In the inscriptions we read
about 'the Jews' who distinguish themselves by means of specific
functions—heads of the synagogue, the elders, a priest, or by means
of a profession—a head of practitioners of medicine. There is no
evidence that the Jews were divided internally in larger or smaller
groups. In this respect the inscriptions about 'the Jews in Ephesus'
are not very relevant in this study.

Clearer and with demonstrating more interferences with John's text are the texts about Greek-religious groups: the groups of Demeter and Dionysus especially and the combination of these two, precisely because they are a model for many more particular groups of this kind:
—a steady kernel as basis for the group;
—a division of roles in various functions for the various members;
—a continuing, but also marginal, change in the composition of the group;
—the social composition of the group;
—the freedom to act as a group in public as well as in private, in houses;
—the communal involvement with a particular doctrine regarding this particular deity;
—the special cohesion as group as result of these activities.

4.2.3.2 *The beloved disciple*

The Johannine story presents the group of disciples as a community of friends among whom Jesus selected one to be his beloved friend: 'the disciple whom Jesus loved'. In my interpretation of the texts about this beloved disciple, the author of the Johannine Gospel made a selection from what in the Greek-Hellenistic culture is a form of *paiderastia*: a teacher who, from among the group of his disciples, selects one to whom he gives his special love. In Greek-Hellenistic literature we find abundant texts which demonstrate this typical phenomenon.

The question which this study evokes is whether this is true also for Ephesus. That is not self-evident. There is a lack of extended biographies of 'famous people' which could have told us something about this kind of relations. Yet, the picture is not completely blank. There is a sufficient number of texts and images which make it clear that in Ephesus too, or with people who have some relation to it, such relations between men do exist.

a. From the *Anthologia Graeca*:

There are innumerable poems about the love for boys. They are collected in the *Musa Puerilis* (book 12) of which Strato is the most important author. In 12.226, Ephesus is mentioned:

All night long, my dripping eyes tear-stained,
I strive to rest my spirit that grief keeps awake—
Grief for this separation from my friend since yesterday,
When Theodorus, leaving me here alone,
Went to his own Ephesus.
If he come not back soon I shall be no longer able
To bear the solitude of my bed.

Strato is a poet who, probably, lived in the era Trajan-Hadrian and who wrote all kind of poems about the love of a man for a boy, not only from his own experience, but, as he says in his closing poem, also on commission by other people. With the words of this poet, these people give expression to their own experiences of love. The one above is an example of this.

Rufinus is another love-poet from the time of Hadrian.[35] As is clear from the Anth. Graeca he worked also in Ephesus: because of the separation from his beloved Elpis, the I-figure in poem 5,9 "visits tear-wet the Koressos Hill and the temple of Artemis".
    Rufinus wrote two poems about the relation between love between boys and love between girls:

boy-mad no longer
        as once before
        I am called
woman-mad now
        from scabbard to thimble
instead of boys' unalloyed skin
        I go in for
chalky complexions
        and the added-on crusts
                of cochineal
dolphins shall pasture
        in the Black Forest
and nervous deer
        in the grey sea.   (5,19; transl. A. Marshfield)

---

[35] For the dating of this poet see esp. Robert 1989, 777ff.

And about the theme of a boy who gets hair on his cheeks and who, therefore, is no longer attractive (5,28):

Now, you so chary of your favours, you bid me good-day
when the more than marble smoothness of your cheeks is gone;
now you dally with me, when you have done away
with the ringlets that tossed on your haughty neck.
Come not near me, meet me not, scorner!
I don't accept bramble for a rose.

b. From the novel *Ephesiaca*:

The text which we possess of this novel is, probably, only a summary from a much later date. The supposition is that the text itself was written in the time of Hadrian. In any case Ephesus plays a main part. There is the beginning of the separation of the two lovers: Habrocomes, the most beautiful boy in Ephesus, and Anthia, the most beautiful girl in Ephesus, who found one another during a procession of Artemis. As in all classical novels, the main plot consists in the separation and the re-finding of the lovers. The story ends, therefore, again in Ephesus where all live in peace and love. In the meantime there has been a long journey with storms at sea, pirates, bandits, battles, imprisonment and rescues. An important figure in these sub-stories is Hippothōs, a bandit who leads a group of robbers; he has a tragic history. He has been in love with the beautiful boy Hyperanthes, but it did not bring him much luck. He had to murder an important man from Byzantium who was his competitor in love. During his flight his friend drowned in a storm. On Lesbos he erected a small burial monument for his friend, but since then he has had to earn his living thieving and robbing. On these trips he meets Anthia, the heroine of the story. He falls in love with her but, notwithstanding all his efforts, he loses sight of her. In Sicily they find each other again and tell each other their true stories. Hippothōs, then, respects Anthia's love for Habrocomes. He himself falls in love again, after a good marriage with a rich woman, now with the boy Clisthenes. Together with him and Anthia they go in search for Habrocomes. In Rhodes they all meet again. They go back to Ephesus. Everyone is happy and the novel ends with the words:

Hippothōs decided definitively to live with them.
Without further delay he went to Lesbos and erected a
beautiful monument for Hyperanthes. Then he adopted
Clisthenes as his son and lived with Anthia and
Habrocomes in Ephesus. (Ephesiaca 5.15.4)

c. From the *Oneirocritica* of Artemidorus:

Artemidorus, inhabitant and citizen of Ephesus, who wrote his book
of dreams in the middle of the second century, gives many
examples of dreams about sexual contact between man and man
(son, father, disciple, teacher, slave, lord, friend, enemy, lovers).
The very first dream runs as follows: "in this way, for example,
the lover dreams necessarily about a being together with his lover-
boy; the man plagued by fear about the object of his fear etc."
(1.1). Also further on in the book, homo-sexual dreams are a
constant topic, running more or less parallel with hetero-sexual
dreams. It indicates how 'normally' people of that time related to it.
As far as I have been able to discover the author never specifically
mentions Ephesus.

d. From the *Vita Sophistarum* by Philostratus:
The Life of Scopelian, the legate of Asia who in the name of the
province protests against Domitian against his decree to make all
vineyards outside Italy illegal, ends:

How great a reputation he won in this contest on behalf of the
vines is evident from what he said, for the oration is among
the most celebrated; and it is evident too from what happened
as a result of the oration. For by it he won such presents as
are usually given at an imperial court, and also many
compliments and expressions of praise, and moreover a
brilliant band of youths fell in love with his genius and
followed him to Ionia. (I.21.520)

e. From the *visual arts* in Ephesus:

Two types of images are linked to this form of friendship:
1. the image of Ganymedes, the lover-boy of Zeus—who plays an important role also in poetry (see the numbers 101, 102, and 103 in Aurenhammer 1990);
2. the beautiful image of Androclos as Antinous, the beloved of Hadrian who has passed away (see Inan I, no. 37, plate XXIV; and Clairmont 1966). It is a monument which makes clear that the love of the emperor for his friend has divine proportions, but it clarifies also how the city tries to link Hadrian to its own history.

f. From *epigraphy* one can point to a number of inscriptions in which 'friends' speak to each other:

—the statue for M. Aurelius Cotta, "the friend and benefactor" of Alexander, the son of Memnōn (VII-1-3022, Tiberius era);
—the statue for Gaius Julius Cleon, "the high priest and friend" of Alexander Eumeneus, son of Menander (III-688, Nero era);
—the statue for M. Arruntius Claudianus, "the friend and benefactor" of C. Vibius Salutaris (III-620, Trajan era);
—the statue for Veturius Paccianus, "the friend" of Fl. Damianus (III-735, Hadrian era);
—the statue for Gn. Pompeius Quartinus, "the friend" of L. Gerellanus Rufus Slavianus (III-710; SEG 1986, 1018, after the second neocorate).

Even if from these inscriptions it is not clear what kind of 'friendship' is meant, the ease with which friends honour each other shows again that in Ephesus friendship is also a living and felt experience.

In his *Histoire de la sexualité* , Foucault (1976-1984) takes as his point of departure that the *Erotikos* by Plutarch is a last, and rather lost reflection on the relationship of male love for boys and for girls. The high point of 'Greek love' would have been in the 5th/4th century BC and it was not repeated. The multitude of indications, as given above, and these seen as related to one city only, make it clear that this presentation of reality is wrong. In the first and second century AD relationships between men and boys are also 'naturally accepted': imaginarily, poetically, emotionally, and factually. The story about the disciple of Jesus, who, during the last meal is allowed to lie down on his lap, who under the cross of Jesus hears that Jesus' mother will become his mother; who, after Jesus' death, gives active witness about Jesus' life and death, and of whom it is said that he is the real author of the book about Jesus, is a story which seamlessly fits with other stories which in Ephesus are being told about this kind of love-relationship. It interferes with them; it gives colour and form to the stories which in Ephesus are being told about these love-relationships and it is better understood by them. In short, it supports them and is supported by them.

4.2.3.3 *The position of women in Ephesus*

As far as it is possible to abstract the narrative position of the women in John from their narrative involvement with the main character Jesus, women are given a very special position in John's text. They do not escape completely the male cultural supremacy, but they are presented as persons with some independence. It can be shown that this part of the women's position in John, runs parallel with what happens in Ephesus with and around women. Ephesus participates in what in the whole of Asia Minor is visible with regard to the prominence of women in the first two or three centuries AD.[36] As in John's text one should not look primarily at the number as well as at their public function. In Ephesus too women are numerically under-represented: in the period we are studying, there are some 775 names of Greek inhabitants, of which some 75 are women who are explicitly mentioned by name, plus some 25 instances where a woman is implicitly supposed to be part of the inscription as in "this tomb belongs to Gaius Julius and his wife", i.e. 10%-14% instead of 45%-55%. The public function they exercise is in no relation to this number. Women have access to the highest functions. Obviously, we are talking about rich people but that is not different for the men.[37]

---

[36] Cf. Trebilco 1991, 104ff.

[37] In the surrounding cities the same percentages are sometimes true, but sometimes they are quite different, at least according to the 'archives' I made myself of the surrounding cities in about the same period of time:
- in Pergamum there are 45 women (the names are there especially because of the priesthood in Athens) out of a total of 253 names, i.e.

Priesthoods

1. Artemis was responsible for the fact that women were given special attention in Ephesus. Artemis has a preference for women in leading positions in her temple. Women are mentioned as such, as independent persons of a family which, 'normally', is exclusively male-oriented.

Factually, there are three functions which are given to women: priestess (ἱέρεια), high-priestess (ἀρχιέρεια) and adorner (κοσμητείρη). As priestess they are responsible for the cult: to lead in the *mysteria* in a sacred manner and to take care that the daily sacrifices are offered. The title 'high-priestess' begins—as we said—probably in competition with the title 'high-priest of Asia'. That would place it in 88/89 AD. As appears in the inscription about Claudia Tertulla δίς ἀρχιέρεια (III-643C), the function of high-priest is limited in time, probably, as other high-priesthoods, to a year. As 'adorners' the women are responsible for the safe-keeping and preservation of the temple treasures: the gold and silver and bronze statues of the temple; the wreaths and the various offerings; and especially dressing Artemis when she is brought into the city in a solemn procession: to Hestia, to the sea, and to the amphitheatre. Artemis had many and costly garments and jewelry which were shown to the people several times a year with a good deal of pride. The care of these was entrusted to the rich women in

---

20%;
- in Magnesia there are 6 females out of a total of 48 preserved names, i.e. 12-13%;
- in Miletus there is only one woman among the 58 names of this period;
- in Smyrna the situation is in a way the most favourable as far as the percentages are concerned. There are, relatively, many sepulchral inscriptions preserved or brought to the surface and there are fewer 'politically oriented' inscriptions. In the sepulchral inscriptions we have some 275 names of which at least 188 are explicitly about women and at least another 25 implicitly, as we said in relation to the formulation "this tomb belongs to Gaius Julius and his wife". That means that the percentages male to female are about 60% to 40% or 55% to 45%. In the 'political' texts, I can speak of 133 inscriptions of which 21 are explicitly about women, i.e. about 16%. If one adds all this, one must say that in Smyrna of a total of 608 names, 234 deal with women: i.e. some 37-38%.

the city alternating frequently—again on a yearly basis? The title itself is apparently given for life. As is clear from the inscriptions, it is seen as a great honour by the people involved, an honour which they fulfilled not without great financial sacrifices.

In fact we find the following people:

The following are named *priestess*:

—Timantheia, at the measuring of the area of Artemis under Augustus (VII-2-3513; SEG 1986, 1026):
—Vipsania Olympia, daughter of a father *and* a mother mentioned by name (III-987: time of Augustus-Tiberius);
—Vipsania Polla, her sister (were they priestess in the same year?) (III-988);
—Clodia, the mother-in-law (of Menikiōn?) in the list of donors (to the temple of Tiberius in Smyrna?) (SEG 1989, 1176);
—Tryphosa, the wife of Heras, at the signing of the decree about the contribution (to the temple of Tiberius in Smyrna?) (SEG 1989,1176);
—Stertinia Marina, the daughter of Stertinius Orpex (II-411, Nero era);
—Claudia Trophime, daughter of a father *and* mother mentioned by name (II-508; IV-1012; 92/93 AD);
—Vedia Marcia (IV-1017, Domitian-Trajan era);
—Helvidia Paula at a construction inscription about the restoration of the theatre (II-492; 492A, Domitian era);
—Tryphosa (VII-1-3239A; SEG 1981, 958, Trajan-Hadrian era, found in Büyük Kale);
—Julia Polla, sister of C. Antius A. Julius Quadratus (III-980; II-989A);
—Ulpia Junilla, daughter of a father *and* mother mentioned by name (III-989A, Trajan era);
—Fl. Attalis (III-992; IV-1026, Trajan era);
—Mindia Menandra and her daughter Claudia (III-992A+B; III-792 maybe; Trajan era);
—Claudia Procula, daughter of a father *and* mother mentioned by name (SEG 1983, 936, mentioned between 114-116 AD)
—Hordeonia Paulina, daughter of a father *and* mother mentioned by name (III-690; III-981, Trajan era);
—Paula (IV-1044, Hadrian era);

—Quintilia Varilla (III-986 after the second emperor temple but still in the time of Hadrian).

The following are named *high-priestess of Artemis*:

—Julia Lydia Laterane (II-424; 424A, Trajan era);
—Julia Polla, sister of C. Antius A. Julius Quadratus (III-980; III-989A, Trajan era);
—Mindia Potentilla (III-980, Trajan era);
—Julia Pisonis (IV-1030, Hadrian era);
—Claudia Tertulla twice; her husband (or father) Ti. Cl. Italicus has no title (III-643C, Hadrian era);

The following are named *adorner of Artemis*:

—Julia Polla, sister of C. Antius A. Julius Quadratus (III-980; III-989A, Trajan era);
—Mindia Potentilla (III-980, Trajan era);
—Fl. Attalis (III-992; IV-1026, Trajan era);
—Claudia, daughter of the priestess Mindia Menandra (III-992A+B, Trajan era).

2. As we have already said, there was at least one woman from Ephesus, Vedia Marcia (IV-1017), who was "high-priestess of Asia", i.e. who fulfilled the highest function in the emperor cult. In 130/131 AD another woman from Ephesus, Skaptia Phirmilla (II-430) is given the function. In the period in between there are some other women from other cities who reached that position: Stratonike from Teos, the wife of Tib. Kl. Pheseinos (IGR IV-1571); their daughter Klaudia Tryphaina (IGR IV-1571); and Flavia Ammion Aristion, the wife of Ti. Fl. Kalvesianos Hermokrates (IGR IV-1323/1325). In the discussions about this topic, one assumes that the function was fully exercised by the women and that in the relevant years there is no male high priest in function.[38]

3. The *first* woman who reached the position of high priest of Asia —and who presents herself as such in the inscription—is Juliane,

---

[38] Cf. Friesen 1993, 185.

daughter of Eustratos, wife of Alkiphrōn from Magnesia (I.Magn. 148, time of Tiberius-Caligula). This refers, probably, to the emperor temple in Smyrna. This woman is interesting also for Ephesus because she calls herself also "priestess for life of Demeter in Ephesus". It shows the importance of this special priesthood. When Servilia Secunda in Ephesus is called "priestess of Demeter" in VII-2-4337 in connection with the veneration of Livia Augusta (and the abortive attempt of Ephesus to obtain the emperor temple for Tiberius), this priesthood should be evaluated on a rather high scale.

Women as prytanis

In a way even more important for the city was a completely different function. The city council was presided over by a select group of seven people who were elected yearly: six *kouretes* as we said already, with at their head a *prytanis*. The *prytanis* is the one finally responsible for the city hearth, the fire of the city which must be kept alive for ever in order to remain in the favour of Hestia. As the most important function in the city the *prytanis* gives his or her name to that year: "In the year that Claudia Trophime was *prytanis*, the city council decided that ..."

Because so many lists have been preserved, we can see how many women had this function. As regards our period the following women were *prytanis*:

—Kourtia Postoma in the time between Augustus and Nero (IV-1004);
—Claudia Trophime in the year 92/93 (II-508; IV-1012; 1062);
—Julia Helias in the time of Domitian-Trajan (IV-1047);
—Vedia Marcia in the time Domitian-Trajan (IV-1017);
—Julia Lydia Laterane in the time of Trajan (II-424; 424A; V-1601E);
—Julia Polla in the time of Trajan (III-980; 989A);
—Fl. Attalis in the time of Trajan (III-992; IV-1026);
—Julia Pisonis in the time of Hadrian (IV-1030);
—Paula in the time of Hadrian (IV-1044).

This relatively high number is, probably, due to Artemis because a good number of the same people are also known as priestess of Artemis. Artemis was in contact with Hestia. As a sign of this good relationship, Artemis went once a year to Hestia, the *prytaneum* in the centre of the city, in a solemn procession in which the *prytanis* was accompanied by a group of city slaves who were experts in the ritual: a herald for the sacrifices, a judge of the sacrifices, a lute player of the sacred music and a man for the incense: indications of the way this yearly feast was celebrated.

In this way we know more or less how this rite was celebrated. From a text dated to the 2nd-3rd century AD[39], it is clear that the cultic function of the *prytanis* was not limited to this one day. He or she must pay for 365 sacrificial animals which, according to custom, will be offered in various places and times with a lot of incense and herbs. Paeans are sung, hymns in honour of Apollo and Artemis; festive processions and nightly celebrations are kept; there are prayers for the people of Rome and the people of Ephesus; there is a hierarchy within the college of *kouretes* which must be respected. The *prytanis* of the city fulfils a public function which ensures that the person is seen every day and is kept busy.

Because so much of the historical Ephesus has been preserved, we can be even closer to it. Two poems have been handed on, short songs about the fire of the hearth as a spark/trace of the heavenly fire, probably sung as paean: they are by Claudia Trophime, one of the female *prytaneis*, to be precise in the year 92/93 AD:

> Claudia Trophime, priestess and *prytanis* wrote for Hestia the following hymn:
>   'Let her satisfy the blessed deities;
>   Let her preserve the fiery light of the city.
>   To you, sweetest spirit, new shoot of the cosmos,
>   ever-streaming light,
>   To you who preserve on the altars a spark from heaven.'

---

[39] I-10, for a commentary of the text, see Knibbe 1981, 57ff.

The same *prytanis* wrote:
'As a thief in the night Pion drinks the rain
which falls from heaven;
On all sides it contains water, as much as the sea.
Would that someone would reveal of you,
who maintain the divine fire,
how you in yourself maintain a trace of the beautiful
measure.'

Claudia is the first theologian of the city, in the original sense of the word: someone who knows how to sing about God. Hestia is for her a spark from heaven, a trace of the beautiful order which makes the cosmos whole.[40] The fire on the altar is like the fire of the hearth, the source of light and life. It contains divine mysteries which are unknowable. It can be compared with the earth which receives the rain water and yet does not drown in it. The fire is of divine origin, a sacred rest of the good measure and order which dominates the cosmos. We can think of Heraclites of Ephesus for whom the cosmos came from the fire and will return to it. City traditions sometimes have deep roots. The Johannine way of speaking about light and life, which, even though not dependent on this, runs parallel with this idea, will ensure that this theology will have a long future.

Claudia Trophime is also a very interesting woman from a different perspective. When she is *prytanis*, she erects a statue for the combination 'Artemis-Domitian-people of Ephesus' (II-508): she has made it clear to the city council that the new emperor temple, which two or three years earlier had been erected by the city with a lot of ceremony, should link up with Artemis. This will be deleterious for Artemis because the female god will lose out to the male one. The restoration of the statue in later years by the city-scribe Julius Titianus could not change that.

The execution of the *prytanis* function by Vedia Marcia, Julia Polla, and Attalis also shows the preference of these women for

---

[40] In the first poem δαλός is parallel with λείψανον from the second poem; therefore, I think that Kearsley, *New Doc* 1992, 199 with his translation of δαλός as 'light' is not close enough to the light-cosmos theory which is basic to the poems.

Artemis. They all erect statues for Artemis priestesses: Vedia Marcia for Kl. Prokla (SEG 1983, 936); Julia Prokla, the sister of the famous senator with the long name—C. Antius A. Julius Quadratus—for Junilla (III-989A); Attalis for two others who apparently were her predecessors (III-992, for Mindia Menandra and her daughter Claudia). Here too the council and the people of Ephesus are directly involved.

By mentioning Julia Laterane—the most important woman of the city at the end of the first/the beginning of the second century—I want to point to another reality. When she is *prytanis* of the city, she is the protectress of the association of the "initiated of Dionysus before the city". This is a group of people which, maybe, shows the closest similarity to what we visualize as a Johannine community and from which, as we said, the readers of the Johannine Gospel in Ephesus imagine the group around Jesus in the Gospel text. It is a small group of people who are not too rich (most of them are not yet Roman citizens); who meet before the city to celebrate the *mysteria* of Dionysus. There is clearly a leader who takes care of the sacred activity. There is a priest for the sacrifice, someone who plays the instrument which runs on water, and there is someone who speaks the sacred words.

Because of the fragmentary character of the inscription, it is not entirely certain, but still rather probable, that a woman had a functional role in this religious association. The name with the ending "-lissa" who fulfils the role of priest is almost certainly a woman: "Melissa, the priestess" has been proposed. If this is true, the patronage of Julia Lydia proves that *she* at least thought it self-evident that women from less well-to-do circles could obtain relatively high positions (see V-1601C).

The other liturgies
Apart from the high positions, women are responsible also for somewhat less important liturgies:

1. *Gymnasiarch*
Of three women it is said that they took on the function of gymnasiarch: the responsibility for the maintenance and the

functioning of a gymnasium;[41]
—Tryphosa, the daughter of Artemas and Diadoumenis (VII-1-3239A, time of Trajan-Hadrian, found in Büyük Kale);
—Paula, when she is *prytanis* (IV-1044, time of Hadrian);
—Flavia Myrton (V-1500, time of Trajan) in an interesting inscription. Flavia is, together with her husband, elected gymnasiarch for the sixth time in the name of the perpetual gymnasiarchate of Artemis, and probably even at the expense of Artemis.

2. *Member of the gerousia*
The title which Julia Spendousa has is very rare. In an inscription for her forefather G. Julius Pontianus (she is called his ἔκγονος, i.e., he is her grandfather or great-grandfather), she is called πρεσβύτερα. Parallel to the πρεσβύτεροι who appear at other places in Hellenistic texts, Julia Spendousa must have been a member of the *gerousia* (III-690; Julius Pontianus is from the time of Trajan).

3. *Member of the Roman Senate*
Unique for Ephesus is the title of Fl. Cornelia Caecilia Menestrates, the mother of Demeas Caecilianus. In III-708 (time of Domitian-Hadrian), she is called συγκλητική, that is to say that she has senatorial rank. A few times this title is given to women in the Roman Empire. Do they, then, have all the rights of the male senators?

4. *Constructions*
Several women are mentioned as (co-)financiers of the larger city edifices. These are constructions which usually are started on private initiative from one's own interest or for one's own honour and pride:
—Ophellia Bassa, the wife of Sextilius Pollio (time of Augustus) is mentioned together with her husband as the builder of the royal stoa (II-404; SEG 1989, 1210) and of an aqueduct (VII-1-3092);
—Claudia Metrodora builds together with her husband a gate in the *agora* (VII-1-3003, Nero era);

---

[41] Cf. Trebilco 1991, 117ff.

—Stertinia Marina is mentioned, together with her father, the freed-man Stertinius Orpex, for the construction of the stadium (II-411, Nero era);
—Helvidia Paula, the daughter of Poplios pays for the restoration of the theatre (II-492; 492A, Domitian era);
—Julia Lydia Laterane builds, together with her husband Tib. Cl. Aristion the nymphaeum for Trajan that is part of the water provision for the city (II-424; 424A);
—Varilla, the daughter of Publius Quintillus Valens Varius builds a θᾶκος (a toilet); a παιδισκεῖον (II-455; Hadrian era) and, even more majestic, the temple of Hadrian (II-429).

5. *Financing*
Foundations and contributions to large projects show that women (sometimes) have the chance to decide about (sometimes large) sums of money:
—In the list of contributors in the time of Tiberius (for the temple in Smyrna?) independent women are mentioned twice (+ 20 times together with a man, her husband, father, or brother and 18 times anonymously in the formation "Gaius Julius with his wife"). The independent women are Vedia Secunda who on her own pays 2500 denarii (SEG 1989, 1176) and Mindia Helena who has subscribed 35 denarii (SEG 1987, 883). Obviously, there are rich women and less rich ones.
—Stertinia Marina subscribes together with her father a foundation in favour of the council, the priests, and the *gerousia* (VII-2-4123, Nero era);
—Julia Spendousa, member of the *gerousia*, pays on her own for the foundation of her forefather G. Julius Pontianus, a foundation which pays for sacrifices and which frees money for councillors and priests (III-690, two or three generations after Trajan).

A number of women are, therefore, very visible in Ephesus. That is true also in another respect. As we have said, the city is ornamented with hundreds of statues. In no small measure—it is a pity that we cannot make an accurate accounting—this relates to women: statues of the goddesses Artemis, the Magna Mater, Demeter, Persephone and Kore, Nike, Silene, Hygeia etc.; statues of the female branch of the imperial family: Octavia, Livia, Agrippina, Domitia, Plotina, Sabina; statues of the richer couples from the city as for example the statues of Sextilius Pollio and his wife Ophellia Bassa (II-407); statues of women as girls, as wife, or as matron.[42] In this regard there is a form of equal opportunity which approaches even an equal proportion.

The same is more or less true in the tomb inscriptions. In the edition of the inscriptions of Ephesus, no attempt has been made to date them even generally, so that I could not use them for this research. But the situation will not have been much different from the sepulchral inscriptions from Smyrna. In Ephesus too (see VI-2100-2580), we see all kinds of links: women as wives, as mothers of children, as independent owners of the tomb or the sarcophagus. In an indirect way these texts make it clear that the independent position of the richer women from the city includes sometimes the lower echelons of society.

All in all, it means that there is a great measure of similarity between what the Johannine Gospel says about women and their social position in Ephesus. Special is the mixture of a form of behaviour which is in line with the ideology of the *oikos*—the woman as the one responsible for the functioning of the *oikos* in itself—and the form of behaviour which (at least seemingly) escapes from this—the woman as responsible for the functioning of the access in the *polis*: religiously, politically, and financially. In line with the readers' own evaluation of this social system, they (men and women) will judge positively or negatively the activities of these women and will underline one side or the other. Remembering the ambiguity with which the text of John has treated the various relationships of Johannine women with the main character Jesus, it is—sad to say—not too strange that, in the later reception of the text of John, the woman-promoting side of the text has not been carried forward.

---

[42] Cf. Inan 1966 and 1979; Kruse 1975; Aurenhammer 1990.

CHAPTER FIVE

THE PASSION NARRATIVE AND THE GOD EMPEROR

Not many readers of John's text will be surprised when they see that the *emperor* is involved in the story of Pilate and Jesus. This happens on various levels of the text: Pilate brings him in indirectly, "do you not know that I have the power to set you free and the power to have you crucified?" (19:10). The high priests do it directly, "if you let him go free, you are no friend of the emperor. Whoever makes himself king is against the emperor" (19:12); and, "we have no king other than the emperor" (19:15). Such dialogues and discussions are not found in the other evangelists. They give a special colour to the story of John. First of all, therefore, I want to deal with the special structure of John's passion narrative in relation to the role given to the various actors.

5.1 *The questioning of Jesus by Pilate (Jn 18:28-19:16)*

That within the telling of the passion story a new scene is opened in Jn 18:28 is made clear by the change to another place (the praetorium), the introduction of a new character (Pilate) and a new time setting: "it was early in the morning", at the opening of the passage (in 18:28) and "it was the day of preparation for Easter, it was about the sixth hour", at the end (in 19:14) (this means six o'clock in the morning, because no Roman senator will ever be working on a trial till twelve noon).[1]

---

[1] Brown 1994, 846 deals with all the difficulties of this determination of time 'the sixth hour', in the supposition that the text of John says that Jesus was condemned around noon; he deals specifically with the difficulty of how this can be combined with the time indication in Mark 15:25,33

The praetorium is the meeting place. For the *Ioudaioi* it is taboo because it is the day of preparation for Pesach. They do not enter it, since they want to slaughter and prepare the lambs in purity at the end of the day.[2] Jesus is brought in, tied up (18:24). Pilate is the link between inside and outside. The positions of the actors create a special structure in this episode. Originally the narrator respects the inside and the outside position of the characters, but when the scene of derision by the soldiers has been told, that ends. Even when Pilate and Jesus are inside (in 19:8-12) the *Ioudaioi*, who stay outside, take part in the dialogue and react to what is happening inside. That is to say: the soldiers scene is very important and determines in its own way the course of events.

With a number of exegetes,[3] I take the following order:

18:28-32: Pilate and the *Ioudaioi* outside of the praetorium
18:33-38: Pilate and Jesus inside the praetorium
18:38-40: Pilate and the *Ioudaioi* outside of the praetorium
19:1-3:   Jesus and the soldiers
19:4-7:   Pilate, the *Ioudaioi* and Jesus outside of the praetorium
19: 8-12: Pilate and Jesus inside, the *Ioudaioi* outside
19:13-16: Pilate, the *Ioudaioi* and Jesus outside of the praetorium

---

and 34: Jesus is crucified, there, at the third hour; the darkness falls over the land at the sixth hour and he dies at the ninth hour i.e. 9 a.m., 12 noon, and 3 p.m. The point is that John's text (probably) follows the Roman way of counting the hours of the day; the sixth hour is, then, 6 a.m. (or, as in the story of the Samaritan woman, 6 p.m., see Jn 4:6) and so all discussion about a lack of harmony between Mark and John disappears, in the same way, by the way, as the 'theologizing' about a special way of Johannine time-indication.

[2] That, at least, is the intention of what is said in the text, although, as far as we know, according to the Jewish halacha the house where gentiles walk is not impure, unless one is invited for a meal.

[3] Cf. e.g. Blank, 1959, 61; Meeks 1967, 62 who adds the crucifixion scene as the eighth scene (Jn 19:17-22); Brown 1970, 859; 1994, 743ff; 758; Rensberger 1988, 91; Brodie 1993, 532.

1. *The accusations (18:28-32)*

From the start it is clear that the story is an apologia. Jesus' death is not in contradiction with his life's mission: to be in this cosmos a witness of a different world. For the moment, however, Jesus is not much more than a subject of discussion, the centre of a discussion between Pilate and the *Ioudaioi*.

Pilate starts his investigation correctly as a judge: an investigation into the accusation, the *cognitio* because the judge must know what he is to judge.[4] And, even though the *Ioudaioi* have accused Jesus all through the story of many things (that he works on the Sabbath, that he calls his own father God and so makes himself equal to God, that he presents himself as bread from heaven, as water—equal to the spirit of God—as messiah and as son of God), all that is not now expressed. They say: "if he had not done anything wrong we would not hand him over to you" (18:30). This is clearly a lie, a kind of answer to the question which Jesus asked the servant of the high priest during the interrogation by Annas (18:22ff). They do not offer witnesses. They only make a declaration. Pilate has to take them at their word. This is about power, about the question who will accept responsibility.

For the time being Pilate is not ready to do that: "take him and judge him according to your own law" (18:31). Jesus is pushed back and forth. Pilate still acts in his role as Roman procurator: do not start a case if the local authority is competent and if there are no Roman interests involved. But the *Ioudaioi* know this game. They need Pilate to fulfil their desire: "we are not allowed to put anyone to death" (18:31). This is sometimes seen as historical information. Whether it is correct or not, the literary-strategical function of this sentence is far more important: ἀποκτείνω in the ambiguous sense of 'to kill' or 'to condemn to death': "we are not allowed to kill someone/to condemn anyone to death". The *Ioudaioi* want to act according to the law, but in truth they plan a judicial murder. They desire the death of their brother and so repeat the history of Cain and Abel. They prove the truth of what Jesus said before: "your father is the devil and you want to make real the

---

[4] See for far more juridical details, Sherwin-White 1963, 24ff and the commentary by Brown 1994, 710ff.

desires of your father: he was a *murderer* from the beginning, and
he was not *on the side of truth*" (8:44).

2. *The truth of the kingship (18:33-38)*

Pilate only asks questions. When he is alone with Jesus he spouts a
whole lot of them: are you the king of the *Ioudaioi*? Do you think I
am *Ioudaios*? What did you do? Are you a king? What is truth? He
is a judge and he wants to know why Jesus stands before him.

The point of departure is the title which Pilate attributes to Jesus:
are you the king of the Jews? There has been a change of scene.
Pilate has re-entered the praetorium and he has Jesus brought before
him (φωνέω as the technical term for charging an accused person)
to ask him the definitive question which will determine the rest of
the passion story: are you the king of the Jews?

Jesus answers with a question of his own, necessary because of a
narrative defect in the story: how did Pilate know about this title?
(18:34). The title did play a role in the foregoing story: as
profession of faith by Nathanael, at the very start of the story
(1:49); as popular desire after the events of the people's meal
(6:15); at the entrance into Jerusalem when the people hailed him as
King of Israel (12:13,15), something which evoked the wrath of the
Pharisees and introduced the Greek scene, but to this point it has
never been mentioned that this title could lead to a death sentence,
nor that it would be contrary to Roman power pretensions.

In his answer Pilate rejects this. In the only indicative sentence
which he speaks in this passage he says: "Your people and the high
priests handed you over to me", implying that they have the right
to do so. But Pilate surrounds this sentence by questions: Is he a
Ioudaios? The people and the high priests have handed Jesus over
to him and (therefore) he must ask the question: what did you do?
(18:35). For the moment Pilate still acts as a man who is open-
minded. The people and the high priests (the high priests in the
name of the people?) are proposed as the ones truly responsible for
the trial. Jesus is responsible for what he has done.

Jesus is being tried and must answer: about his kingship and
about the nature of his kingdom; about his mission in this cosmos
and how this is to be understood as a witness for truth: all juridical
terms which fit in the context of a trial.

In the meantime Jesus gives witness about himself. My kingdom
is not of this world or my servants would have fought for me

(18:36). Jesus defends a point of view which is pacifist in the extreme.[5] The absence of any means of power, the absence of fighting servants as demonstrated in the story of his capture, his open surrender, the protection of his followers, the rejection of Peter's sword, they are all proof of the origin of his kingdom and of its content: resist the powers of the cosmos in powerlessness.

For this he came into the world, to give witness to the truth (18:37): that his kingship is from God and that it cannot be brought about by human power, by the force of weapons and soldiers. Only those people can listen to his voice who are "from the truth" i.e. people who know how God looks at the power of the cosmos. Pilate refuses to consider this—what is truth?—proving in this way that he is outside of truth.

3. *Not Jesus but Barabbas (18:38-40)*

Pilate discontinues the interrogation and returns to the *Ioudaioi*. He has found no fault in Jesus. I suppose that this declaration of innocence and its consequence—the desire to let Jesus go and the recognition that he is king—are narratively trustworthy. The answer of the *Ioudaioi*, then, becomes truly grotesque. Out of the blue they present another alternative: they want to exchange Barabbas, a bandit i.e. someone who uses violence, for Jesus, their king, someone who does not use violence. Because they want to condemn an innocent man they opt for the liberation of a guilty one. They go from bad to worse and Pilate becomes more and more caught in the web of injustice. His attempt to do justice is frustrated time and again by new proposals from the *Ioudaioi*. The liberation of Barabbas seals the fate of Jesus.

---

[5] In exegetical literature the term 'pacifist' is hardly ever used because of the political implications, even though this is the consequence of the factual *and* imaginary appearance of Jesus. It is (probably) still a message for possible Roman readers: as Jesus, Christians also will not use force. In Hengel's study about the passion story in John (Hengel 1991), attention is drawn, apart from the powerless way of Jesus' actions, to the present realization of Jesus' kingship: Jesus is king here and now and Pilate cannot grasp this. Jesus' kingship is, according to his own words, 'not of this world' but it is 'in this world'.

4. *The soldier's ridicule (19:1-3)*
Looked at from the point of view of the characters in the story, this
scene stands all by itself. Pilate and the *Ioudaioi* disappear for the
moment from the scene to make room for Pilate's soldiers. It is a
decisive turning point in the story: Jesus is publicly acknowledged
as king.

In the foreground of the story, on the level of communication
between the characters themselves, it is a scene of ridicule: the
crown of thorns on his head, the purple cloak of a soldier, the
mocking homage ending in a slap in the face make clear what
soldier's humour is all about.

It leads to a confession of faith: hail, king of the Jews. The
context makes it clear that they do not believe it, but everyone who
hears the story realizes that the soldiers are making the mistake of
their lives.

5. *Jesus' humiliation (19:4-7)*
From now on the three parties—Jesus, Pilate, and the *Ioudaioi*—
are together, notwithstanding the place where they are. Pilate acts
as if he is Jesus' herald. He goes before him; Jesus comes out in a
way which fits a king (see the similarity between 19:4 and 19:5).
The episode itself is a double story of which the second part echoes
with reverberations from the first part. In the second part (about
Jesus as the son of God) the first part (about Jesus as man) still
resounds.

The story starts with the proof of the possible innocence of
Jesus. That is clear from Pilate's words to the *Ioudaioi*. It is also
the meaning of the attributes which adorn Jesus: the crown and the
purple cloak. That is the meaning of what Pilate says about Jesus to
the crowd: see the man. This scene has made a real impression in
the reception of the Johannine Gospel. In the context of the
characters of the story, this is about the humiliation and the
elevation of Jesus. It is a new appeal to the *Ioudaioi* to recognize
the truth of Jesus, now expressed in the ridiculing attributes and the
consequence of the flagellation, expressed in a way in which human
weakness itself is verbalized.

But compassion no longer has a hold on the people. The high
priests and their servants come centre stage and scream for his
crucifixion. Is it the intention of the narrator that the listeners will
take note of the change in person to make clear that not the people

but the leaders are the ones truly responsible for Jesus' death? That does not seem to be wholly unlikely. In any case Pilate accedes to their request. He hands Jesus over to them.

And still it is not enough. They want Jesus to be put to death "according to the law". What is the meaning of this? Possibly the *Ioudaioi* ask that Jesus be stoned because that is the punishment which Jewish law exacts in the case of blasphemy. But more probably they demand a judicial verdict.

The man Jesus has made himself son of God. Finally, the accusation which Pilate asked for from the beginning is there. The question naturally is whether this accusation is true: did Jesus make himself son of God? On the level of communication between narrator and listeners this is not true: Jesus did not *make* himself son of God; his doctrine and his activity, his words and his deeds proclaim that he *is* the son of God.

6. *The power from above and the power of the emperor (19:8-12)*
The narrative situation is not described so clearly. Pilate enters the praetorium. Without it being mentioned, it appears that Jesus is there too and at the same moment the *Ioudaioi* know what is being discussed.[6] The three parties remain together.

The story is told in a threefold dialogue:
—19:8-9: Pilate is filled with fear in reaction to the accusation of the *Ioudaioi* that Jesus made himself son of God. He takes the accusation seriously and recognizes the truth of the accusation of it. That is clear also from his question, "From where are you?", a question which is very important in the Johannine Gospel, but which is not answered here. Jesus is silent. He has told Pilate from where his kingship is. He will not repeat it.

—19:10-11: This brings Pilate to talk about his power, the power which has been the basis of his actions up to now and which has

---

[6] Brown 1994, 843 has a slightly different division of episodes. Because the *Ioudaioi* in 19:12 react to what is said between Jesus and Pilate, Brown supposes that in 19:12 Pilate is outside again. In my supposition we should not insist too strictly on the opposition between 'inside' and 'outside'. In 19:8,9 Jesus seems to be inside too even though it is not said explicitly; in 19:12 the *Ioudaioi* react to what happens between Jesus and Pilate; in the same way as in 19:13 Pilate reacts to what is being said 'outside'.

brought him into an ever deepening dilemma: "Do you not know that I have the power of life and death?" Indirectly he brings up the power of the emperor. Pilate received this "power of life and death" from his emperor. He believes that he can threaten Jesus with this but in ambiguous words, so characteristic of the Johannine Gospel, Jesus deflates this pretension. Pilate's power over Jesus comes "from above". Jesus is not subject to Pilate. The reverse is true. If he allows Jesus to be crucified he does what is in God's plan. Through Jesus, Pilate is subject to this "power from above" (see also 3:27). That is the reason that his sin is less grievous than the sin of the people who handed Jesus over to him.

—19:12: Pilate knows that Jesus is king; he has found no fault in him, he realizes that he is subject to a "power from above" and he wants to set Jesus free; but more and more he finds himself caught in the web of the necessity of evil. The *Ioudaioi* confront him with his own position. If he is a "friend of the emperor" he cannot identify with someone who made himself a king, because that goes against the emperor's interests. This is the first time that 'the emperor' is mentioned in John's text in a formulation which carries historical reminiscences: Pilate as the protégé of Seianus who, through this friendship, has access to the emperor—a privilege he does not want to lose;[7] and Jesus' kingship which is made dependent on the approval of the emperor. The discussion runs along the same lines as the discussion about Jesus as son of God: did Jesus make himself king as the *Ioudaioi* say or is Jesus 'king in God's name', a kingship to which even the emperor is, in a way, subject.

Pilate faces a dilemma because of what the *Ioudaioi* say to him: if he condemns Jesus he acts unjustly; if he sets him free he is guilty of lese-majesty. He must choose between Jesus and the emperor. He opts for the emperor and thus for injustice. Pilate did not solve his dilemma very well.

7. *The king Jesus versus the king emperor (19:13-16)*
The many indications of time and place underline the importance of this episode. He (Pilate and/or Jesus) sits down on the seat which is

---

[7] See esp. Bammel 1952; J.P. Lémonon 1981, 221ff; 275ff is more careful with this connection; see also recently Brown 1994, 693ff.

called Lithostrotos, in Hebrew Gabbata. It is the day of preparation for Easter. It is about the 6th hour. For the last time Pilate speaks his confession: "See, this is your king". Jesus is present as king.

But the *Ioudaioi* want none of it. Again they reject him: "crucify him", now complemented with "away, away with him". The last, questioning, confession of Pilate "should I crucify your king?" is erased by the high priests in their answer "we have no king but the emperor".

This is the second time 'the emperor' is mentioned. There is again a remarkable change in person: only the high priests say that they do not know any other king but the emperor. In the context of this story it is a very important statement. Saying this, the high priests not only renounce their political independence but they also no longer profess that God is the only king of Israel. In this way the dilemma 'Jesus or the emperor' is not only Pilate's dilemma; it is just as much the dilemma for the leaders of Israel. And they too do not solve it well.

5.2 *The emperor and the emperor cult in Ephesus*

The emperor, the imperial family and the interests of the emperor
play a special and very important role in Ephesus. The emperor,
concentrated in the cult of the emperor, is massively present in the
city. To make this clear I need to develop this reality. It may be
correct to write such a sentence but it does not evoke as such the
ubiquity of the emperor. The emperor is linked to all realities in the
city. This needs fleshing out. In this construction interferences are
present on all levels: in the necessary presence of the emperor in all
questions of importance for city and country; in the oppositions
between Pilate and the Jews; in the connection between the high
priest(s) and the imperial interests; in the imperial titles which are,
positively and negatively, attributed to Jesus, where we need to
look more broadly at the total Johannine text; in the availability of
the soldiers and the role they play; in the relation between Pilate
and his emperor and the relations of the high priests and their
emperor. The presence of the emperor is powerful. The
interferences with the Johannine text are, therefore, tightly present.

5.2.1 *The emperor in the city*

Let us start with the presence of the emperor in the city. At first
sight this may seem to be rather removed from possible
interferences but it is the basis for all that follows. All through the
first century the name of the emperor is omnipresent: on the large
buildings, in the houses, in and around the many statues, at all
events in the city—processions, feasts, sacrifices, games—in the
case of inheritances and in city politics. I will develop this. The
emperor is there. He is present also in his historical succession.
The history of the Roman emperors is linked with the history of the
city. From dedications of all kinds of people to the various
emperors, the history of the city can be reconstructed *grosso modo*,
as can be various involvements of the emperors in city affairs.

Buildings
The large public buildings are often dedicated to the emperor.
Obviously not everything has been preserved and it is not always
clear to which building a specific fragment belonged. In other cases
it is clear:

—the monumental gate of Mithradates and Mazaios, dedicated to Augustus and his family (VII-1-3006/7);

—the *stoa basilikē* of G. Sextilius Pollio, dedicated to Augustus (II-404);

—the toll house of the fishermen and the fishmongers in honour of Nero (I-20);

—the side wall of the doric gallery on the *agora* in honour of Nero (VII-1-3003);

—the majestic buildings on the *agora* by Ischyrion and Isidoros in honour of Trajan where the *stoa* is tiled with marble and the *exedra* is adorned with statues and ornaments (VII-1-3005);

—the building of the 'workshops' dedicated to Trajan, places where sellers of food and craftsmen can ply their trade, near to the bath of Varius (II-421);[8]

—the covering of the halls of Verulanus in honour of Hadrian (II-430), a renovation of the large harbour gymnasium of Domitian, built in the year that Tib. Kl. Aristion was *prytanis* (II-427).[9]

These are all buildings which mark the city and which, publicly, proclaim the homage to the emperor (and to Artemis as we will see).

Sometimes there is mention of a certain continuity, of a rebuilding, an expansion, a beautification. In the course of the century the city expands and becomes richer and that expresses itself also in its buildings. The stadium and the theatre are good examples of this. Stertinius Orpex of Nero's time is the first man of whom a dedication has been preserved (II-411). In Domitian's time there are already new expansions: the *skēnē* and the northern wing are revised (VI-2034/35). And in Trajan's time Ti. Fl. Montanus builds a new vaulted ceiling in the theatre and dedicates it to this emperor (VI-2037).

On a smaller scale too we find such revisions, such as the wall between the Augusteum and the Artemision. When this is erected in Augustus' time (V-1522), repair is mentioned in the same year (V-

---

[8] See also II-443 where 'workshops' are dedicated to Artemis and the Sebastoi near to another gymnasium.

[9] A text which, in addition to Friesen (1993, 122) is possibly of importance in dating this complex.

1523).[10] In any case, such repair does occur in Titus' time (II-412). It is said "that the dividing wall of the Augusteum, fallen into disrepair, is repaired". It is celebrated with a feast. The expenses for the dance are paid by the legate Pomponius Bassus from the income of the temple of Artemis.

The temple of Artemis enjoyed evidently always the interest of the emperors. Apparently there was continual discussion about the limits of the area which belongs to Artemis. There are marker stones from the time of Augustus (VII-2-3501/02); of Domitian (VII-2-3506/10; III-853) and of Trajan (VII-2-3511/12). The texts of the time of Domitian are interesting because there is mention of the presence of successive proconsuls, probably there personally to inspect the work. But the emperors also have other interests in the temple: the right of asylum in Augustus' time (V-1520), the organization of the income of the temple, the priests, slaves, and other personnel in Augustus' and Claudius' time (I-17-19), the singers of hymns in Tiberius' and Claudius' time (VII-2-3801), and the processions in Trajan's time (I-27-37). In short, all activities of the temple are under the supervision of the emperors. We will see that there is a specific, special reason for this and that it has consequences.

Finally, the city profited in two ways from the typical Roman input in the construction work of this time: the attention to road-building and water-provision.

Road-building often occurs anonymously but, in a number of cases, the builder believes it important to mention his own name as well as the names of the emperors. In this form, there are inscriptions from the time of Augustus (II-459), of Claudius (VII-1-3163) and of Domitian (II-263; 263A+B). In the city itself there is also an inscription about the beautification of the *embolos*, the longest and widest street of the city. M. Tigellios gives the honour for that to Domitian (VII-1-3008).

The watersystem is, obviously, more important still for the life of the city. Those responsible do not keep this a secret. In this way we know that large aqueducts were built: by Augustus (II-401 which carries the name 'aqua Iulia'; see also II-414); by the builder Sextilius Pollio with a large fountain in the city (II-402) which in

---

[10] But it is a term which Augustus uses easily cf. *Res Gestae*,24.

the time of Domitian is given new connections with the rivers Marnas and Klaseas.[11] In Trajan's time, Aristion and his wife Julia Lydia Laterane provide a new aqueduct of 210 stadia (II-424; 424A) where the name of the emperor again shines. At the same time several 'fountains' are constructed in the city as public watering places. The Pollio monument plays an important role here visually. Domitian is given his own place in the form of a nymphaeum (II-413; 419). Trajan follows that example in honour of the God Nerva (II-420) at the so-called nymphaeum of Trajan which is built by Aristion and Julia Lydia Laterane as the conclusion of their aqueduct in honour of Trajan (II-424; 424A). The builders of these magnificent constructions know that the emperor will in this way receive the gratitude of the population and that this will be beneficial for all kinds of people in many different ways.

The games
It is not only these buildings, generally large, that proclaim the glory of the emperors. As we mentioned already, we find the names of emperors in many places. The games, which are organized either every year or every two or four or five years, become more important in and for the city and also for the emperor cult with which they are linked in a special way. In the inscriptions of Ephesus the memory of these games is well preserved.[12] A small number mention the name of an emperor and thereby show the special relation between these games and the various emperors.

It is interesting that they also mention parts of the ritual—albeit somewhat shortened:
—In the time of Augustus, G. Julios Nikephoros, a freedman of Augustus, informs us that he has spent money for the yearly ἀγών τῶν 'Ρωμαίων, for the sacrifice to "[Rome, Augustus and] Artemis" (III-859A). He is a man with lots of money who, as πρύτανις διὰ

---

[11] II-415/6; II-419; 419A; see also SEG 1984, 1122 from the time of Nero.

[12] See the texts about the Dionysia, the Sebasta Epheseia, the Artemisia, the Balbilleia, the Olympia, the Pythia, the Isthmia, the Hadrianeia.

βίου, probably had much influence in the city. His financial contributions to the games set the tone for the rest of the century.

—That is clear from an inscription from the time of Claudius. When Alexander Memnōn combines the leadership of "the games of the emperor" with the secretariat of the city, he erects a statue for the wife of Claudius (for Agrippina or Messalina) (II-261). It is important for the city that the emperor maintains this link with the games.

—Friesen[13] has shown that, in the time of Domitian, a large gymnasium-palaestra complex was constructed near the harbour in the style of Olympia and with the intention to have the Olympics in Ephesus. A coin of Domitian has been preserved on which, on the obverse, Domitian's head can be seen together with his name, and on the reverse there is an image of Zeus Olympios with in his right hand the statue of Artemis, with the inscription Ζεύς 'Ολύμπιος 'Εφεσίων. From inscriptions from Iasos, it is clear that, in the time of Domitian, Olympics were organized in Ephesus,[14] which, after a break, only came back under Hadrian and which are again to be linked to the titles of Zeus Olympios, now attributed to Hadrian. From the place where some inscriptions are found in this spot (IV-1125 and 1155), Friesen shows that these are the βαλανεῖα Σεβαστῶν/Σεβαστοῦ, linked with xystoi, colonnaded halls arranged around an open courtyard.[15]

Additional to this thesis of Friesen, we can point to IV-1124, an inscription which has been found also in the ruins of the harbour complex. As in IV-1104.1125.1155, it is also about a 'high priest of the xystos' who is also 'xystargēs for life'. The inscription is interesting because the man, Tib. Kl. Artemiodoros, is also a winner in Olympia and is now given a statue in Ephesus because of his victory, a statue which is dedicated to Artemis, Nerva, and the people of Ephesus. That is to say that, after Domitian, the games went on even though no longer under the name of Olympia.

—In the time of Trajan, the city again takes the initiative of honouring the emperor in connection with games (IV-1122). There are the imperial Balbilleia. Organized by a member of the Balbilli

---

[13] 1993, 117ff.

[14] Knibbe 1980, 775; Friesen 1993, 117.

[15] Friesen 1993, 135.

family (see VII-1-3041/42), these were held in Ephesus for the fourth time between 97 and 102. All those involved probably had their name mentioned in this inscription but the stone is broken after the third name. The names of the leader of the games,[16] of the *grammateus of the synodos*, and of the first *archōn* have been preserved so that we know how the games were organized.

—In a last inscription of the time of Hadrian (II-276), it becomes clear how the priesthood and the games are linked. The priests and the *hieroneikai* (people who have won in some sport in the games), who carry the gold adornment of the goddess in the procession of Artemis, honour Hadrian. It is an inscription which was made at an important moment in the history of the city. Pompeius Falco is proconsul and Hadrian visits the city for the first time. There is hope that he will give permission for a new emperor temple. The homage is probably set up before they receive the negative answer. The group which is brought together—the priests of Artemis and the victors in the games—shows how people express their expectations. The games, Artemis, and the emperor form a close combination.

Foundations, statues, and inheritances
Above we already saw inscriptions in which people were linked to the emperor on a more personal title. Usually this is personally motivated. One is linked to the emperor as senator, as member of the equestrian rank, as an official of the emperor, as a freedman of the emperor, or simply because one has obligations relating to the emperor, or one is bound to the emperor because the connection will give certain advantages. All motivations are valid and apparently they were legion.

In the long text of the foundation of Vibius Salutaris, the personal link to the emperor is broadly elaborated. He belongs to the equestrian rank and is, according to the text, "honoured with military functions and procurations by our Lord and emperor" (I-27). That appears from his *cursus honorum*. He was *promagister* of the harbours and the corn for Rome in Sicily; he was prefect and military tribune in the army and *subprocurator* in Mauretania and Belgium. This is repeated in every inscription—at least 14 times—

---

[16] Probably an Apellas, see Halfmann 1979, 137.

so that it cannot be overlooked (I-28-37). This is a man of great merit who owes everything to the emperor. For the context in which this foundation is now mentioned, it is interesting that he submits his plan not only to the city council but also to the Roman proconsul and the legate, who, as if they were "true citizens of our city" (I-27 line 80) give their consent orally and in writing to the great plan of Vibius Salutaris. Their separate letters to the city council have been preserved. Both show that they have friendly relations with Vibius: "he is one of my closest friends", writes the proconsul (I-27 line 340); "because he is a man who is dear to us and who is important ... who showed himself to be one of our best and closest friends", writes the legate (I-27 line 376). And when, a couple of years later, there are problems with the execution of the plan, the consent of the then ruling proconsul and the legate are asked for again and are again given whole-heartedly (I-35).

The text makes clear that the proconsul especially, as the direct representative of the emperor, is actively involved with the homage given to the emperor. In a number of the foregoing inscriptions such an involvement can be supposed, in others it is explicitly stated.

This is most remarkable in some inscriptions of statues, which we have not discussed yet and where one would not expect that a proconsul or a city council would be involved. In the same year that Vibius Salutaris sets up his foundation, Sex. Atilios Amarantos and his daughter Atilia Maximilla erect a group of statues of Theseus. In the Greek inscription (there is also a Latin text), the proconsul is surprisingly mentioned. He is even called "benefactor of the city of Ephesus" which makes one think that the decision about the foundation of Vibius Salutaris has already been passed by the city council (II-509). A year earlier T. Fl. Epagathos, a freedman of the emperor, had also erected a group of statues together with his wife Manlia Procula. In the Latin text, the proconsul is mentioned; in the Greek text, the proconsul and the *grammateus* of the city are mentioned (III-858). Something similar is the case with the statue of Athamas erected by Tib. Kl. Hermes. Only the Greek text gives the name of the proconsul and the *grammateus* of the city (III-857). It is very remarkable that, in this sort of 'apolitical' statues, there is an involvement of the highest authority in state and city.[17]

I close this series of emperor dedications with two inscriptions about inheritances. Often we find a foundation connected with an inheritance. In this case it is about emperor statues. In II-259B the heirs erect a statue for Claudius in accordance with the testament of Tib. Kl. Damonikos. In II-262 Eutaktos, a freedman of the emperor,[18] executes the testament of Kl. Summachos by erecting a statue for Titus. The phenomenon of the emperor cult comes closer with these statues.

5.2.2 *The emperor and his family*

Before showing in what large numbers they are present, something else must be clarified. Practically all the emperors have their immediate relatives play a role in the promotion of the imperial interests. The members of the *familia* increase the influence of the *pater familias*. Certainly in the time of Augustus and Tiberius, the emperors are actively involved in this. Augustus has a large family and promotes his succession. Tiberius continues this policy, at least at the beginning of his time as emperor. The later emperors of the Julio-Claudian dynasty and the Flavii no longer mention their male relations. Their wives then take the main position and, quite remarkably, there is attention to the collection of the Sebastoi, the existing and dead Venerable Ones.

Augustus
The inscriptions which have been preserved are a short history of the politics Augustus played in securing his succession. The triumphal arch for Augustus on the south side of the *agora* sets the tone. It was erected in 3 BC and all important members of the

---

[17] However remarkable, the procedure is not totally necessary, as appears from the statue of Daedalus and Icarus in II-517. The text consists of an emperor dedication and a *cursus honorum* of the founder but without mention of other authorities.

[18] Maybe he is the procurator in charge of the vectigal of the XX hereditatium who takes care that 5% of the inheritances is given to the state, see Hirschfeld 1963/3, 93; Eck 1979, 125ff; cf. Weaver 1972, 276.

family are named: Augustus and his wife Livia; Agrippa, the beloved son-in-law of Augustus who even has the title of *Imperator* here and his wife Julia. On the pedestal of a statue, which certainly was part of the arch, the son of Agrippa and Julia is mentioned, Lucius Caesar —with the addition 'son of Augustus', because Augustus had already adopted him.[19]

He shares this honour with another grandchild of Augustus, Gaius Caesar (cf. Tac. Ann. I.3). It is a privilege which, at least in the province, made a deep impression.[20] Many statues of him and his brother have been preserved. In Ephesus there are two inscriptions which mention their names. II-253 is a text of dedication to Augustus, Gaius Caesar, Lucius Caesar, and Marcus Agrippa, another son of the son-in-law Agrippa. It is probably part of a pedestal for a group of statues. The inscription may have been made while Gaius and Lucius were still alive. That is not so for III-719 where the personal physician of Trajan calls himself priest of "Gaius and Lucius, descendants of Augustus". The text proves that until the second century there was a cult around these Sebastoi who died young. It had its origin in this time when Augustus still hoped that his succession would be fairly straightforward.

As is well known, Tiberius became the next emperor. Augustus prepared this succession too. In Ephesus they knew this. Three texts express the co-principate. On the *stoa basilikē*, on the aqueduct of Sextilius Pollio, and on the bridge of this aqueduct, the dedication is for Augustus as well as Tiberius (II-402; 404; VII-1-3092). He is called 'the son of Augustus', because he was adopted by Augustus just like Lucius and Gaius and was made co-regent as the successor (cf. Tac. Ann. I.3).

Tiberius
The first man who has the favour of Tiberius is Germanicus. The story of his journey to the East, which ended so famously and sorrily, and of his arrival in Colophon to hear from the oracle what

---

[19] VII-1-3006/07; for Lucius Caesar, see also II-408.

[20] See Magie 1950, 481/82; for the area which concerns us see for Miletus I. Miletus Delphinion 127 p. 148; for Sardis I. Sardis 8 and for Pergamum I. Perg. 384 and 475.

is awaiting him, and where his death is predicted,[21] has left traces behind in Ephesus. There are two dedications for him alone (II-255 and 255A) and four for his family.[22]

Finally, there is probably also a dedication to the man who will be Tiberius' successor. It is a short inscription, "C. Caesari pontifici maximo" (II-259), which probably is meant for Caligula; but the connection with Ephesus is not too clear. This inscription may be connected with the visit of Germanicus to Colophon, because Caligula is with Drusus and Nero the third son and he has been in Asia with Germanicus.[23] Be that as it may, there is agreement with Augustus' politics even though the material is limited. The family of the emperor represent the emperor.

This is most clearly expressed in the honorary decree of the devotees of Demeter (VII-2-4337). This religious organization decides to make an image of Livia Augusta (Tiberius' mother) in the form of Demeter, and an image of the then newly born twins Germanicus and Tiberius, Tiberius' natural grandchildren, in the form of two young Dioscuri. This plan is probably conceived in reaction to Tiberius' decision not to give the emperor temple to Ephesus but to Smyrna. When the city was not allowed to build an emperor temple, one could still pay homage to his immediate family and hope for the future by setting up an eternal priesthood and a public exposition.

Claudius-Hadrian
When Claudius accedes to the throne, dedications to male members of the imperial family stop. The reason cannot be that there were none. That may be true for Claudius and Nero but certainly not from the time of Vespasian on and with Trajan. The dynasty of the Flavii (via father and sons) and the adoption system for the succession from Nerva's time on were sufficiently developed to

---

[21] For the literary data about this trip, see Magie 1950, 497/99; Halfmann 1986, 168/70.

[22] II-256 for his wife and two children, Drusus and Nero; II-257 for himself, for Drusus, the son of Tiberius and for Tiberius himself; in II-258 and in SEG 1983, 934 there is another, separate dedication for Drusus, the son of Tiberius.

[23] Cf. Halfmann 1986, 171.

ensure that there was no danger to the succession. But this did not result in inscriptions which appear before the succession as happened in the time of Augustus and Tiberius.

The fact that the wives attract more attention in this period is remarkable. In the time of Claudius there is (most probably) one inscription for his wife. Because the opening text is lost, it is not clear whether it relates to Messalina or to Agrippina (II-261). The text speaks about the games of Augustus and relates thus directly to the imperial cult.

The mention of Nero's mother is special to Nero. It shows that the imperial history is known even in the far away provinces. It probably is a result of the influence of the proconsuls on the formulation of important texts. Concretely these are about the dedication for two important public buildings:

—the toll house for fishery, dedicated to Nero, to Julia Agrippina Sebasta, his mother, to Octavia, the wife of the emperor, to the Roman people and to the people of Ephesus. Note the position which the mother is given in this text, named in second place, immediately after Nero and before Octavia (I-20);

—the southern wall of the *agora* which Claudia Metrodora and her husband dedicate to Artemis, the God Claudius, Nero, Agrippina Sebasta, and the people of Ephesus (VII-1-3003). Nero's wife is not even mentioned here.

After Nero, the first dedication to a member of the imperial family is in the time of Domitian and it is again the wife who receives the honour. The people of Ephesus honour "Domitia Sebasta, the wife" (II-263C), a formulation which makes one suspect that a statue of Domitian stood next to it. The title Sebasta indicates that the emperor and his wife claim the same divine rights. One can point to the coin from the time of Domitian where on the obverse side Domitia is seen with the inscription Δομιτία Σεβαστή and on the reverse side Ἐφεσίων Δ[ὶς Νε]οκόρων, "from the Ephesians who are twice keepers of the temple", i.e. of Artemis as well as of the imperial family.[24] That is not only the case in Ephesus. When in the time of Domitian the emperor temple is erected, "a priest and warden for life of the temple of Domitian, of Domitia Sebasta, of their *oikos* and of the Senate" comes from

---

[24] Friesen 1993, 56.

Tmolos (II-241). In the time of Domitian it becomes most clear that the imperial family is a gathering of Sebastoi.

Even if there is no dedication, the statues of Plotina, Trajan's wife, which are mentioned in the foundation of Vibius Salutaris, belong in this same series. There is the silver statue of Plotina that is carried along in the Artemis procession together with the five silver statues of Trajan—there must be a difference—and there is the silver statue of her (and Trajan) which Salutaris kept at home (I-27 line 150ff). A title for her has not been preserved but perhaps one can call her Sebasta, with the editors of IE (I-27 line 153).

Finally, in the time of Hadrian, the wife Sabina appears in several inscriptions. There is, first of all, the special dedication to Sabina as Hera Sebasta, probably as wife of 'Hadrianus Zeus' (VII-1-3411). Then there are six inscriptions which honour Sabina as Thea Sebasta and which show every time that the complete political structure of the city is involved in such a dedication: the city council, the people's gathering, the proconsul, the *grammateus* of the people and the supervisor of the work.[25]

The Sebastoi
I have pointed out several times that, apart from the individual attributions to the various emperors and their family, there is a tendency to gather the emperor dedications under the term 'the Sebastoi'. That is not unique to Ephesus,[26] but because many more inscriptions have been preserved in Ephesus, it is easier to trace this aspect of the emperor cult in Ephesus. Doubtless there is a connection with the expansion of the emperor cult to the closer members of the family of the emperor; there is the possibility also to attribute divine qualities to the man as well as to the woman. When this begins—and, as we showed, that is already in the time of Augustus—one begins to speak of the "*oikos* of the Sebastos", the house of the Venerable One. Whenever the wife of the emperor is

---

[25] II-278; 279; 441; VII-2-4334; VII-2-4108.

[26] See for example Pergamum AthMitt 19, 1904, 8 dedicated to Θεοῖς Σεβαστοῖς καὶ Ἑρμεῖ καὶ Ἡρακλεῖ (= to Augustus and Julia) and I. Perg. Askl. 36 for a priest τῆς τῶν Σεβαστῶν Εὐσεβείας, which texts probably originate in the time of Claudius.

given the title Sebasta (respectively Augusta), one can speak of
Sebastoi.

After the death of Augustus—it is not clear whether it was soon
after or some time later—the high priests of the emperor temple in
Pergamum make the decision to celebrate with great pomp the
birthday of Augustus (IV-1393). It is a pity that we have only a
fragment of the inscription. What is clear from it is that every high
priest pays 1000 denarii for the festivities surrounding the birthday
of the God Sebastos. This is to pay for the expenses of the
"sacrifices and libations in favour of ($\upsilon\pi\acute{\epsilon}\rho$) the [Sebastos?] and the
house of the Sebastos". It is a kind of foundation which derives its
importance from its founders, the high priests of the past era who
actively promoted the interests of the emperor, which they extended
to include those of the whole of his family.

In the time of Claudius this combination becomes even more
explicit. Two more important decrees have been preserved.

The edict of Paullus Fabius Persicus (I-17-19) ends, in the
reconstruction of the editors of IE, with the words:

> Because the Imperator Sebastos [.....] gave Julia Sebasta
> divine adoration equal to that of others and which is due
> her for such a long time already, one must attribute to
> those who sing the hymns for her the same rights as have
> those who sing hymns for the divine Sebastoi, since the
> Senate and the God Sebastos thought that she, who had
> been honoured with sacred law before she became
> immortal, was worthy of deification and deified her.

The Imperator Sebastos is Claudius who, together with the
Senate allowed Julia, the wife of Augustus, the apotheosis. When
she died in 29 Tiberius did not want this, even though the Senate
asked for it. Claudius 'restores' this defect in 42. The result of this
deification is now (in 44) that the hymn-singers receive the same
rights as the singers of hymns for the divine Sebastoi (at least
Augustus, Tiberius, and Claudius, who in this text is called the God
Sebastos). Not without reason Julia is in this decree addressed with
the title Sebasta.[27]

---

[27] See Price 1984, 70.

In VII-2-3801.2, there is mention of the honour given to the deceased Tiberius. In content, the text is parallel to IV-1393. The singers of hymns of the emperor-temple take the decision in Pergamum to celebrate in perpetuity the birthday of Tiberius. They recognize the need to honour the house of the Sebastos; they will sing in honour of the house of the Sebastos; they will offer sacrifices for the divine Sebastoi and they will celebrate with a festive meal.

Whether there is mention in this text of the Σεβαστοὶ Θεοί depends on how one fills the lacuna in the text. From I-17-19, where the Σεβαστοὶ Θεοί are explicitly mentioned, it cannot be excluded, but the reconstruction is definitely not certain. In fact all it says is:

καθυ-
[μνοῦντες τὸν Σεβα]στὸν οἶκον καὶ το[ῖς]
[Σεβαστοῖς θεοῖς θυσία]ς ἐπιτελοῦν[τες]
[καὶ ἑορτὰς ἄγοντες καὶ ἐσ]τιάσεις

Sing[ing hymns for the Vener]able House and sacrificing [offerings for the Venerable Gods and celebrating feasts and] festive meals.

The title Sebasta is settled from this time on. As we said, from the time of Nero, several imperial women are given this title in Ephesus already while still alive: Nero's mother, the wife of Domitian, the wife of Trajan, the wife of Hadrian. In the time of Domitian it becomes most clear that the imperial family is a gathering of Sebastoi. That has everything to do with the neocorate in Ephesus, as the first emperor-temple is erected in Ephesus.

In all the texts which deal with these events, the temple is given the special title ναῶι τῶι ἐν Ἐφέσωι τῶν Σεβαστῶν κοινῶι τῆς Ἀσίας, "the naos of the Venerable Ones in Ephesus which belongs to the community of Asia" (II-232-242; V-1498; VI-2048). It appears from two texts that the various visiting cities think that this veneration of the Sebastoi does not belong to Ephesus alone. The people of Philadelphia let it be known about themselves that they honour this temple διὰ τε τὴν εἰς τοὺς Σεβαστοὺς εὐσέβειαν, "because of the (=their) piety for the Venerable Ones" (II-236) and the people of Stratonikeia let the same thing be noted down and also that they are free and autonomous τῆι τῶν Σεβαστῶν χάριτι, "out of the goodwill of the Venerable Ones" (II-237).

In the letter which L. Pompeius Apollonius writes to the proconsul Mestrius Florus—a proconsul who is involved in the neocorate—there is also mention of a cult (*mysteria* and sacrifices) for Demeter and the Sebastoi (II-213). That means that the initiated ones of Demeter have linked their cult with the cult of the Sebastoi.

There are two lines, a link with the emperor cult and a link with the cult of the Gods, which run through the texts of a later time. They are about dedications to emperors and members of the imperial family and the cult of the Sebastoi is mentioned almost in passing:

—from the time of Trajan, an inscription in which the medicine men call themselves "the ones offering sacrifice to Asklepios and the Sebastoi" (III-719);

—an inscription in which 'work-places' are dedicated to "Artemis and the Sebastoi" (II-443);

—from the time of Hadrian, inscriptions in which several persons are called νεοκόρος τῶν Σεβαστῶν (III-710; VI-2069).

The emperor temple, Artemis, Asklepios and Demeter are linked to the Venerable Gods.

5.2.3 *The emperor and the cult*

We come closer and closer to the emperor cult itself. It is clear that the emperors have found a place in the centre of city life. Therefore, it is natural that they linked themselves with a central aspect of city life: religion as it is given form and substance in the city. The emperor cult is a specific but diffuse phenomenon. It is specific in as far as the emperor becomes an explicit object of the cult. It is diffuse, because the veneration is embedded in a multitude of practices: when the emperor is seen in his relation to other divinities; when certain statues of the emperor are given a specific cultic function; when religious overtones appear in the modes of address, sometimes very general, sometimes relating specifically to the service of the explicit emperor cult. We need to develop these aspects further:

The emperor in combination with other divinities

In the foregoing text I have indicated several times that dedications to the emperor are linked with dedications to other divinities: to Dionysus, Demeter, Asklepios, Hera, and in Ephesus especially and rather exclusively to Artemis. When Pergamum gets its emperor temple, Augustus does not want it to be dedicated to him alone (Tac. Ann. 4,37). He wants his name linked to *Dea Roma*. This combination appears several times in Pergamum[28] and in Sardis[29] in an important inscription.

In Ephesus one does not find the same picture.

In Augustus' early years, the *prytanis* fulfils the function of leadership of the games for Dionysus as well as the priesthood of Rome (ἱερεὺς τῆς ᾿Ρώμης). That goes back to a time before Augustus (51/50 BC) and goes on till 40/39 BC. After that the priesthood of Rome disappears in the list of names which runs from 51/50 yearly till 18/17 BC. The *prytaneis* are still leaders of the Dionysia but they are no longer called 'priests of Rome'.

III-859A is probably from the time of Augustus. In the restored text there is mention of payment for a sacrifice for Rome, Augustus, and Artemis, but, in fact, this ᾿Ρώμηι καὶ Σεβαστῶι is an addition by the editors of IE. From the edition of the text it is not at all clear that such a large piece of the fragment has been broken off.

In VII-2-3825, a decree to honour a certain Theophrōn and his family, erected by the *koinon* of the Hellenes in Asia, the high priest Gaios Ioulios Pardalas carries the title ἀρχιερεὺς καὶ διὰ βίου ἀγωνοθέτης θεᾶς ᾿Ρώμης καὶ Αὐτοκράτορος θεοῦ υἱοῦ Σεβαστοῦ. But this text was not found in Ephesus, but in Hypaipa. Theophrōn himself comes from Sardis and furthermore there is one Ti. Ioulios Pardalas known from Sardis, so that it is not improbable that Gaios Ioulios Pardalas is also from Sardis.

In the only remaining text (as far I have been able to discover), there are similar problems (VII-2-3801.2). Again this concerns an ἀγωνοθέτης about whom the text—with additions!— says: διὰ βίου

---

[28] See I. Perg. 269; 374; AthMitt 24, 1899, 30; 32, 1907, 50; see also I. Perg. Askl. p. 165; AthMitt 37, 1912, 25; see Ohlemutz 1968, 276.

[29] I. Sardis 8, line 83.

ἀγων[οθέτου Θεᾶς ʿΡώμης] καὶ Θεοῦ Σεβαστοῦ Κα[ίσαρος Διὸς].
Considering I. Smyrna 591 and IE VII-2-3825, these additions are
probable, but again this is not a text from Ephesus but from
Hypaipa.

Be that as it may, the combination of the name of an emperor
with Artemis is found in Ephesus in large numbers. Almost all the
emperors are linked to Artemis. Sometimes the link is indirect
because the emperor takes monies from the Artemis-temple to
provide for certain needs in the city (water, buildings, boundaries),
but mostly there is a direct combination, in the formula: to Artemis
Ephesia and the Autokrator Kaisar N.N.:

—for Artemis, Augustus and Tiberius: II-404; VII-1-3092;
—for Artemis and Tiberius (or Claudius): IV-1398;
—for Artemis, Claudius, Nero, and Agrippina: VII-1-3003;
—for Artemis and Nero: II-411; II-413; SEG 1984, 1122; cf. also
    the Nero-coin;[30]
—for Artemis and Domitian: II-418; II-508; VI-2034; VI-2047;
    VII- 1-3005; VII-1-3008; cf. also the coin of Domitian and
    Artemis and of Domitian, Artemis and Zeus;[31]
—for Artemis and Nerva: IV-1124;
—for Artemis and Nerva or Trajan: II-264B;
—for Artemis and Trajan: II-421; II-422; II-424; II-470; II-509; II-
    517; III-857; III-858; IV-1208; VI-2037;
—for Artemis, Trajan and Plotina: I-27;
—for Artemis and the Sebastoi: II-443;
—for Artemis and Hadrian: II-273; II-274; II-430;

I said that the supervision of all the activities of the Artemis-
temple were in the hands of the emperor. The multitude of
inscriptions makes clear what is the reason for this and what are the
consequences. In these many inscriptions, the emperor is
exclusively linked to Artemis. If the greater number of inscriptions
can lead us to draw conclusions, this is certainly true for the time
of Domitian and Trajan, but, as has been shown, there is no lack
even under other emperors. The emperor is the σύνθρονος of

---

[30] Karwiese RE Suppl. 330; Friesen 1993, 53.
[31] Karwiese, RE Suppl. 331; Friesen 1993, 56 and 119.

Artemis. One must understand this correctly. Hanfmann, Vermeule, and Price[32] have pointed out that the emperor does not in this way push out the local deity. We must remember that, certainly in Ephesus, Artemis is always mentioned first and that in the temples the statue of Artemis functions as cult object, if not alone then in combination with the statue of the emperor. Artemis is the primary deity. That the emperor associates himself (or is associated) with the divinity is good for both.[33]

In Ephesus we find the exclusive combination with Artemis. Except in the case of Hadrian (more about this in the history of the emperor temples), the emperors are never linked to another deity. There are a couple of (apparent) exceptions:

—the combination of (probably) Augustus with Zeus in VII-2-3801.2 (see also I. Smyrna 591) is because this decree was written in Pergamum where Zeus plays an important role;

—Tiberius is linked to Hermes in VII-1-3420, but that inscription is from Metropolis;

—Trajan is linked to Dionysus in VII-1-3329, but that inscription is from Thyaira (Tyre).

—The only real exception seems to be the coin on which, on the reverse side, Domitian identifies himself with Zeus Olympios. One must not forget that, even in this case, there is an association with Artemis. The Zeus image carries in its right hand the Ephesian Artemis instead of a Nikē.[34]

If other divinities are mentioned in the inscriptions—and this does happen a few times—they are always members of the imperial family: Livia with Demeter; the young children of Drusus, the grand-children of Tiberius with the Dioscuri (VII-2-4337) and Sabina with Hera (cf. the combination of the Sebastoi with Demeter and Asklepios above). Individual emperors link themselves exclusively with Artemis.

---

[32] Hanfmann 1975, 73; Vermeule 1977; Price 1984, 149/150.

[33] See Hannestad 1986, 55/57; 99/100; 113; recently Friesen 1993, 146ff and passim; he emphasizes over against Price that, in these combinations, it is not a question of making ontological judgments about the divinity of the respective emperors.

[34] Karwiese RE Suppl. 331; Friesen 1993, 119.

In a few cases, a third dedication is added to this unbreakable couple: to the people or the city of the Ephesians. That practice starts already in the time of Augustus (II-404 and VII-1-3092) and continues till the time of Trajan. When the emperor temple has been founded, we find the addition νεωκόρος: "to the people/the city which is the keeper of the (emperor) temple".[35] In this way the aspect of the emperor cult is given a special accent.

The question is whether one can/must attribute a 'divine' quality to this dedication. It is, in fact, in line with the phenomenon from the beginning imperial era that abstract realities can be given superhuman attributes: the priest of the εὐσεβεία τῶν Σεβαστῶν, of the piety of the Sebastoi (I. Perg. Askl. 36); the statue of the holy Senate which is erected in the time of Trajan (V-1499); the statues in front of the library in Ephesus which express the Wisdom of Celsus, the Virtue of Celsus, the Knowledge of Celsus, and the Insight of Philippus (VII-2-5108-11). The most remarkable example in Ephesus is the enormous collection of statues of the Vibius Salutaris foundation (I-27ff): apart from the statues of Artemis, Trajan, and Plotina, there are statues of the Senate, of the Roman nobility, of the City of Ephesus, of the People, of the six Clans of Ephesus, of the City Council, of the Council of Elders and the Union of the Ephebes, of the Temple Servants, of the People who carry the golden statues, of the Kouretes etc. The abstract reality is made concrete in these statues. Whatever associations the inhabitants of Ephesus may have made, the explicit mention of the people/the city in these dedications brings emperor and city even closer to each other.

The statues of the emperor
Ephesus is a city filled with statues. There was a kind of industry: one could order a statue, there were statues in series, statues of which only the head needed to be changed to be current again.[36] In our period of time there are dozens statues of the emperors and their family.

---

[35] In the time of Domitian: II-492; 508; VII-1-3005; VII-1-3008; and in the time of Trajan: II-470; II-509; III-857; III-858; VI-2037.

[36] See Richter 1951; Clairmont 1966; Hanfmann 1975; Bieber 1977; Vermeule 1977; Aurenhammer 1990.

For the first time there is mention not just of memorials, inscriptions which refer to those absent. A number of emperor statues have been preserved till today, spread all over the world's museums. A catalogue which tries to be exhaustive, with images and descriptions has been edited by Inan-Rosenbaum.[37] The following statues or pieces of statues have been preserved from Ephesus of the first century (the precise place where it is found is not always known):

—Augustus (large head: Inan II.2; Vermeule 381)
—Augustus (colossal seated statue: Inan II.3)
—Livia (colossal seated statue: Inan II.5)
—Livia (statue for house cult: Robert 770)
—C. or L. Caesar (bust: Inan II.9)
—Tiberius (head: Inan I.15; Vermeule 385)
—Tiberius (statue for house cult: Robert 770)
—Members of Julio-Claudian family (heads: Inan I.21; I.25; II.18)
—Nero, son of Germanicus (head: Inan II.19)
—Domitian (colossal head and arm; the height of the whole was some seven to eight metres: Inan I.27; cf. Price 187; according to Friesen 1993, 62 this is an image of Titus)
—Trajan (heads: Inan II.39; II.41)
—Trajan (relief portrait, cuirassed imperator: Vermeule 107)
—Hadrian (head: Inan I.33; Wegner 38,59,116; Vermeule 392)
—Hadrian (relief portrait: Inan I.34; Wegner 38,63,66,116; Vermeule 109/110)
—Sabina (relief portrait and upper part of the body: Inan II.52; Wegner 89,129; Vermeule 112)
—Antinous as Androclus (statue: Inan I.37; Clairmont 1966).

This list alone makes clear that there are all sorts of statues. In his *Res Gestae*,[38] Augustus distinguishes between statues where he appears standing, sitting on a horse, or driving a chariot. In modern research one distinguishes among the complete statues, those where the emperor is seen as the commander of the army, standing and

---

[37] 1966 and 1979; see also Wegner 1956; Vermeule 1968; Robert 1989.

[38] *Res Gestae*, 24.

with military attributes; where he is seen naked in the form of some divinity; or as citizen in a toga or *himation*. More important is the distinction because of the function of the statue, expressed by the names given to it. The statue has a cultic function if it is indicated as ἄγαλμα (see e.g. III-690: τὰ ἀγάλματα τῶν θεῶν καὶ τόν βωμὸν). All other names (ἀνδρίας, εἰκών, ἀπεικόνισμα, σύμπλεγμα (to limit myself to words which appear in Ephesus in this time), are only contemporary descriptions, even if not always very clear to us.[39]

It is difficult to give a complete overview of all emperor statues because it is not always clear from the inscriptions whether this or that pedestal supported a statue of the one dedicating or of the one to whom it was dedicated. That is true sometimes of the statues which have been preserved, e.g. the equestrian statue of Celsus Polemaeanus (respectively of Tib. Aquila) about which Hanfmann[40] says: "Having carefully looked at the statue in the Istanbul Museum, I think it is really a statue of the emperor Hadrian". I have no pretensions that I would be able to provide a comprehensive list.

The following seems to me to be more important: of a number of statues one can say with some certainty that they have been used as a cult statue. Of those which are preserved this is true of the colossal seated statues of Augustus and Livia;[41] the statues of Livia and Tiberius which have been found in a private house;[42] probably, the statue of Antinous as Androclus, the mythical founder of Ephesus; the colossal statue of Domitian which stood in the emperor temple. Friesen,[43] basing himself on Daltrop-Hausmann-Wegner,[44] supposes that this is a statue of Titus. He links it with other colossal statues such as that of Augustus and Livia in Ephesus and the statues of Claros and Sardis, and he supposes that in the temple itself similar colossal statues of the other Flavii were present: of Vespasian, Domitian, and maybe also of Domitia.

---

[39] Cf. Price 1984, 176.
[40] 1975, 65.
[41] Cf. Price 1984, 255.
[42] Robert 1989, 707.
[43] 1993, 62.
[44] 1966, 26,38,86.

From the inscriptions a number of other cult statues are known:
—a statue of Augustus which was erected together with a τέμενος by Apollonios Passalas, *prytanis* in 19/18 BC (III- 902);[45]
—a statue of Augustus as God, erected by the θίασος τῶν νέων, when Herakleides Passalas is gymnasiarch (II-252);
—(maybe) a silver statue of Augustus, which Vibius Salutaris had made in the time of Trajan, to be placed in the theatre (I-28);
—(maybe) the εἰκόνες γραπταί (= paintings) of Livia and the sons of Drusus (VII-2-3437);
—(maybe) a statue of Domitian in the theatre, erected by the νεοποιήσαντες (VI-2047);
—(maybe) a statue of Domitian in the theatre, in the form of the dedication of the people of Synaitos to the emperor temple (VI-2048);
—a statue of Domitian near to the nymphaeum of Domitian (II-413);
—the statues of Domitian near the harbour complex, erected by Nysios (II-518) and Klaudia Trophime (II-508);
—a statue of Nerva, with the text θεὸν Νέρβαν near the nymphaeum of Trajan (II-420);
—a colossal statue of Trajan near the nymphaeum of Trajan (II-424);
—the statues of Trajan and Plotina which Vibius Salutaris keeps at home for the house cult (I-27 line 150ff);
—the statues of Hadrian which honour him as Zeus Olympios and which are often used for the house cult (II-267-272);
—a statue of Hadrian as σύνθρονος τῷ Διονύσῳ (II-275);
—a statue of Sabina with the text Ἥρᾳ Σαβείνῃ Σεβαστῇ (VII-1-3411).
The place-determination of the statue determines this choice.
The emperors were venerated:
—in temples: in the Sebasteion respectively the Augusteum near the Artemis-temple; the τέμενος on the agora; in the temples of Domitian/the Sebastoi and of Hadrian;
—in the cult-places of other gods such as Demeter, Dionysos, Asklepios;

---

[45] According to Price 1984, 254 the head has been preserved, see Inan II.2.

—in the various gymnasia;[46]
—on the market cf. the colossal seated statues of Augustus and
 Livia which stood near the *stoa basilikē*;
—near the public 'fountains', especially the nymphaeum of
 Domitian and Trajan;[47]
—in the theatre in various situations—even though it is impossible
 to point to concrete statues; from the list above, the statue
 erected by the νεοποιήσαντες stands the best chance to have been
 a cult statue;
—and in private houses of which some statues have been
 preserved; possibly the preserved terra cotta statuettes of the
 emperor and his family were used for a house cult.
 The city in all its aspects radiates cult.

The titles of the emperor

We must speak here also about the titles which the emperor and the
imperial family attributed to themselves in connection with Artemis
and other deities. In chapter 2, I developed this and there is no
need to repeat that here. In John's passion story the title 'king' for
Jesus stands central: it is not unimportant to see that the title in
John's text is also used by the high priests for the emperor: "we
have no other *king* but the emperor" (Jn 19:15).
  The title is much used in the provinces as is clear from the use
of 'king' for the Roman emperors in Josephus (Bell. Jud. 3,351;
4,569; 5,563); from the development of the theme of kingship in
relation with 'king Trajan' by Dio Chrysostom (especially in Or.
1,3 and 62); and from some papyri.[48] Such abundance is not
apparent from the inscriptions in Ephesus. Apart from some later
texts about the Byzantine emperors, only Hadrian (I-20 line 20
indirectly), Antoninus Pius (I-20), and Lucius Verus (VII-1-3072)
are called 'king'. That is not to say that the statement of the high
priests before Pilate would have been unintelligible for the readers
in Ephesus. As with the use of 'saviour', the title has the potential

---

[46] See esp. Hanfmann 1975, 65.
[47] Cf. Ginouvès 1962, 364-73.
[48] In Bauer, Wb s.v. βασιλεύς are mentioned: P.Oxy. 33 II, 6.35
verso 1; BGU 588,10; ZP 4,2448; in Preisigke-Kießling also SB 8545 B.

to be understood also in later times. When the title 'king' becomes common for Hadrian and the later emperors, the text in John gets a new and up-to-date meaning.

5.2.4 *The emperor and his promoters*

The emperor cult in all its aspects is the work of people. Actual people take the initiative to build the holy places and the temples; it is actual people who commission the emperor statues, who take care of the cult and participate in it. Up to a point an inner circle of these people has been preserved in the inscriptions: via the mention of their names and via the titles which they gave themselves and each other to indicate the functions which they fulfilled in the emperor cult.

In the system of titles the various emperor temples play an important role. The titles (usually) indicate functions which are directly linked to the temple. As with the cult itself, there is again a combination with the cult of Artemis. The μολποί, λευκοφόροι and χρυσοφόροι carry the statues of the emperor from now on (I-27 line 437ff), or they take the initiative to bring homage to the emperor (II-276ff), or a priestess of Artemis brings Artemis and the emperor together (II-508). As soon as the emperor cult becomes explicit, there is a link with one of the emperor temples. For Ephesus this means that these indications of function grow enormously in quantity after the erection of the emperor temple there.

The epithets φιλοσέβαστος, νεωκόρος and φιλόκαισαρ
I start with three words which—as adjectives—do not indicate a function but give a description of the (desired and/or actual) relation to the emperor. The word φιλοσέβαστος is often combined with εὐσεβής: "pious and loyal to the Emperor". It is clear that this word has a stronger religious connotation than esp. φιλόκαισαρ. This must, probably, be seen in connection with the difference in meaning between the use of the words Σεβαστός and Καῖσαρ.

In Ephesus the word φιλοσέβαστος became a craze. If I counted well, it is attributed to people at least 132 times in our period, sometimes collectively to a group of *kouretes*: "these are the pious *kouretes*, loyal to the emperor", followed by the six names; it is often an epithet for individual persons. Then it is used a number of

times as epithet for other collectives: the city council, the council of
elders, the *stratēgoi*, and sometimes the people of Ephesus.

It looks as if the use of the word has a history. In the early
period—till more or less the time of Domitian—it is seldom used:
—in two texts from the time of Augustus (in VI-2033 as epithet for
   the *prytanis* and in II-442 as epithet for the *gerousia*;
—on the tomb inscriptions of M. Antonius Albus and his wife
   Laevia Paula, probably from the time of Claudius-Nero (in II-
   614C as epithet for the *boulē* and the *grammateus* of the people;
   and in II-614B as epithet for the *boulē* and the *dēmos*);
—on the statue for Agrippina or Messalina from the time of
   Claudius (in II-261 as epithet for the man who commissioned the
   statue).

All other texts where the word is used are from the time of
Domitian or later. There is reason to suppose that the concern to
obtain the permission for the emperor temple created an explosive
use of the word. It even seems that the very extensive use of the
word can be used as a secondary way to date some texts.[49] From
the time of the dedication of the temple in Ephesus, a large number
of people and a (limited) number of institutions claim the right to
honour themselves with this epithet.

In fact, there develops a use of the word which is not without
hierarchical implication. The *gerousia* (II-442), the *stratēgoi* (II-
449; IV-1024), the yearly *kouretes*,[50] and the *boulē*[51] call themselves *filosebastos*.

The use of the epithet for ὁ δῆμος is special. A number of times
'the people' in combination with 'the city council' is called
φιλοσέβαστοι.[52] One time, at the mention of the institution 'the
people', the word φιλοσέβαστος is combined with the title

---

[49] For the dating of the lists of the *kouretes* this could be so: IV-1008
is then not from the time of Nero, but comes after VI-1011; and what
about IV-1005?, see Knibbe 1981, 17f.

[50] IV-1008,1012-1018,1020-1024,1028-1030.

[51] II-266,278-280,441,449; III-644A; V-1500; VII-1-3060; VII-2-
4101A; 4333.

[52] II-449; III-614B; IV-1024,1385; VII-1-4101A, see also I-27 lines
4,132.

νεωκόρος.[53] For the rest where there is mention of 'the people', it is always said that it is νεωκόρος, usually in the following combination: ἡ φιλοσέβαστος Ἐφεσίων βουλή καὶ ὁ νεωκόρος δῆμος, the Council of the Ephesians who is loyal to the Emperor and the People which is warden of the temple.[54] The people must care for the temple. The city council is concerned about the cult—and the high priests are the highest representatives of that.

The word νεωκόρος—when used as an adjective, because it is also an indication of function for individual persons—is a very old title which belongs to Ephesus from of old because of Artemis.[55] We find two (or three) references to this in Ephesus in the first century. On a coin of Nero a temple is shown on the reverse side which can be seen as the Artemis-temple with the inscription Ἐφ[εσίων] νεωκόρων: from the Ephesians who are the keepers of Artemis. And in Acts 19:35, the *grammateus* of the city says to the people who for two hours have been shouting against the Jew Alexander "great is Artemis of Ephesus": "who under the people does not know that the city of the Ephesians is the *guardian* of the great Artemis and of the statue which came down from heaven?" The third reference has a different status: it is about two coins from the time of Domitian of which one has the image of Domitian on the obverse side and on the reverse Artemis with two pillars and the inscription Ἐφεσίων Β Νεοκόρων, while the other coin shows on the obverse side Domitia and on the reverse Artemis and her temple with the inscription Ἐφεσίων Δ[ὶς Νε]οκόρων. This must be about the double *neocorate* of Ephesus, that of Artemis and that of the Sebastoi.[56]

---

[53] In II-236: 'the people who is warden of the Temple and loyal to the Emperor'; in IV-1238 there is a similar combination with the word *polis*. In II-263C the editors of IE filled the existing lacuna as [ὁ φιλο]σέβαστος Ἐ[φεσίων δῆμος]. More probably, similar to II-266,278-280,441; III-644A; V-1500; VII-1-3060 and VII-2-4333 [ἡ φιλο]σέβαστος Ἐ[φεσίων βουλή] should be put here.

[54] I-36A-D; II-266,278,279,280,441; V-1500; VII-1-3060; VII-2-4333.

[55] See e.g. the *neokoros* of Artemis who returns to Xenophon in Olympia his deposit for Artemis, Xenophon Anab. 5.3.4-6. This text is about a functionary and here it is not in apposition to some noun.

[56] Cf. Friesen 1993, 52-56.

In the inscriptions in Ephesus, the term is never from then on used in connection with Artemis. The link to the emperor temples is from this point on exclusive. As we said, the word has spread mostly as epithet for 'the people', 'the *polis*', and 'the metropolis': the People, the City, the Metropolis "which is the warden of the temple", and, when the temple of Hadrian has been built, the People, the City, the Metropolis "which is the warden of the temple for the second time".[57] The massive use of the word makes it clear how proud Ephesus was to present its own emperor temple to anyone who wanted to hear it or read about it.

It is different with the epithet φιλοκαῖσαρ. The word itself is not used all that often but for the interference with the Johannine Gospel it is much more important. Friesen[58] writes about the use of the word by the city of Aphrodisias in its dedication text to the emperor temple (II-233), "The Aphrodisians added φιλοκαῖσαρ to emphasize Caesar's role in the acquisition of free status". If I understand him well, he links the expression with the historical Caesar and not with the *Kaisar* who is alive then. In his vision "the addition [is] unusual in a late first century CE inscription honouring a Flavian emperor". But this does not seem correct if one looks at all the texts where φιλοκαῖσαρ is used. A number of times people who were of great importance to the history of the city are called φιλοκαῖσαρ:

—the master of the coinage Lucius Cusinius (III-716 from the time of Claudius who is mentioned in at least 5 other inscriptions; his wealth appears especially in VI-2246A where four freedmen are mentioned);

—the high priest Anaxagoras from Pergamum who proposed the decree about the singers of hymns for Tiberius (VII-2-3801.2 from the time of Claudius);

—the builder M. Tigellius Lupus, who probably received this title because he was so actively involved with the building of the temple

---

[57] - with ὁ δῆμος: II-236,266,278,280,415/6,429,430,441,449,508, 517; III-857/8; IV-1385; V-1500; VII-1-3060; VII-2-4333;

    - with ἡ πόλις: II-233,237,264,415/6,422,509; III-793; V-1499; VI-2034; VII-1-3005.3008;

    - with ἡ μητρόπολις: IV-1238; VI-2069; VII-2-4342.

[58] 1993, 38.

of the Sebastoi (II-449). In every inscription with his name φιλοκαῖσαρ is added (II-446, the restoration of a building; VI-1-3008, the embellishment of the *embolos*; III-793 a statue set up under his direction);

—the equestrian Vibius Salutaris who is called several times φιλάρτεμις καὶ φιλόκαισαρ (I-27 line 452; I-33 line 16; I-36A-D).

—an anonymous man from Larisa (of his name only An[   ] has been preserved), who erected a statue for Hadrian and dedicated a μάκελλον to him (VII-1-3271).

These are all people who are actively involved in the promotion of the emperor cult or in any case in the promotion of the interests of the emperor in the city.

The functionaries

Slowly it becomes clear how intensively and extensively the inhabitants of the city are involved in everything which has to do with the emperor and his family and how sensitively people follow the life of each emperor. That is even more true for the people who are directly involved in the emperor temples. In a large number of texts it is clear that there are different functions which suppose a different commitment. Before giving a description of the history of the temples, I want to indicate briefly these different functions and show how they have become part of the city hierarchy.

The singers of hymns

Because in the course of the century the rules about hymn-singers, the people who sing hymns in honour of the emperor, were changed, we know something about the history of this special group. Pergamum organized a choir when they erected the first emperor temple. Augustus decreed that these people would individually receive a sum of money and that the province was responsible for that, not Pergamum by itself. Furthermore, the sons of these people were given a right of succession. Ephesus paid its own people.

The regulation could not be followed completely. In Claudius' time already, it is determined that only the ephebes are allowed to sing, and only for free (see I-17 line 52-62).

Whenever a new temple is erected a new choir is organized: the singers of hymns for Tiberius (VII-2-3801);[59] for Domitian[60] and for Hadrian, indirectly in IV-1145 where we read, "while the emperor listened, the ephebes sang beautiful songs in the theatre" (IV-1145). For Ephesus it is remarkable that in the existing inscriptions we do not find names;[61] this by contrast to the inscriptions from Pergamum[62] and Smyrna.[63]

The temple officials and the temple wardens
The emperor temples come ever more clearly into focus. Two terms express a direct relation with the temples: the persons who call themselves νεωποιοί (or νεοποιοί), the officials of a temple, and the persons who rank in the temple hierarchy, the νεωκόροι (resp. the νεοκόροι), the wardens of the municipal or imperial temple(s), which, as an adjective as we just indicated, is used also as epithet for 'the people' and 'the city'.

Obviously, there are many officials. The function in Ephesus (and in other places) is not limited to the emperor temples. Artemis employs people and it is not always clear whether the νεωποιοί exercise their function for Artemis or for the Sebastoi. If there is an apposition, as e.g. τῆς Ἀρτέμιδος, it is clear.[64] But with the two νεοποιοί about whom in the foundation of Vibius Salutaris we find continual mention,[65] it is more difficult to determine. These are two persons in a larger group (it is said time and again "two of the νεοποιοί"), who must take care that the gold and silver statues of

---

[59] Should we not suppose εἰς Σμύρναν in VII-2-3801.2 line 16?, though as a decision which is taken in Pergamum see 3801.1. line 11.

[60] At least not improbable; I-27 line 267 and I-34 line 23 is certainly about the hymn-singers for Artemis but is this true also for I-27 lines 146 and 296?

[61] See the later inscriptions about M. Ant. Aristides Euandros who is called 'the hymn-singer of the temple of God Hadrian' (III-921).

[62] See I. Perg. 374 with a long list of names of hymn-singers for the God Sebastos and the goddess Rome, from the time of Hadrian.

[63] I. Smyrna 594 where there is mention of 24 hymn-singers, see I. Smyrna 697.

[64] See in II-712B and VII-1-3080; in II-233 an official of the Goddess Aphrodite is mentioned.

[65] I-27 lines 48,94,147,209,423,544,560; I-34, 36A-C.

Artemis and the Imperial House are safe, during and after the various processions.

The title of the statue from the Salutaris collection—συνεδρίον τῶν νεοποιῶν—indicates that the officials act as a group. That is clear also from other inscriptions. In the time of Domitian the συναγωγή τῶν νεοποιῶν takes care of the water provision (II-419). And the more indeterminate indication οἱ νεοποιήσαντες is responsible for the statue of Domitian in the theatre (VI-2047). There are all sorts of lists of names of νεοποιοί, although except for maybe the list of V-1578A, none is demonstrably from the first century. That says something about the socio-cultural place which these νεοποιοί have in the life of the city.

If we go from here to the texts which mention the νεωκόροι,[66] we find a different atmosphere. This is much more about individual persons who in the city itself have an important social and political position.

These concern:

—Tib. Kl. Ariston who is often called νεωκόρος,[67] and who made a name for himself with the emperor temple of the Sebastoi;

—G. Kaskellios Politikos (III-904) who as legate for the city went to Hadrian in connection with important financial problems in the city. Hadrian demands in a letter to the city that the city will pay for the legation—unless he himself had promised to do this on his own (V-1486);

—several members of the Gnaei Pompeii family[68] who play an important role in the city in the second century.

Friesen[69] supposes that this function was created when the emperor temple was erected. He even believes that he knows the exact date and the first functionary: Tib. Kl. Ariston in the period

---

[66] See also Kearsley 1992, 203.

[67] II-237,241,424,424A; III-638; by the editors of IE filled out in VII-2-4105.

[68] Hermippos (III-710; VI-2069); Kouartinos (III-710; IV-1238) and his friend L. Gerellanos Silvianos (III-710); Antonios Amoinos (III-710B; VII-1-3038.

[69] 1993, 46-49.

between summer 90 and September 90.[70] It is certain that all other
names which are known come from a later time, but there is a gap
in time between Aristion and Kaskellios which does not look good
when we are dealing with such an important function. From II-424
and 424A it is, anyway, clear that Aristion still fulfils this office in
the time of Trajan.

The high priests
The highest functionaries in the emperor temples are 'the high
priests of Asia': men and women who are ready and able to take on
this expensive liturgy. In the foregoing chapters we have met them
several times. It is clear that they play an indispensable role also
here, in this chapter about the relation between the passion narrative
and the imperial cult. The high priests of the imperial temples are
fully in service to the imperial cult. In the inscriptions which they
erect they want this to be known.

In addition to what already has been said, and which should fully
be taken into account here, I want to point to two images: the statue
of Damianus, the sophist, which was found in the palaestra of the
East Gymnasium, where he is dressed as a high priest. Especially
important is the crown on his head which is closed with a ring of
busts which (probably) show emperors; and parallel to this another
statue of an anonymous high priest who also has such a crown with
12 busts of emperors.[71] These images make clear, in still a new
way, how close the relation between the high priesthood and the
imperial cult is.

5.2.5 *The imperial temples*
From the foregoing it is clear how closely the erection of imperial
temples determines the history of the city; they are undisputed high
points of city politics. They stimulate the building activity
enormously and cause a reorganization in the social relations in the
city. They give the city importance in relation to other cities, first

---

[70] But what should one do with the man from Tmolos from II-241
who, precisely in this time, is also called *neokoros* of Domitian, Domitia,
their house and the Senate?

[71] See Inan I, 151 and 143 and his commentary on this kind of crown;
Robert 1989, 129.

of all in relation to Pergamum, Smyrna, and, slightly less, in relation to Miletus, but also in relation to many other smaller cities. The erection of the imperial temples is the most important topic of the city's history of this era.

The history of these events has recently been recorded several times: by Knibbe (1980), by Price (1984), and by Friesen (1993). I will relate what is relevant for my perspective in this research. It can be seen in four periods:

The time of Tiberius
While Pergamum already has had an imperial temple in its area since 29 BC, imbedded in a large organization in which it has a place of honour in the yearly celebrations of the γενεθλία of the emperor, a place of honour which remains so at least until the time of Claudius (see VII-2-3801); while the first high priests since the beginning of the province of Asia are elected yearly (and Ephesus can only take a minor place in that); when an enormous earthquake has hit the region and emperor Tiberius in common with the Senate has whole-heartedly offered support (Tac. Ann. II.47); when furthermore the emperor and the Senate have heard the complaints of the province about the misconduct of the proconsul C. Silanus (20/21 AD) and the procurator Lucilius Capito (21/22 AD), the province decides one year later (in 23 AD) to erect an imperial temple for Tiberius, his mother, and the Senate (Tac. Ann. III. 66; IV. 15). It will take some years before the next step is taken. In 26 AD legations from eleven cities are present in Rome to defend their interests in the Senate. The province has apparently not been able to determine the place where the temple is to be built because each city defends itself as the best place, knowing that whoever gains the right to a temple will obtain a position of honour and monopoly in relation to other cities. In the gripping story of Tacitus about these events (Ann. IV. 56/7), one can see how the deliberations go: the city of Hypaipa, Trallus, Laodicea, and Magnesia lose out because they have no political clout; Troy because it can only speak about its own history; Halicarnassus because all it has to offer is solid rocky ground which has not suffered an earthquake for 1200 years; Pergamum already has its own imperial temple; Ephesus and Miletus lose out because the cult of Diana (=Artemis) and Apollo should be enough for them; Sardis could have a chance considering its long history and its important position of power, but Smyrna

wins the battle because it has always chosen the side of Rome since
the time of Sulla. The report of this consultation makes clear that
the building of an imperial temple is a very important political act,
not only seen from the position of the city itself, but also from the
position of the centre of power in Rome.

Not all that much is known about the temple. Rome gave a
subsidy for the building. The proconsul Manius Lepidus is given an
additional legate—probably because he was not the most energetic
of men (Tac. Ann. IV. 56, see also III. 32). It is not improbable
that Manius Aemilius Proculus, the *praefectus fabrum* of Lepidus
helped in the construction. Pergamum put up an altar with his name
(I. Perg. 635) which shows that Pergamum reacted favourably. In
Smyrna itself a coin was found with the image of the temple. It is a
coin from the time of Petronius (29-35 AD) where on the obverse
side Livia and the Senate can be seen and on the reverse side a four
column temple with the statue of Tiberius as priestly offerer.[72]
The temple is as one had imagined it: a temple for Tiberius, his
mother, and the Senate.

The long list of contributors in Ephesus[73] which is headed by
and ends with the mention of an (now anonymous) ἀρχιερεὺς τοῦ
Σεβαστοῦ Τιβερίου Καίσαρος which, not improbably, gives the
names of the people who contributed somehow to the temple in
Smyrna, shows the reaction of the people in the province.
Something similar must have happened in the other places. In the
case of Ephesus one must ask also when and why the people who
venerated Demeter start a cult for the mother of Tiberius and his
grandchildren as Δημήτηρ Καρποφόρος and νέοι Διόσκυροι. Is this
after the birth of the twins in 19 or 20 or after the death of one of
them in 23 or after the death of Livia in 29? It cannot be after the
death of the other of the twins (in 37) because he was murdered by
Caligula. I ask this question because any dating between 23 and 37
makes the institution of this cult a political act as a reaction to the
veneration of Tiberius, Livia, and the Senate in Smyrna. The cult is
organized with the agreement of the city council and the people of
Ephesus and makes it clear that Tiberius himself cannot have been
venerated as a God in Ephesus.

---

[72] See Price 1984, 258; Friesen 1993, 19ff.
[73] See V-1687; SEG 1987, 883; 1989, 1176 (and III-1396; III-1404).

The time of Caligula
In the time of Caligula the province was involved once again in the building of a temple: the ναός of Miletus. Not much is known about it. Not much is left over from it: only the base of the statue for the God Gaius together with the names of the first two high priests, the *neokoros* and the *neopoioi*. It was found in Didyma and the text of Dio Cassius—"Gaius ordered that a sacred precinct should be set apart for his worship at Miletus in the province of Asia (τέμενός τι τεμενίσαι)...because he desired to appropriate to his own use the large and exceedingly beautiful temple which the Milesians were building to Apollo" (59.28.1)—makes it not improbable that the ναός, which is mentioned in the inscription, does not signify much more than a τέμενος (cf. the Sebasteion in the Artemis-temple of Ephesus). Friesen[74] thinks that "Dio was probably not accurate when he linked the Didyma precincts to the provincial cult of Gaius. Provincial cults did not normally convert existing facilities for the use of the new cult. Rather, a new temple accompanied the new cult."

That this is not always so, especially with Caligula, is clear from the history of Israel under Caligula. There too we find mention of the combination of the emperor cult and the city temple. Josephus relates that Caligula, "because he wishes to be considered God and to be hailed as such" demands that a statue of him (statues, in the plural, in the parallel text Bell. Jud. II.184ff) will be placed in the temple in Jerusalem. A popular opposition develops which the legate Petronius takes seriously. He writes a letter to Caligula who takes this amiss and commands him to commit suicide. According to Josephus it is thanks to God's intervention that this letter arrives later than the official communication about the emperor's death so that the people of Israel and Petronius are saved (Jos. Ant. XVIII. 261ff).

In Miletus too the cult for Gaius cannot continue after his premature death. Because there are no later references it is better to see the history of this 'temple' as a short-lived interruption.

---

[74] 1993, 25.

The time of Domitian

Not so with the temple which Ephesus builds for Domitian. But, even though there is an abundance of epigraphic material, the occasion which led to the construction is still not known. But we may venture a guess. If one sees what happened in Ephesus—the construction of a large palaestra where the Olympic Games in honour of Zeus will be celebrated and the construction of a temple where the Sebastoi will be venerated—it looks like a replica of what happened in Rome. In 86 Domitian initiates the Capitoline Games to commemorate the reconstruction of the temple of Jupiter which burned down, and in 87 he builds a temple for Vespasian and Titus in the forum. The temple in Ephesus can be dated between the end of 88 and the beginning of 89. The first legations which arrive in Ephesus and erect a statue to honour the new temple, mention the proconsul Mestrius Florus who exercised his office in Ephesus from the summer of 88 till 89. And even though it is not probable that the city could have been reconstructed in one year, the similarity between Rome and Ephesus can hardly be accidental. The events in Rome may not have been the occasion for the request to build an imperial temple, but they did give form and substance to the plans.

From the inscriptions which are preserved something more can be said about the history of this temple. Twelve cities sent delegations and commissioned an inscription of honour. Under the proconsul Mestrius Florus the first delegations arrive: from Synaitos (VI-2048) and from Keretapa (II-234); when Fulvius Gillo (89/90) is proconsul, (probably) the delegation from Teos, and those of Klazomenai, Hyrkanis, Kyme, Aizanoi, Aphrodisias, and Silandos; and when Luscius Ocra (90/91) is proconsul, the delegations from Stratonikeia and Tmolos (II-230-242).

They all have their inscriptions made and they all give honour to Domitian for the ναῶι τῶι ἐν Ἐφέσωι τῶν Σεβαστῶν κοινῶι τῆς Ἀσίας, mentioning the respective high priests in Ephesus—Tib. Kl. Aristion who later on is the *neokoros*, Tib. Kl. Pheseinos, and Tib. Julius Damas Claudianus—together with the priestly functions of all kinds of legates, adding priesthood to priesthood for the greater glory of the God Emperor, Sebastos with the Sebastoi, represented by a series of enormous statues which are higher than those of other gods, in a temple in the middle of the renovated city. Because they are not just building a new temple, they are also renovating old buildings. The *embolos* is covered in marble (VII-1-

3008) and "the renewal of the old buildings is fitting for the νέα τῶν Σεβαστείων ἔργων μεγέθη", "for the new, large works of the imperial deeds" (II-449). By these buildings Tigellius Lupus shows that he is a 'friend of the emperor'.

Looking at the list of names of the legations, it is remarkable that the big cities are not there: Pergamum, Smyrna, Sardis, and Miletus. Maybe it is accidental, or, more probably, maybe it is true for these names—as was the case in Miletus[75]—that the preserved cities represent the various districts of the province. Hyrkanis belongs, according to Schuchhardt,[76] to the διοίκησις of Pergamum; Synaitos to the district of Sardis (see I-13), as also does Tmolos.

There is one other item. In Smyrna as well as in Pergamum interesting coins have been preserved. In Smyrna there is a coin with on the reverse side an image of a temple and the words "under the proconsulate of Mestrius Florus", and on the obverse side the image of a woman (=Asia) and the inscription "the Smyrnians (dedicated) Asia to Domitian Caesar Sebastos".[77] In Pergamum we have similar *homonoia* coins. On the reverse side is an image of Artemis and the obverse side an older man with a beard and a sceptre in his hand who can be interpreted to represent Zeus.[78] In that case it would be Zeus as the city god of Pergamum, but an (ambiguous) association with Domitian cannot be excluded (cf. the Ephesian coin with Domitian as Zeus). At least indirectly, therefore, all the important cities are represented. That is not without importance because the supposition is[79] that the cities have contributed to the building of the temple.

It is interesting that—parallel to the reaction in the time of the construction of the temple in Smyrna—the devotees of Demeter are heard of again. Through L. Pompeius Apollonius they write a letter to the proconsul Mestrius Florus to ask him to participate in their μυστήρια καὶ θυσίαι in honour of Demeter and the θεοὶ σεβαστοί (II-213). The association of Demeter with Livia and the

---

[75] See Robert 1949, 226-238.
[76] 1912, 143.
[77] See Friesen 1993, 67 note 59.
[78] Ohlemutz 1968, 89,261.
[79] Price 1984, 129.

grandchildren of Tiberius has become an association of Demeter with the Sebastoi.

It is an understandable change but that does not take away from the fact that during his life-time Domitian in the company of the Sebastoi is the most important divinity. All dedication-inscriptions are addressed to him, as is the altar which is filled with military symbols—which obviously can be transferred to other emperors.[80] His name was to be deleted when he is condemned after his death. Based on the veneration of the Sebastoi, his name can be exchanged with that of his father, the God Vespasian. It could have been a great deal worse for Ephesus because the city can proudly retain the title *neokoros*.

Habicht[81] discovered that precisely the use of this title by Ephesus was not without a consequence within the province. It helped Pergamum to stand out more clearly. Pergamum had an imperial temple already in 29 BC but the city had never prided itself on it. Till the time of Trajan the city describes itself as ἡ βουλὴ καὶ ὁ δῆμος, but from the beginning of the time of Trajan this is changed to ἡ βουλὴ καὶ ὁ δῆμος τῶν νεωκόρων Περγαμηνῶν.[82] And from the year 102 they add πρώτων: ἡ βουλὴ καὶ ὁ δῆμος τῶν πρώτων νεωκόρων Περγαμηνῶν.[83] When, in the time of Trajan, in 114, a second imperial temple is built, it is added that they are twice *neokoroi*: ἡ βουλὴ καὶ ὁ δῆμος τῶν πρώτων καὶ δὶς νεωκόρων Περγαμηνῶν.[84] Especially remarkable is that the reaction does not begin in the time of Domitian, but only later when Ephesus continues its temple cult in the time of Nerva and Trajan. It shows again how important the emperor cult is for the individual cities.

The time of Hadrian
The competition is fierce and does not diminish in later years. As we have said, in 114 Pergamum gets a new imperial temple. The

---

[80] See Price 1984, 157.

[81] 1969, 158ff.

[82] I. Perg. 461; AthMitt 32, 1907, 62,63; AthMitt 35, 1910, 58,59; I. Perg. Askl. 157.

[83] AthMitt 32, 1907, 64,65,66,68; I. Perg. 438; 441; 441B; 550.

[84] I. Perg. 395; 397; 520; AthMitt 37, 1912, 26.

other cities must then try their best to get one too. Smyrna and Ephesus fight each other for it and Hadrian must decide which one should be given preference. The history of the imperial temples is linked with the travels of Hadrian in the East, with his first visit in 124 and his second visit in 129.

When Hadrian visits Asia in 124,[85] he goes first to Smyrna where the famous sophist Polemon makes sure that the city gets its second *neocorate*. Although, because of the special archaeological situation of Izmir, there are not too many inscriptions of Smyrna preserved, this second *neocorate* is very clearly traceable. There is a letter from Hadrian in which he allows the building of a temple so that sacrifices can be offered for the perpetual wellbeing of the Roman Empire (I. Smyrna 594); there is a text of dedication of some city or other—parallel to the one in Ephesus—in which Polemon is mentioned (I. Smyrna 676); and in a long list of foundations the merits of Polemon are expressed: he made sure that the Senate gave permission for the second *neocorate*, that there were a holy *agōn*, tax freedom, theologians and singers of hymns, a foundation of 1.500.000 denarii, and pillars for the space where people are anointed.[86] A magnificent feast was celebrated in Smyrna on the occasion of Hadrian's visit and the city calls itself right away δὶς νεωκόρος.

That cannot have been very nice for Ephesus. Again they are last in line. Already in the first years of Hadrian, Publius Quintillius Valens Varius took the initiative as a private citizen to dedicate his own temple to Artemis, Hadrian, and the people of Ephesus. But it never got provincial recognition. When in August 124 Hadrian visited Ephesus after Smyrna,[87] the expectations must have been very high indeed. Records have been preserved of a number of events which took place during his visit. Q. Roscius Murena Pompeius Falco is the person first responsible in the city as proconsul. In his proconsulate gold-bearing priests and the winners in the games erect a statue for Hadrian (II-276); the initiated of

---

[85] And not (see Halfmann 1986, 200) in 123 as was previously thought.

[86] I. Smyrna 697; in Philostr. Vita Soph. 1.25.531; 533 one finds even more fantastic figures.

[87] See Halfmann 1986, 201.

Dionysus make Hadrian σύνθρονος τῷ Διονύσῳ (II-275); the ephebes sing sweetly in the theatre in the presence of the emperor (IV-1145),[88] people from far-away Samaria come to be present when the homage is offered (III-713), and the inhabitants of Ephesus have put all their hope in Favorinus, the sophist in conflict with Polemon.[89] But notwithstanding all this Ephesus does not get its new temple.

The city has to wait till Hadrian visits it for the second time in 129. He has been honoured in Athens as Zeus Olympios and has come directly from Eleusis to Ephesus. It seems that Hadrian is more actively involved in Ephesus. He asks the city whether his captains, who brought him safely from Ephesus to Rhodes and now from Eleusis to Ephesus, can become councillors (V-1487/8). In the inscription of 129 to honour the merits of Hadrian for the city, many other matters are mentioned: his care for Artemis, for the finances of the city, the grain brought from Egypt, the dredging of the harbours and rivers (II-274). Things are looking up for Ephesus.

Tib. Kl. Piso Diophantes is, probably, the finally successful promoter. In an inscription of honour from a somewhat later date it is said of him that under his high priesthood the temple of Hadrian was dedicated, "which he as the first asked of the God Hadrian and got" (II-428). It is not clear in the text whether "as the first" refers to his high priesthood or to the temple—that he asked for this as the first. Be that as it may, the permission to build the temple was given and as in Athens, Hadrian is now venerated as Zeus Olympios also in Ephesus. From 129 on there is a veritable explosion of dedications which honour Hadrian as Zeus Olympios (II-267-273; SEG 1989, 1212), not paratactical as was usual with Artemis: "for Artemis and Hadrian" but in dedications which use this divine name as a proper name: "for the Autokratōr Hadrianos Zeus Olympios" parallel to the title "for Hera Sabina Sebasta" (VII-1-3411) as dedication for the divine spouse. The blocked Zeus tradition of Domitian is taken up grandiosely under Hadrian. It is from this moment that the Olympics are restarted and that the city can call itself δὶς νεωκόρος τῶν Σεβαστῶν.

---

[88] See Knibbe 1980, 784.

[89] Philostr. Vita Soph. I.8.490; I.25.531; see also Keil 1953,7.

5.3 *The interferences with John's text*

The emperor in particular as represented in the cult of the emperor, is massively present in Ephesus. The inhabitants of the city are confronted with the emperor in a limitless number of places, times and events, very often in the form of a public or private cult. The multiplicity of the emperor's presence in John's text fits with that and causes a number of interferences for the readers in Ephesus. In the passion narrative the emperor is expressly present too: in person, in his representative Pilate, and in those who take care of his interests: the high priests. I think this is true on various levels of reading and that, therefore, the religious connotations are not lacking from a certain point of view.

5.3.1 *The proclamation of Jesus as king in God's name by the soldiers, the people, and the Senate*

It has always drawn the attention of the commentators that the narrator of the passion story managed to convey his story with such eloquence on different levels. Whether one sees this as a game of irony and facticity, as a mise-en-scène with foreground- and background-events, or as an exchange of the process of communication between narrator and listeners with that of the implicit author and readers, it is a fact that John's text can be read on different levels: as a story of a trial in which Jesus is condemned to death by Pilate at the instigation of the high priests, and as a story of an enthronement in which Jesus is made a king by the soldiers, by Pilate, and by the people: Jesus is made the king of Israel and against the background of the competition with the Roman emperor he is preferred. In the story we find constantly new statements which ring out on this level: Jesus himself confirms that he is king and knows himself thereby to be a witness for truth (18:36ff); Pilate declares that Jesus is innocent and recognizes Jesus as king (18:38,39; 19:4,14,15); the *Ioudaioi* and the high priests bring up the position of the emperor and the opposition this evokes between Jesus and Pilate (19:12,15).

It is important to see that the story is given a different dimension with the scene of the soldiers. We said already that this is the breaking point of the story, because in this scene Pilate as well as the *Ioudaioi* are absent *and* because, from that moment on in the story, the three parties—Jesus, Pilate, and the *Ioudaioi*—are not separated again, notwithstanding the going in and out of Jesus and Pilate.

1. *19:1-3: The enthronement of Jesus as king by the soldiers*

If one looks at this 'second' meaning of the story one must give different titles to the scenes too. Instead of 'ridicule', it is an 'enthronement of Jesus as king'. For the listeners to the story the ridicule by the soldiers is sick humour. They realize the truth of what the soldiers are doing: Jesus is made a king by them. The crown and the purple cloak are royal attributes. And the individual homage which the soldiers bring by greeting him as king of the Jews is their oath of loyalty, their *sacramentum* with which soldiers offer their service to their king. The soldiers think they are ridiculing him but actually they are prophets of truth. From this moment on Jesus will not take off his royal clothes.

2. *19:4-7: The epiphany of Jesus for the people*

Jesus' solemn exit, preceded by Pilate as his herald, means for the listeners to the story the epiphany of Jesus: Jesus appears before the people. His exit has royal overtones (see the similarity between 18:29,38 and 19:4) and Pilate acts as his herald: See the man, who made himself son of God. The verses 19:5 and 19:7 belong together. On this level of the story it is not a scene of humiliation and accusation; rather the opposite: in this man as he appears here the son of God manifests himself. This does not speak about an extreme incarnate humiliation (see how deeply the son of God humiliates himself in his humanity, see how far the son of God is willing to go). The humiliation is his greatness and the accusation is false. This man did not make himself into the son of God, he *is* the son of God. See how in this man God's kingship becomes visible in the cosmos.

3. *19:8-12: The discussion about power with a member of the Senate*

The perspective changes again. On the level of the story as told Pilate is convinced of his own power and of the emperor's power over life and death. The truth of the scene is different. Not Pilate nor the emperor but only God is the source and origin of power. Everyone is subject to that. Jesus too, but he has a special place in the sharing of power. God has transferred to him the participation in the divine power. Through Jesus, Pilate (and thus also the emperor) is bound by the dominion of God.

4. *19:13-16: The proclamation of Jesus as king*
The background and the foreground of the story meet again in this scene. Also the people in the story know what is at stake now. Jesus sits on (or stands next to) the seat of judgment. The hearers of the story understand that the high priests have made the wrong choice. Jesus goes to his death as king, a glorification which will lead to the glorification of his father.

These scenes, read in this way, have a real significance in the contemporary life of the Roman Empire. These are situations which occur at assumption of power amongst the Roman pretenders to emperorship: the soldiers, the people, and the Senate determine in a laboriously arranged process who will be the next Roman emperor. Especially in Tacitus one can read how with the various pretenders to the throne the take-over happens: via the oath of loyalty by the soldiers and the installation as emperor as its consequence; via the epiphany to the people and the acclamations by the people and via the discussions which take place or do not take place in the Senate, and its final transfer of power.[90]

Obviously, the question is how far this was known in Ephesus. The need to go to the Roman administration for every dedication to the emperor, makes it more than probable that there was an acute awareness of the happenings in Rome. As we have already seen, the inscriptions follow the chronological events in Rome meticulously and they adjust immediately to every change in power (even if it is a palace revolution). One can suppose at least that, out of pure self interest, people were interested and it is this knowledge which makes such a possible reading important.

The question is only in how far there were also religious connotations which played a role.

---

[90] See in Otho, Historiae 1,36 (the installation by the soldiers); 1,45 (the epiphany to the people); 1,47 (the transfer of power); with Vitellius: 1,56; 2,89.90; with Vespasian: 2,79; 4,6.7; with Piso: 1,17.18.

5.3.2 *Pilate as friend of the emperor and the power from above (Jn 19:8-12)*

The first time that the emperor is named in John's text is in the discussion about the power of Jesus and of Pilate: "Where is Jesus from? Where does Pilate's power come from? In whose name is Jesus king?" Pilate is addressed by the *Ioudaioi* as 'friend of the emperor'. That has political implications, as we developed in the last chapter. In scholarly exegesis the expression is seen as a possible historical reference to the friendship between Pilate, Seianus, and Tiberius.

Against the background of Ephesus another reference plays a role. It interferes there with the people who are honoured as φιλόκαισαρ. These are always people who are actively involved in the emperor cult: the high priest Anaxagoras in the decree about the singers of hymns for Tiberius; the mint master Lucius Cusinius from the time of Claudius; the builder of the temple of the Sebastoi in the time of Domitian; Vibius Salutaris with his innumerable statues of emperors which bring solemnity to the processions in which the high priest of the year fulfils his first ceremonial duty; the man from Larisa who dedicates a slaughter-house to the Sebastos Hadrian. The threat of the *Ioudaioi* that Pilate acts too little as "friend of the emperor" means in the context of Ephesus that Pilate does not sufficiently respect the divine qualities of the emperor: if he accepts Jesus as king, he cannot be a friend of the emperor.

It is clear that this 'interpretative interference' fits extraordinarily well in the context of the scene. The discussion between Jesus and Pilate is precisely about the divine origin of power. Jesus tells Pilate that he would have no power over Jesus if it were not given to him 'from above', a power which is more than the emperor's and which relativizes that power of the emperor on which Pilate depends, in relation to the power which Jesus has received from God. If Pilate recognizes that Jesus is king in God's name, he cannot be a 'friend of the emperor' because he cannot combine it with the conviction that the emperor is elected by God to be the one and only leader of the people.

5.3.3 *"We have no king but the emperor" (Jn 19:15)*

The second time the emperor is mentioned goes hand in glove with this. The high priests—in Ephesus the highest representatives of the

imperial cult—come to their conclusion about the divine kingship of
the emperor and the fake kingship of Jesus. They present this to
Pilate as a dilemma. Twice Pilate introduces Jesus to the *Ioudaioi*
as their king: the first time in an affirmative sentence "see, this is
your king" (19:14) parallel to the foregoing "see, this is the man"
(19:5); the second time in an ironical question "should I have your
king crucified?" (19:15). The high priests then speak the sentence
which we are now discussing: "we have no king but the emperor".
To what extent are messianic overtones present here?

It is clear that the high priests force Pilate into a corner with
their political dilemma but, in the story as told, it is not all to their
advantage. To get what they want they have to give up their
political independence. And, what is worse, they cannot go on
confessing that only God is the king of Israel. The exegesis of this
is, up to this point, fairly common and unanimous. But should we
not go a step further, against the background of the history of
Ephesus and John's theology? Jesus' kingship (cf. Jn 19:22) is, in
the eyes of the high priests, a pretence, but the kingship of the
emperor is real: i.e. the high priests exchange Jesus as king, king
in God's name, for the Caesar as king in God's name. This way of
thinking can be historically placed, as is clear from the first four
Discourses of Dio Chrysostom, where among others the kingship of
Trajan is compared with and evaluated from Zeus' kingship. In
fact, it is the origin of the emperor cult itself: the emperor makes
God (in his or her various forms) present in his imperial function,
in his titles, statues and images. Anyway, people in Ephesus will
not have found it strange that precisely the high priests of the
people are presented as the advocates and spokesmen of the divine
kingship of the emperor.

This position is strengthened by two further specifications in
John's text: by the use of the word cosmos in the story about the
interrogation by Annas and by Pilate, and by the Thomas
confession at the end of the story as the model for every future
confession of faith.

The word cosmos is used in a double sense in the Johannine
Gospel. This appears, for example, from the use of the word in the
narrative of the Last Supper of Jesus and his disciples. The
connection between 15:18-19 and 16:1-2 makes clear that there is
an identification between 'the cosmos' and 'the *Ioudaioi*': the hatred
of the cosmos shows in the persecution by the *Ioudaioi*; they will

eject the followers of Jesus from the synagogue and they are ready
to commit murder. But this identification seems to disappear in the
subsequent narrative. In chapter 17 the word 'cosmos' is used in a
much broader sense: the whole range of the anti-divine forces
which threaten the work of Jesus and his disciples in any way they
can. In the passion story this double identification plays a role too.
When Jesus is brought before the high priest Annas, who inter-
rogates him about his doctrine and his disciples, Jesus says that he
"spoke openly *to the world*. I have taught in a synagogue and in the
temple" (18:19-20); i.e., the openness to the world (the cosmos) is
confined to synagogue and temple; to the world of the *Ioudaioi*. But
when Jesus is brought before Pilate and Pilate asks what Jesus has
done, Jesus begins to speak about "his dominion which is not from
this world"; and about the fact that "he has come into this cosmos
for the sake of the truth" (18:31-37); i.e., Jesus' kingship has
consequences for the whole of the cosmos. Jesus who as king of the
Jews has been rejected by *the cosmos of the Ioudaioi*, posits his
kingship before *the cosmos of Pilate*.

How the readers should handle this can be found at the end of
John's story. Just before the first closing of the book, as the stories
of the apparitions have been told and the group of the disciples,
through Mary Magdalene, through Jesus' commission to his
disciples, and through the indisputable proof of the truth of Jesus'
resurrection has been gathered anew, the profession of Thomas
resounds: "My Lord and my God". And even if, as we said, this
confession may not interfere unequivocally with the 'dominus et
deus' confession of Domitian in the temple of the Sebastoi, it is a
direct reference to all imperial cults which use these divine titles.
Before all the Roman pretence of imperial divinity, it is true for
every reader of the book that for him or for her Jesus must be *my*
Lord and *my* God.

Different from the foregoing realities the interference between
text and social reality is in this case only negative. The Roman
emperors do not merit any form of divinisation because in this
cosmos God has made himself visible only and exclusively in Jesus.
The importance and possible consequence of this confession appear
in the story about Jesus himself, who is rejected and executed by
the high priests of the people. The conflict with the cosmos of the
Jewish world becomes a conflict with the cosmos of the Roman

the Roman world. It is clear that this will go on also without the influence of the Jewish high priests and is not restricted to the area of Ephesus. Perhaps I may be permitted to point to a last text, the *Martyrdom of Polycarp*, as an expressive example of what I am trying to say. After his arrest Polycarp is asked by the *eirenarchos* Herod: "But what harm is it to say, 'Lord Caesar' (Κύριος Καῖσαρ), and to offer sacrifice, and so forth, and to be saved?" (8:2). And when Polycarp has entered the arena and is interrogated by the proconsul, he answers: "For eighty and six years have I been his (= Christ's) servant, and he has done me no wrong, and how can I blaspheme *my* King (τὸν βασιλέα μου) who saved me ?" (9:3). And the text concludes with: "Polycarp was arrested by Herod, *when Philip of Tralles was high priest*, when Statius Quadratus was proconsul, but Jesus Christ was reigning (βασιλεύοντος) for ever" (21:1). The readers of the Johannine story enter into a dangerous world, when they finish their reading and are going to confront their daily city life.

SELECT BIBLIOGRAPHY

Alzinger W., 1962, *Die Stadt des siebenten Weltwunders. Die Wiederentdeckung von Ephesos*, Wien, Im Wollzeiler Verlag

Alzinger W., 1974, *Augusteische Architektur in Ephesos,* Wien, Verlag der Österreichischen Akademie der Wissenschaften

Arnold C.E., 1989, *Ephesians: Power and Magic. The Concept of Power in Ephesians in Light of its Historical Setting*, Cambridge, Cambridge University Press

Ashton J., 1991, *Understanding the Fourth Gospel*, Oxford, Oxford University Press

Aurenhammer M., 1990, *Die Skulpturen von Ephesos*, Wien, Verlag der Österreichischen Akademie der Wissenschaften

Bammel E., 1952, Philos tou Kaisaros, in, *Theol. Lit. Zeitung* 77, 1952, 205-210

Bauer W. & Paulsen H., 1985, *Die Briefe des Ignatius von Antiochia und der Polykarperbrief*, Tübingen, Mohr

Becker J., 1979, *Das Evangelium nach Johannes*, Gütersloh, Gerd Mohn

Beutler J., 1972, *Martyria. Traditionsgeschichtliche Untersuchungen zum Zeugnisthema bei Johannes*, Frankfurt a.M., J. Knecht

Beutler J. & Fortna R.T., 1991, *The Shepherd Discourse of John 10 and its Context*, Cambridge, Cambridge University Press

Bianchi B.R., 1975, *Die römische Kunst. Von den Anfängen bis zum Ende der Antike*, München, Beck'sche Verlagsbuchhandlung

Bieber M., 1967, *Entwicklungsgeschichte der griechischen Tracht. Von der vorgriechischen Zeit bis zum Ausgang der Antike*, Berlin, Verlag Gebr. Mann

Bieber M., 1977, *Ancient Copies. Contributions to the History of Greek and Roman Art*, New York, New York University Press

Bittner W.J., 1987, *Jesu Zeichen im Johannesevangelium. Die Messias-Erkenntnis im Johannesevangelium vor ihrem jüdischen Hintergrund*, Tübingen, Mohr

Blank J., 1959, Die Verhandlung vor Pilatus. Joh 18,28-19,16 im Lichte johanneischer Theologie, in, *Bibl. Zeitsch.* 3, 1959, 60-81

Botha J.E., 1991, *Jesus and the Samaritan Woman. A Speech Act Reading of John 4:1-42*, Leiden, Brill

Brodie T.L., 1993, *The Gospel According to John. A Literary and Theological Commentary*, Oxford, Oxford University Press

Broer I., 1983, Noch einmal: Zur religionsgeschichtlichen "Ableitung" von Jo 2,1-11, in, *Studien zum Neuen Testament und seiner Umwelt*, 8, 1983, 103-123

Broughton T.R.S., 1959, Roman Asia Minor, in, *An Economic Survey of Ancient Rome, Vol IV, Africa, Syria, Greece, Asia Minor*, ed. by T. Frank, Paterson, Pageant Books

Brown R.E., 1966-1970, *The Gospel according to John*, I, 1966; II, 1970, Garden City, New York, Doubleday

Brown R.E., 1979, *The Community of the Beloved Disciple. The Life, Loves, and Hates of an Individual Church in New Testament Times*, London, Chapman

Brown R.E., 1994, *The Death of the Messiah. From Gethsemane to the Grave. A Commentary on the Passion Narratives in the Four Gospels*, New York-London, Doubleday

Bühner J.-A., 1977, *Der Gesandte und sein Weg im 4. Evangelium*, Tübingen, Mohr

Campbell J.B., 1984, *The Emperor and the Roman Army. 31 BC - AD 235*, Oxford, Clarendon Press

Caragounis C.C., 1977, *The Ephesian mysterion: Meaning and Content*, Lund, Gleerup

Carson D., 1991, *The Gospel according to John*, Leicester-Grand Rapids, Eerdmans

Chamay J. & Frel J. & Maier J.L., 1982, *Le monde des Césars. Portraits romains*, Genève, Journal du Genève

Clairmont C.W., 1966, *Die Bildnisse des Antinous. Ein Beitrag zur Porträtplastik unter Kaiser Hadrian*, Neuchâtel, P. Attinger

Cullmann O., 1975, *Der johanneische Kreis. Zum Ursprung des Johannesevangeliums*, Tübingen, Mohr

Culpepper A., 1983, *Anatomy of the Fourth Gospel. A Study in Literary Design*, Philadelphia, Fortress Press

Culpepper A., 1994, *John, the Son of Zebedee. The Life of a Legend*, Columbia, South Caroline, University of South Caroline Press

Davies M., 1992, *Rhetoric and Reference in the Fourth Gospel*, Sheffield, Sheffield Academic Press

Deininger J., 1965, *Die Provinziallandtage der römischen Kaiserzeit von Augustus bis zum Ende des dritten Jahrhunderts n. Chr.*, München-Berlin, Beck'sche Verlagsbuchhandlung

Dodd C.H., 1968/8, *The Interpretation of the Fourth Gospel*, Cambridge, Cambridge University Press

Doer B., 1974/1937, *Die Römische Namengebung. Ein historischer Versuch*, Stuttgart, Kohlhammer

Döring K., 1979, *Exemplum Socratis. Studien zur Sokrates-Nachwirkung in der kynisch-stoischen Popularphilosophie der frühen Kaiserzeit und im frühen Christentum*, Wiesbaden, Steiner Verlag

Duprez A., 1970, *Jésus et les dieux guérisseurs. A propos de Jean, V,* Paris, Gabalda

Eck W., 1979, *Die staatliche Organisation Italiens in der hohen Kaiserzeit*, München, Beck'sche Verlagsbuchhandlung

Finley M.I., 1975, *The Ancient Economy*, London, Chatto and Windus

Fleischer R., 1973, *Artemis von Ephesos und verwandte Kultstatuen aus Anatolien und Syrien*, Leiden, Brill

Foucault M., 1976-1984, *L'Histoire de la sexualité*, Paris, Gallimard

Friesen S.J., 1993, *Twice Neokoros. Ephesus, Asia and the Cult of the Flavian Imperial Family*, Leiden, Brill

Gagé J., 1971/2 (1964), *Les classes sociales dans l'empire Romain*, Paris, Payot

Ginouvès R., 1962, *Balaneutikè. Recherches sur le bain dans l'antiquité Grecque*, Paris, Ed. de Boccard

Hafner G., 1954, *Späthellenistische Bildnisplastik. Versuch einer landschaftlichen Gliederung*, Berlin, Gebr. Mann

Hagenow G., 1982, *Aus dem Weingarten der Antike. Der Wein in Dichtung, Brauchtum und Alltag*, Mainz, Ph. von Zabern

Hahn F., 1964, *Christologische Hoheitstitel: ihre Geschichte im frühen Christentum*, Göttingen, Vandenhoeck & Ruprecht

Halfmann H., 1979, *Die Senatoren aus dem östlichen Teil des Imperium Romanum bis zum Ende des 2.Jh.n.Chr.*, Göttingen, Vandenhoeck & Ruprecht

Halfmann H., 1986, *Itinera principum. Geschichte und Typologie der Kaiserreisen im Römischen Reich*, Stuttgart, Fr.Steiner Verlag

Hanfmann G.M.A., 1967, *Classical Sculpture*, London, Michael Joseph

Hanfmann G.M.A., 1975, *From Croesus to Constantine. The Cities of Western Asia Minor and Their Arts in Greek and Roman Times*, Ann Arbor, University of Michigan Press

Hannestad N., 1986, *Roman Art and Imperial Policy*, Aarhus, Aarhus University Press

Hemer C.J., 1986, *The Letters to the Seven Churches of Asia in Their Local Setting*, Sheffield, Sheffield Academic Press

Hengel M., 1975, *Der Sohn Gottes: die Entstehung der Christologie und die jüdisch-hellenistische Religionsgeschichte*, Tübingen, Mohr

Hengel M., 1991, Reich Christi, Reich Gottes und Weltreich im Johannesevangelium, in, *Königsherrschaft Gottes und himmlischer Kult im Judentum, Urchristentum und in der hellenistischen Welt*, Hrsg M. Hengel & A. M. Schwemer, Tübingen, Mohr

Hengel M., 1993, *Die johanneische Frage. Ein Lösungsversuch*, Tübingen, Mohr

Himmelmann N., 1980, *Über Hirten-Genre in der antiken Kunst*, Opladen, Westdeutscher Verlag

Hirschfeld O., 1963/3 (1905/2), *Die kaiserlichen Verwaltungsbeamten bis auf Diocletian*, Berlin, Weidmannsche Verlagsbuchhandlung

Horsley G., 1981-1992, *New Documents illustrating Early Christianity. A Review of the Greek Inscriptions and Papyri*, Macquarie, Ancient History Documentary Research Centre

Horsley G., 1992, The Inscriptions of Ephesos and the New Testament, in, *Nov. Test.* 34, 1992, 105-168

Inan J. & Rosenbaum E., 1966, *Roman and Early Byzantine Portrait Sculpture in Asia Minor*, London, Oxford University Press (= Inan I)

Inan J. & Alföldi-Rosenbaum E., 1979, *Römische und frühbyzantinische Porträtplastik aus der Türkei. Neue Funde*, Mainz, von Zabern (= Inan II)

Inscriptions of Aizanoi:
- Naumann R., 1979, *Der Zeustempel zu Aizanoi*, Berlin, W. de Gruyter
- Le Bas P. & Waddington H., 1972 (1870), *Inscriptions grecques et latines recueillies en Asie Mineure, Vol II*, Hildesheim-New York, Olms, 234-257 (= Le Bas-Waddington + number)
- *Inscriptiones ad Res Romanas Pertinentes*, Vol IV, nr 557-591

Inscriptions of Ephesus:
- Wankel H. & Börker C. & Merkelbach R., u.a., 1979-1984, *Die Inschriften von Ephesos*, Bonn, Habelt Verlag (= IE + volume + number)
- *Supplementum Epigraphicum Graecum* 1981-1990 (= SEG + year + number)

Inscriptions of Magnesia:
- Kern O., 1900, *Die Inschriften von Magnesia am Meander*, Berlin, W. Spemann (= I. Magn. + number)

Inscriptions of Miletus:
- Hülsen J., 1919, *Das Nymphaeum von Milet*, Berlin, de Gruyter (= I. Miletus, Nymphaeum + page)
- Kawerau G. - Rehm A., 1914, *Das Delphinion in Milet*, Berlin, Reimer (= I. Miletus, Delphinion + page)
- Knackfuss H., 1908, *Das Rathaus von Milet*, Berlin, de Gruyter (= I. Miletus, Rathaus + page)
- Knackfuss H., 1924, *Der Südmarkt und die benachbarten Bauanlagen von Milet*, Berlin, von Schoets-Parrhysius (= I. Miletus, Südmarkt + page)

Inscriptions of Pergamum:
- Fränkel M., 1890-1895, *Die Inschriften von Pergamon = Altertümer von Pergamon VIII.1 + VIII.2*, Berlin, W. Spermann (= I. Perg. + number)
- Habicht C., 1969, *Die Inschriften des Asklepeions = Altertümer von Pergamon VIII.3*, Berlin, W. de Gruyter (= I. Perg. Askl. + number)
- Mitteilungen des kaiserlich deutschen archäologischen Instituts, Athenische Abteilung = *Athenische Mitteilungen* (= AthMitt + 24, 1899; 17, 1902; 19, 1904; 32, 1907; 33, 1908; 35, 1910; 37, 1912 + number)
Inscriptions of Priene:
- Hiller von Gaertringen F., 1906, *Inschriften von Priene*, Berlin, de Gruyter (= I. Priene + number)
Inscriptions of Sardis:
- Buckler W.H. - Robinson D.M., 1932, *Sardis. Greek and Latin Inscriptions, Part I, Vol VII*, Leiden, Brill (= I. Sardis + number)
- Robert L., 1964, *Nouvelles Inscriptions de Sardes*, Paris, A. Maisonneuve (= I. Sardes Nouv. + number)
Inscriptions of Smyrna:
- Petzel G., 1982, *Die Inschriften von Smyrna*, Bonn, Habelt Verlag (= I. Smyrna + number)
Inscriptions of Tralleis:
- Poljakov F.B., 1989, *Die Inschriften von Tralleis und Nysa*, Bonn, Habelt Verlag (= I. Tralleis + number)
Jameson M.H., 1988, Sacrifice and Animal Husbandry in Classical Greece, in, *Pastoral Economies in Classical Antiquity*, Ed. by C.R. Whittaker, 87-119, Cambridge, Cambridge University Press
Jobst W., 1977, *Römische Mosaiken aus Ephesos I: die Hanghäuser des Embolos*, mit einem Beitrag von H. Vetters, Wien, Verlag der Österreichischen Akademie der Wissenschaften
Jonge M. de, 1973, Jesus as Prophet and King in the Fourth Gospel, in, *Eph. Theol. Lov.* 32, 1973, 160-177
Jonge M. de, 1977, *Jesus: Stranger from Heaven and Son of God*, Missoula, Scholars Press
Jonge M. de, 1988, *Christology in Context: the Earliest Christian Response to Jesus*, Philadelphia, Westminster Press
Kajanto I., 1965, *The Latin Cognomina*, Helsinki, Keskuskirjapaino
Karwiese S., *RE Suppl* s.v. Ephesos
Keil J., 1953, Vertreter der zweiten Sophistik in Ephesos, in, *Jahreshefte des Österreichischen Archäologischen Instituts in Wien*, 40, 1953, 5-26

Klauck H.-J., 1982, *Herrenmahl und hellenistischer Kult. Eine religionsgeschichtliche Untersuchung zum ersten Korintherbrief*, Münster, Aschendorff

Knibbe D., 1978, Ephesos—nicht nur die Stadt der Artemis. Die 'anderen' Ephesischen Götter, in, *Studien zur Religion und Kultur Kleinasiens*, Fs f. F. K. Dörner, 489-503, Leiden, Brill

Knibbe D. & Alzinger W., 1980, Ephesos vom Beginn der römischen Herrschaft in Kleinasien bis zum Ende der Prinzipatszeit, in, *Aufstieg und Niedergang der römischen Welt VII.2*, 748-830

Knibbe D., 1981, Der Staatsmarkt. Die Inschriften des Prytaneions. Die Kureteninschriften und sonstige religiöse Texte, in, *Forschungen in Ephesos IX/1/1*, Wien, Verlag des Österreichischen Archäologischen Instituts

Knibbe D., *RE Suppl* s.v. Ephesos

Kraabel A.T., 1971, Melito the Bishop and the Synagogue at Sardis: Text and Context, in, *Studies Presented to G.M.A. Hanfmann*, Ed. by D.G. Mitten et al., 1971, 77-85, Mainz, von Zabern

Kreiler B., 1975, *Die Statthalter Kleinasiens unter den Flaviern*, Augsburg, Blasaditsch

Kruse H.-J., 1975, *Römische weibliche Gewandstatuen des zweiten Jahrhunderts n. Chr.*, Göttingen, Boenecke

Kuhn H.-J., 1988, *Christologie und Wunder. Untersuchungen zu Joh 1,35-51*, Regensburg, Pustet

Lampe P., 1987, *Die stadtrömischen Christen in den ersten beiden Jahrhunderten*, Tübingen, Mohr

Laubscher H.P., 1982, *Fischer und Landleute. Studien zur hellenistischen Genreplastik*, Mainz, von Zabern

Le Bas P. & Waddington W.H., 1972 (1870), *Inscriptions grecques et latines recueillies en Asie Mineure, Vol I-II*, Hildesheim-New York, Olms

Lémonon J.-P., 1981, *Pilate et le gouvernement de la Judée. Textes et Monuments*, Paris, Gabalda

Leroy H., 1968, *Rätsel und Mißverständnis. Ein Beitrag zur Formgeschichte des Johannesevangeliums*, Bonn, P. Hanstein Verlag

Linnemann E., 1973-74, Die Hochzeit zu Cana und Dionysos, in, *New Test. Studies 20*, 1973-74, 408-418

Loos H. van der, 1968, *The Miracles of Jesus*, Leiden, Brill

Macro A.D., 1980, The Cities of Asia Minor under the Roman Imperium, in, *Aufstieg und Niedergang der römischen Welt VII.2*, 658-679

Macmullen R., 1974, *Roman Social Relations. 50 B.C. to A.D. 284*, New Haven-London, Yale University Press

Magie D., 1950, *Roman Rule in Asia Minor to the End of the Third Century After Christ, Vol I: Text; Vol II: Notes*, Princeton, Princeton University Press

Martyn J.L., 1979, *History & Theology in the Fourth Gospel*, Nashville, Parthenon Press

Mastin B., 1975-76, A Neglected Feature of the Christology of the Fourth Gospel, in, *New Test. Stud* 22, 1975-76, 32-51

Mattingly H., 1960, *Roman Coins from the Earliest Times to the Fall of the Western Empire*, London, Methuen

Mattingly H. & Sydenham E.A., 1968 (1926), *The Roman Imperial Coinage, Vol 2: Vespasian to Hadrian*, London, Spink

Meeks W. A., 1967, *The Prophet-King. Moses Traditions and the Johannine Christology*, Leiden, Brill

Meeks W. A., 1972, The Man from Heaven in Johannine Sectarianism, in, *Journ. Bibl. Lit.* 91, 1972, 44-72

Meinhold P., 1979, *Studien zu Ignatius von Antiochien*, Wiesbaden, Fr. Steiner Verlag

Meshorer Y., 1967, *Jewish Coins of the Second Temple Period*, Tel Aviv, Am Hassefer

Miltner F., 1958, *Ephesos. Stadt der Artemis und des Johannes*, Wien, Deuticke

Moloney F., 1976, *The Johannine Son of Man*, Roma, Libreria Ateneo Salesiano

Mussies G., 1990, Pagans, Jews and Christians at Ephesus, in, P. van der Horst & G. Mussies, *Studies on the Hellenistic Background of the New Testament*, 177-195, Utrecht, Fac. der Godgeleerdheid

Nicol W., 1972, *The sèmeia in the Fourth Gospel. Tradition and Redaction*, Leiden, Brill

Ohlemutz E., 1968 (1939), *Die Kulte und Heiligtümer der Götter in Pergamon*, Darmstadt, Wissenschaftliche Buchgesellschaft

Okure T., 1988, *The Johannine Approach to Mission. A Contextual Study of John 4:1-42*, Tübingen, Mohr

Ollrog W.-H., 1979, *Paulus und seine Mitarbeiter. Untersuchungen zu Theorie und Praxis der paulinischen Mission*, Neukirchen, Neukirchener Verlag

Olsson B., 1974, *Structure and Meaning in the Fourth Gospel. A Text-Linguistic Analysis of John 2:1-11 and 4:1-42*, Lund, Gleerup

Oster R., 1990, Ephesus as a Religious Centre under the Principate, I Paganism before Constantine, in, *Aufstieg und Niedergang der römischen Welt II.18.3*, 1661-1728

Painter J., 1991, *The Quest for the Messiah. The History, Literature and Theology of the Johannine Community*, Edinburgh, T&T Clark

Picard C., 1922, *Éphèse et Claros. Recherches sur les sanctuaires et les cultes de l'Ionie du Nord*, Paris, Boccard

Pleket H.W., 1990, Ephesos: 'De eerste en grootste metropool van Asia', in, *Lampas* 23, 1990, 187-197

Poland F., 1967/1908, *Geschichte des griechischen Vereinswesens*, Leipzig, Zentral-Antiquariat der DDR

Potterie I. de la, 1977, *La Vérité dans Saint Jean*, Tome I-II, Rome, Biblical Institute Press

Price S.R.F., 1984, *Rituals and Power. The Roman Imperial Cult in Asia Minor*, Cambridge, Cambridge University Press

Ramage A. & Ramage N.H., 1983, *Twenty-Five Years of Discovery at Sardis 1958-1983*, Cambridge Mass., Archeological Exploration of Sardis

Rengstorf K.H., 1964, *TWNT*, s.v. σημεῖον

Rensberger D., 1989, *Overcoming the World. Politics and Community in the Gospel of John*, Cambridge, Cambridge University Press

Richter G., 1951, *Three Critical Periods in Greek Sculpture*, Oxford, Clarendon Press

Richter G., 1977 (1959), *A Handbook of Greek Art. A Survey of the Visual Arts of Ancient Greece*, London - New York, Phaidon

Robert L., 1949, Le cult de Caligula à Milet et la province d'Asie, in, *Hellenica* 7, 1949, 206-238

Robert L., 1989, *Opera Minora Selecta V*, Amsterdam, A.M. Hakkert

Runia D.T., 1988, Philosophical Heresiography: Evidence in Two Ephesian Inscriptions, in, *Zeitsch. f. Papyrologie u. Epigraphik* 72, 1988, 241-243

Schaeder H.H., *TWNT*, s.v. Ναζαρηνος—Ναζωραῖος

Schede M., 1964/1962, *Die Ruinen von Priene, durchgesehen und verbessert von G. Kleiner & W. Kleiss*, Berlin, de Gruyter

Schmidt E.M., 1961, *Der große Altar zu Pergamon*, Leipzig, Seemann Verlag

Schnackenburg R., 1967/1971/1975/1984, *Das Johannes-Evangelium*, Vol. I-IV, Freiburg, Herder

Schnackenburg R., 1991, Ephesos: Entwicklung einer Gemeinde von Paulus zu Johannes, in, *Bibl. Zeitschr.* 35, 1991, 41-64

Schober A., 1951, *Die Kunst von Pergamon*, Wien - Innsbruck, Rohrer Verlag

Schuchhardt C., 1912, *Altertümer von Pergamon, Stadt und Landschaft, I,1*, Berlin, G. Reimer

Schürer E., 1973-1987, *The History of the Jewish People in the Age of Jesus Christ (175 B.C.-A.D. 135)*, revised and edited by G. Vermes, F. Millar, M. Goodman, 3 vols, Edinburgh, T&T Clark

Schulz S., 1972, *Das Evangelium nach Johannes*, Göttingen, Vandenhoeck & Ruprecht

Sherwin-White A.N., 1963, *Roman Society and Roman Law in the New Testament*, Grand Rapids Michigan, Baker Book House

Smallwood E.M., 1981, *The Jews under Roman Rule. From Pompey to Diocletian. A Study in Political Relations*, Leiden, Brill

Smith M., 1974-75, On the wine god in Palestine (Gen 18, Jn 2, and Achilles Tatius), in, *Fs. in honour of S. Wittmayer Baron*, II, 815-829, Jerusalem, American Academy for Jewish Research

Stern M., 1976-1984, *Greek and Latin Authors on Jews and Judaism, ed. with Introductions, Translations and Commentary, Vol 1-3*, Jerusalem, Israel Academy of Sciences and Humanities

Stibbe M.W.G., 1992, *John as Storyteller. Narrative Criticism and the Fourth Gospel*, Cambridge, Cambridge University Press

Strocka W.M., 1977, *Die Wandmalereien der Hanghäuser in Ephesos*, mit einem Beitrag von H. Vetters, Wien, Verlag der Österreichischen Akademie der Wissenschaften

Tcherikover V.T. - Fuks A., 1957-1960, *Corpus Papyrorum Judaicarum, I-II*, Cambridge, Harvard University Press (= CPJ)

Thiessen W., 1994, *Christen in Ephesus. Die historische und theologische Situation in vorpaulinischer und paulinischer Zeit und zur Zeit der Apostelgeschichte und der Pastoralbriefe*, Tübingen-Basel, Francke Verlag

Thür H., 1990, *Das Hadrianstor in Ephesos*, Wien, Verlag der Österreichischen Akademie der Wissenschaften

Thylander H., 1952, *Étude sur l'épigraphie latine. Date des inscriptions - Nom et dénomination latine - Nom et origine des personnes*, Lund, Gleerup

Tilborg Sj. van, 1993, *Imaginative Love in John*, Leiden, Brill

Trebilco P., 1991, *Jewish Communities in Asia Minor*, Cambridge, Cambridge University Press

Vermeule C.C., 1968, *Roman Imperial Art in Greece and Asia Minor*, Cambridge Mass., Harvard University Press

Vermeule C.C., 1977, *Greek Sculpture and Roman Taste. The Purpose and Setting of Graeco-Roman Art in Italy and the Greek Imperial East*, Ann Arbor, University of Michigan

Vetters H., 1973, *Ephesos. Vorläufiger Grabungsbericht 1972*, Wien, Verlag der Österreichischen Akademie der Wissenschaften

Weaver P.R.C., 1972, *Familia Caesaris. A Social Study of the Emperor's Freedmen and Slaves*, Cambridge, Cambridge University Press

Wegner M., 1956, *Hadrian, Plotina, Marciana, Matidia, Sabina*, Berlin, Gebr. Mann

Wengst K., 1983/2, 1981, *Bedrängte Gemeinde und verherrlichter Christus. Der historische Ort des Johannesevangeliums als Schlüssel zu seiner Interpretation*, Neukirchen, Neukirchener Verlag

White K.D., 1977, *Country Life in Classical Times*, London, Paul Elek

Winden J.C. van, 1971, *An Early Christian Philosopher: Justin Martyr's Dialogue with Trypho, chapter one to nine*, Leiden, Brill

INDEX OF MODERN AUTHORS

DATE DUE

NOV 0 5 2002			
			Printed in USA